Governing the
EVERGREEN STATE
Political Life in Washington

Governing the
EVERGREEN STATE
Political Life in Washington

EDITED BY
Cornell W. Clayton, Todd Donovan,
AND Nicholas P. Lovrich

WSU
PRESS
Washington State University Press
Pullman, Washington

WSU PRESS
WASHINGTON STATE UNIVERSITY

Washington State University Press
PO Box 645910
Pullman, Washington 99164-5910
Phone: 800-354-7360
Fax: 509-335-8568
Email: wsupress@wsu.edu
Website: wsupress.wsu.edu

Library of Congress Cataloging-in-Publication Data

Names: Clayton, Cornell W., 1960- editor. | Donovan, Todd, editor. |
    Lovrich, Nicholas P., editor.
Title: Governing the Evergreen State : political life in Washington /
    edited by Cornell W. Clayton, Todd Donovan, and Nicholas P.
    Lovrich.
Description: Pullman, Washington : Washington State University
    Press, 2018. | Includes bibliographical references and index.
Identifiers: LCCN 2017047621 | ISBN 9780874223552 (alk. paper)
Subjects: LCSH: Washington (State)--Politics and government.
Classification: LCC JK9216 .G65 2018 | DDC 320.4797--dc23
LC record available at https://lccn.loc.gov/2017047621

Cover photo: Washington State Capitol, Olympia. *iStockphoto.com*

Table of Contents

Foley Institute Sponsorship

The Thomas S. Foley Institute at Washington State University is proud to sponsor this volume. We believe that readers will find it informative, thought-provoking, and an invaluable asset in helping citizens understand Washington State government.

State governments have always played an important role in the political life of our nation, but their role has grown more vital and more complicated during the past several decades. Economic globalization, broad demographic trends, and new forms of community (virtual and otherwise) have dramatically altered the political landscape in the United States. As a consequence of these and other developments, control over a growing number of policy areas has been shifting away from Washington, DC, and simultaneously up toward international organizations and down toward state and local governments. This more complex set of intergovernmental relations greatly complicates the role of state political institutions.

This is the sixth iteration of this important resource on Washington government and politics published by Washington State University Press. The five predecessors were *Governing Washington: Politics and Government in the Evergreen State* (2011), *Washington State Government and Politics* (2004), *Government and Politics in the Evergreen State* (1992), *Political Life in Washington: Governing the Evergreen State* (1985), and *The Government and Politics of Washington State* (1978).

Foreword

This book will provide insight into the dynamics of Washington State's politics and government and how we continue to successfully change and grow with the times.

And it's quite a story. We have a rich, fascinating history—reaching back to our populist founders in the nineteenth century and to the progressive movement in the early part of the twentieth century.

At national meetings and conferences, I became aware of our uniqueness. We have one of the most open systems in the nation.

To run successfully for public office here in Washington State, you don't need to be from the right family or union or business or educational background. We truly have a meritocracy. If you are a community leader and pick the right timing and jurisdiction, develop a cadre of supporters, and campaign hard, you have a chance of being elected.

Anyone of any political party can get on our primary ballot simply by filing for office. There are no restrictions: no need for petitions or party conventions or the blessing of party organizations.

While some states make voters jump through hoops to participate, ours is the opposite. Voters don't have to go to polls and prove who they are. Everyone receives his or her ballot in the mail. To register to vote, you don't need to find the right location, you can do it online.

Our primary election system is the most open in the nation. Voters are allowed to vote for any candidate of any party. This idea is deeply imbedded in our state's political culture and heritage.

And given our populist tradition, we elect everybody—from water districts to port districts to school districts to cities and towns to counties to the state. Here in Washington that includes the judiciary—including the state Supreme Court.

If you have a public policy idea or are opposed to one that the legislature adopted, you can file an initiative or referendum, collect a daunting number of signatures, and get it on the ballot for a public vote.

Our government is wide open too. This state's Open Public Meetings Act (OPMA) and Public Records Act are rigorous. They apply to all government levels, from special taxing districts to the state government.

Unlike most states where legislators redistrict themselves in acts of decennial political cannibalism, this state has a bipartisan commission charged with redrawing legislative and congressional district boundaries. The same is true for establishing and overseeing state salaries.

The end result is a state known for its political mavericks, where independents outnumber Democrats and Republicans and voters take pride in being ticket splitters, and for a political culture that is usually characterized as operating with civility, moderation, and bipartisanship.

Overall, there is much competition among the state's political parties. As in most states, Democrats dominate in the cities, Republicans dominate the rural/natural resource areas, and the suburban/exurban areas are battlegrounds.

Democrats have carried this state for presidential and gubernatorial candidates for the past three decades. But that fact is a little deceptive. In gubernatorial races for open seats, the contests have been very even. For example, in 2012, the Republican candidate came within 1.55 percent of winning. In 2004, the Republican came within 0.01 percent of winning. Republican county officials outnumber Democrats. In the legislature, the parties are close to a tie in both houses. This openness and competitiveness makes for interesting, pragmatic policy making. Washington is known as a bellwether state in public policy—particularly in respect to the environment, elections, and women.

This book will be a valuable guide to our state's politics and government. I've touched on the surface. Now you can dive deep into how our system is working.

Each of the chapters is written independently, by an unusual blend of academics and practitioners. In addition to professors, we have a state senator, a pollster, a newspaper reporter/blogger, a former chief justice of the state Supreme Court, and a court administrator. This combination of perspectives and knowledge has produced an enormously valuable publication.

I hope you find this book as illuminating and interesting as I did.

Sam Reed
Secretary of State, 2001–2013
Olympia, Washington

SECTION I
Political Setting and Behavior

CHAPTER 1

Two Washingtons? Political Culture in the Evergreen State

Nicholas P. Lovrich Jr., John C. Pierce, and H. Stuart Elway

Political Culture

Why is it that when a person relocates to a different area of the country it takes a while to adjust to the new community? Some people describe the experience as "culture shock." The reason for this sensation is often in the difference between the *political cultures* of the former home and the new place of residence. In the case of Washington State, not only does the political culture differ from that of other states, but also there are two distinct political cultures present in different parts of the state itself. But first, what precisely is a political culture?

The term is used to characterize that mix of shared attitudes, values, behaviors, and institutions that reflect a particular or distinctive historical legacy and persistent approach to politics (Sarigil 2015). Such political cultures may be characteristic of people within a particular geographic boundary (e.g., the political culture of a particular state), or ethnic group (e.g., Latino political culture), or other clearly bounded social grouping (Nardulli 1990; Mead 2004). This chapter identifies differences in the political cultures in two different parts of Washington, and explains how those differences likely influence political behavior. It also shows how the political culture in Washington State compares to that present in other places in the United States.

Most research into political culture in the United States focuses upon comparisons at the cross-national, cross-state, or cross-major-city levels (Sharkansky 1969). Political culture is an important aspect of political life because it provides a filter through which leaders and citizens interpret and understand both historical events and contemporary public affairs controversies as they arise. In other words, political cultures provide the framework upon which many attributes of government and societal practices are built (Bannerman and Haggert 2015). Accordingly, *democratic* political cultures—those in which citizens tolerate differences, participate actively in elections, and are informed about important issues—might be expected to be more likely to have governmental structures and feature decisional processes that provide ample opportunities for influence and access by their citizens (Campbell et al. 1960). Among democratic political cultures there are also specific types of cultures reflecting historical legacies and major events. These shape the choices citizens make and the public policies that emerge from those structures and processes, such as statutory provisions for affirmative action, same sex marriage, or the legalization of medical and recreational marijuana.

In his classic work, *The American Mosaic* (1994), Daniel Elazar suggests there are three major types of political cultures in the United States: the *individualistic,* the *moralistic,* and the *traditionalistic.* According to Elazar, every place in the country features a mix of those three culture types, but one is usually predominant and a second is present in less force. An area's particular type of political culture reflects "the streams and currents of migration that have carried people of different origins and backgrounds across the continent in more or less orderly patterns" (Elazar 1994, 229). Political cultures often are seen as "path dependent," meaning that they tend to remain fairly stable across time, even though the forces that shaped them initially may have dissipated (David 2007; Pierce, Lovrich, and Budd 2016). An area's political culture tends to be learned by newcomers and sustained by long-time residents, and thereby comes to have an ongoing impact on politics and policy.

Elazar's *individualistic* political culture features a view of politics as resembling a "free marketplace," wherein the role of government is to be held to the minimum required in order to "encourage private initiative and widespread access to the marketplace" (Elazar 1994, 230). In such individualistic political cultures, politics is viewed as utilitarian and being dedicated primarily to enhancing the satisfaction of individual needs. The *moralistic* political culture, in contrast, emphasizes the "positive potential" of politics, and views the goal of political activity as "centered on some notion of the public good and properly devoted to the advancement of the public interest" (Elazar 1994, 232). Citizens are expected to participate in political affairs, and there is a sense of obligation to intervene in the activities of individuals when necessary to promote the public welfare or common good. Finally, the *traditionalistic* political culture is "rooted in an ambivalent attitude toward the marketplace coupled with a paternalistic and elitist conception of the commonwealth" (Elazar 1994, 234). This political culture is dominated by privileged elites whose primary goal is that of maintaining existing social and political arrangements.

What is the political culture of the two major cities of Washington—Seattle and Spokane—when compared to other cities around the country? Elazar classifies Washington as an "MI" state, one in which the moralistic strain of American political life predominates and the individualistic strain is present in somewhat less force. Table 1 presents Elazar's rating of both the Spokane area and the Seattle area on each of the three major political culture dimensions, and compares these to other U.S. cities. Neither Seattle nor Spokane has any elements of the traditionalistic political culture, suggesting that there is an absence of a dominant elite committed entirely to sustaining the status quo through ongoing political activity. The two principal Washington cities differ from Atlanta in that regard, for example, where traditional, elite-sustaining political values are the major theme of the culture.

According to Elazar, Seattle has only a minor strain of individualistic political culture, while the Spokane area has none. This might seem unexpected in light of the reputation of Spokane as a more conservative city than Seattle, but recall that Elazar is writing about the relative emphasis on the individual as opposed to the common welfare, and also that Seattle and Spokane really are quite similar in one important respect. The shared distinctiveness of Seattle and Spokane may be best expressed in their respective ratings on the dimension of *moralistic political culture*. Both Seattle and Spokane are more like the other Western cities of San Francisco, San Diego, Sacramento, and Salt Lake City than they are like other major U.S. cities. For example, both Seattle and Spokane differ greatly from Atlanta, Houston, Kansas City, and Miami in this respect.

Table 1: Elazar Political Culture Types for Seattle, Spokane, and Selected Other U.S. Cities

	POLITICAL CULTURE TYPES		
	Traditionalistic	Individualistic	Moralistic
Seattle	**None**	**Minor**	**Major**
Spokane	**None**	**None**	**Sole**
Atlanta	Major	Minor	None
Boston	None	None	Sole
Chicago	None	Major	Minor
Denver	None	None	Sole
Houston	Sole	None	None
Kansas City	None	Sole	None
Los Angeles	None	Minor	Major
Miami	None	Sole	None
Minneapolis	None	None	Sole
Salt Lake City	None	None	Sole
San Diego	Minor	None	Major
San Francisco	None	Minor	Major
St. Louis	None	Sole	None

Source: Elazar 1994, 242–43.

Overall, then, the state's two major cities seem similar in their dominant political cultures, as well as similar to other cities of the American West, and similar to Minneapolis, a city that lies in the same immigrant stream that moved across the northern reaches of the country through Minnesota and west to Washington Territory (Elazar 1984). The political cultures of Washington's two major cities differ from many other U.S. cities located in the lower Midwest, the Southwest, the Border States, and the South.

Social Capital

Another important concept in understanding the culture and politics of a place is its level of *social capital*. Social capital refers to the degree to which individuals trust one another and assume good intentions on the part of others generally, a concept often characterized as *diffuse trust* (Fukuyama 1995; Ladd 1999; Putnam 2000; Uslaner 2002;

Hetherington 2005). If people trust each other they are more willing to join in social networks, and the interpersonal interaction from being in such networks in turn serves to increase trust levels. Those trust-based social networks then become a resource (capital) that can facilitate collective action on matters of shared concern in a community.

Individuals who trust other people, especially in groups other than their own, are inclined to invest in interpersonal networks (bridging social capital) that benefit others because they believe others can be trusted to reciprocate when the time comes that their support is needed. This mutual trust binds people together in ways that allow them to exert greater collective influence than they each would have individually. Many scholars argue that social capital is required to ensure democratic political practices featuring genuine and broad-based public involvement (Hendryx et al.; Field 2003; Coffee and Geys 2005). Despite ongoing debate over the meaning and effects of social capital (Paxton 1999; Williams 2006), the concept has attained nearly universal presence in political science, sociology, criminal justice, and other social science literatures where collective action at local levels of government is thought to be of major consequence for societal outcomes of public policy (Woolcook 2010; Kawachi et al. 2010).

Table 2 (on the next page) displays scores for a number of U.S. cities on a measure of political and social trust expressed by citizens in large scale surveys conducted in major U.S. and Canadian media markets. The higher the score, the higher is the level of trust, and thus the higher the level of social capital (see survey items and score calculation in Pierce, Lovrich, and Moon 2002). Seattle's social capital score is among the highest, surpassed only by Minneapolis. Spokane's score, in contrast, is much lower than that of Seattle—although higher than a number of other major U.S. cities such as Miami, Atlanta, and St. Louis. Hence, while Spokane and Seattle share a moralistic political culture, Seattle has greater social capital—and the concomitant higher levels of civic engagement and political participation associated with that trait.

Another recent study of social capital in the U.S. looked less at direct measures of trust, and instead documented the presence of the networks that are said to be both the result and the source of trust (Rupasingha et al. 2006). Calculating social capital scores for every county and state in the U.S., this study reported both a score for the number of different kinds of networks (recreational, civic, religious, etc.) present in each county; and a second *composite social capital score* that combines the network data with several other indicators of trust-based civic behavior such as county voting turnout in presidential elections, the number of tax-exempt nonprofit organizations working on public interest-promoting activities, and the percentage participating in the decennial census household survey process. Table 3 shows the average county network-based composite social capital score for each U.S. state (the table entry is the average of the counties in the state).

Table 2: Political and Social Trust Levels in Seattle and Spokane Compared to Selected other U.S. Cities for 1990–2003

City	Trust Score	City	Trust Score
Seattle	**205.75**	Boston	197.92
Spokane	**195.39**	Atlanta	192.36
Minneapolis	210.08	St. Louis	190.26
Salt Lake City	205.16	Miami	189.13
Denver	200.86	Kansas City	184.66
San Francisco	199.64	Los Angeles	178.94
Chicago	199.01	Houston	176.06
San Diego	198.30		

Source: Data for the calculation of political and social trust scores provided by the Leigh Stowell and Company market research firm of Seattle. Access to digital archives containing these data can be gained through Dataverse at the Institute for Quantitative Social Science at Harvard University.

A score near zero on the network-based measure indicates that the state is about average in social capital. Positive scores for a state suggest social capital levels higher than average, while negative scores indicate a below-average level of social capital. The data displayed in Table 3 indicate that Washington State is *about average* in overall network-based social capital scores (–.038). When compared to other states in the West, Washington scores somewhat higher. Montana and Oregon have higher social capital scores, but Washington State's score is higher than those of Nevada, Alaska, Arizona, California, Idaho, and Utah.

What about variation in network-based social capital within Washington State? Are some counties richer than others with respect to this type of "capital"—a trait shown in many studies to correlate with higher levels of collective action in behalf of shared community goals

Table 3: Network-Based Social Capital Scores for U.S. States[1]

State	Mean	No. of Counties	State	Mean	No. of Counties
Alabama	-.94247	67	Nebraska	1.17583	93
Alaska	-.96884	5	Nevada	-.98276	17
Arizona	-1.52058	15	New Hampshire	.69617	10
Arkansas	-.62678	75	New Jersey	-.26846	21
California	-.42708	58	New Mexico	-.65453	33
Colorado	.57464	63	New York	.17646	62
Connecticut	.54323	8	North Carolina	-.58625	100
Delaware	-.42612	3	North Dakota	2.01996	53
Florida	-.89265	66	Ohio	.42476	88
Georgia	-1.41987	159	Oklahoma	-.23200	77
Idaho	-.38394	44	Oregon	.22675	36
Illinois	.70643	102	Pennsylvania	.17083	67
Indiana	.12158	92	Rhode Island	.32939	5
Iowa	1.31521	99	South Carolina	-1.17862	46
Kansas	1.46926	105	South Dakota	1.79545	66
Kentucky	-.81245	120	Tennessee	-.93035	95
Louisiana	-.54046	64	Texas	-.75784	254
Maine	.86926	16	Utah	-1.03514	29
Maryland	-.35804	24	Vermont	.79796	14
Massachusetts	1.43155	14	Virginia	.14845	134
Michigan	.11274	83	Washington	-.03869	39
Minnesota	1.76876	87	West Virginia	-.56166	55
Mississippi	-.88720	82	Wisconsin	.51446	72
Missouri	.18553	115	Wyoming	1.50388	23
Montana	.99747	56	**Total**	**0.00000**	**3,111**

[1] Hawaii data unavailable

Source: Rapusingha, Goetz , and Freshwater 2006.

and higher quality of life and public policy outcomes (Andrews 2012)? Table 4, containing the summary composite social capital scores for each of the state's 39 counties, indicates that all parts of the Evergreen State feature some counties with high levels of social capital as measured by the Rupasingha et al. index. The two highest network-based social capital scores are found on opposite sides of the Cascade Mountains —namely, in San Juan County (3.19) in the Puget Sound area and in Lincoln County (2.78) in the east-central portion of Washington.

Table 4: Composite Social Capital Scores
for Washington's Counties

(0=National Average, + indicates above average, – indicates below average)

County	Score	County	Score
Adams	–.67	Lewis	–.21
Asotin	–.45	Lincoln	+2.78
Benton	–.61	Mason	–.62
Chelan	+.23	Okanogan	+.02
Clallam	+.12	Pacific	+1.10
Clark	–1.12	Pend Oreille	+.26
Columbia	+1.32	Pierce	–.99
Cowlitz	–.60	San Juan	+3.19
Douglas	–1.03	Skagit	–.28
Ferry	–.30	Skamania	–.45
Franklin	–2.01	Snohomish	–.99
Garfield	+2.61	**Spokane**	**–.51**
Grant	–1.20	Steven	+.34
Grays Harbor	–.35	Thurston	–.19
Island	–.23	Wahkiakum	+.13
Jefferson	+1.35	Walla Walla	–.58
King (Seattle)	**–.27**	Whatcom	–.07
Kitsap	–.21	Whitman	+.35
Kittitas	+.30	Yakima	–1.38
Klickitat	+.28		

Source: The Northeast Regional Center for Rural Development, Pennsylvania State University, 2014.

In summary, social capital is a potential resource arising from the trust-based networks and connections existing among people. Those networks provide a way for citizens to organize and to press claims on governments at all levels. Overall, Washington State is at about the national average in terms of social capital, although it clearly rests near the top of its western state neighbors. Within Washington State there is considerable variation in county social capital levels, with the highest ranking counties spread around the state geographically and differing in terms of geographic size and population. On both the trust-based measure of social capital and the associational density and aggregate civic engagement-based measures of social capital Seattle is higher than its eastern Washington counterpart city of Spokane.

Creative Culture and Vitality

The traditional view of political culture focuses on political attitudes, behavior, and governmental policy and processes. In recent years, though, it has become clear that political culture must also encompass activities and institutions that are not explicitly political but which clearly have noteworthy political implications, what might be called "culture-culture" (Jeannotte 2003). This sense of culture has to do with the mix of attitudes, behaviors, and activities relating to the forms of arts and creativity. Arts and creative activities may not seem to be politically important at first blush, but in recent years the boundaries between the creative arts and a community's economic vitality have become more permeable. Richard Florida (2002), for example, has identified and measured creative lifestyles in American cities, and found that those featuring a large "creative class" tend to be economically better off and politically distinct in terms of both tolerance for alternative lifestyles and innovation in commercial and governmental problem-solving. Other scholars have suggested that a vital and creative arts culture is also important to the development of a community's social capital (Greenwood and Holt 2010). Thus, it is important to understand how Washington State stacks up on creative vitality, and how the 39 counties in the state differ in that regard.

A detailed investigation into the creative vitality of U.S. counties has been conducted by researchers at the Western States Arts Federation (WESTAF), who have developed a Creative Vitality Index (CVI) measure. The CVI is a composite score based in three sets of data: 1) creative industry data collected by the U.S. Commerce Department which reflect the volume of the goods and services related to creative arts, such as art and bookstore sales, art gallery revenues, and performing arts events participation; 2) creative occupation data collected by the U.S. Labor Department which represent scale of employment in occupations reflecting "creative thinking, originality, and fine arts knowledge"; and, 3) nonprofit arts organizations data collected by the U.S. Internal Revenue Service which reveal the "total number of non-profit organizations and arts-active organizations" (WESTAF). The CVI score is constructed so that the national average score is 1.0. Table 5 displays data showing how Washington compares to the other western states on the CVI. The results are in line with our prior analyses of social capital. Washington is near the national average on the Creative Vitality Index, with a score of 1.03. Of the other western states, California is the highest in creative vitality, while Idaho is the lowest. Washington shares its CVI score with its neighbor directly to the south, Oregon.

Table 5: Creative Vitality Index (CVI) Scores for Six Western States

State	Creative Vitality Score
California	1.39
Idaho	.70
Montana	.93
Oregon	1.03
Utah	.83
Washington	**1.03**
U.S. Average	1.00

Source: Western States Arts Federation (WESTAF).

Are there noteworthy variations in the CVI scores among Washington State's 39 counties? Table 6, providing county-level data, indicates clearly that Washington's 39 counties vary significantly in their creative vitality. Only three of the state's counties are found to rank above the national average. Those three are Jefferson County, King County, and San Juan County, all of which are located in the Puget Sound region.

The three counties with the lowest CVI scores (Douglas, Garfield, and Grant) are all found in eastern Washington, in areas not very densely populated and perhaps lacking the critical mass of residents required to provide support for creative activity and performances.

In summary then, two major political culture patterns are present in Washington. The first is that, on the whole, Washington's political culture is dominated by moralistic communitarian values. In terms of both trust-based social capital and associational networks-based social capital, and in terms of creative vitality, Washington is near the average for the country on these measures. However, it is important to note

Table 6: Creative Vitality Index Scores for Washington's Counties

(National Average Score = 1.00)

Adams	.168	Lewis	.334
Asotin	.353	Lincoln	.293
Benton	.662	Mason	.363
Chelan	.891	Okanogan	.423
Clallam	.622	Pacific	.344
Clark	.645	Pend Oreille	.244
Columbia	.566	Pierce	.647
Cowlitz	.341	San Juan	2.137
Douglas	.130	Skagit	.559
Ferry	.296	Skamania	.245
Franklin	.189	Snohomish	.550
Garfield	.182	**Spokane**	**.756**
Grant	.207	Stevens	.273
Grays Harbor	.358	Thurston	.786
Island	.734	Wahkiakum	.268
Jefferson	1.403	Walla Walla	.590
King (Seattle)	**2.080**	Whatcom	.758
Kitsap	.656	Whitman	.695
Kittitas	.432	Yakima	.396
Klickitat	.605		

Source: WESTAF.

that their distribution across the state is not uniform. Hence, the note-worthy second pattern to observe is that significant differences exist *within* Washington in regard to both social capital and creative vitality. It should come as no surprise that Washingtonians who live in central or eastern Washington must have very different political lives than do citizens who live in the King County and the Puget Sound region. Higher social capital, more trusting attitudes, and greater presence of creative vitality characterize the major cities—Seattle in the west, and Spokane in the east—that anchor the state's population on either side of the Cascade Mountain Range. In a direct comparison, however, Seattle outpaces Spokane in social capital networks, trust attitudes, and cultural capital. The different political lives in the regions surrounding Seattle and Spokane are at least in part a direct reflection of the political cultures present in these two areas.

The Public Agenda

What is the impact of political culture differences on how citizens view important questions about how government ought to operate? In the 2010 general election the state's voters were confronted with two important ballot initiatives that clearly reflect central dimensions of political culture. The first, Initiative Measure 1053, imposed a "super majority" (75 percent approval) requirement upon the state legislature for "any increases in taxes or fees." Initiative 1053 passed resoundingly with a 63.75 percent of the statewide vote. It is reasonable to interpret the strong support for that measure as an expression of public distrust of and cynicism toward government and politics, a sentiment widely present across the entire country (Hetherington 2005). The second is Initiative Measure 1098 which represents a form of "Robin Hood" tax. That measure would have imposed an income tax on "the wealthy," defined as those individuals with an adjusted gross annual income of $200,000+, and for joint-filers with an adjusted annual income of $400,000+ (Franko, Tolbert, and Witko 2013). Initiative Measure 1098 received support from only 35.85 percent of the state's voters. It too can be seen as representing cynical or mistrustful views of government activity in the economic sphere, and as a form of opposition to using the increased tax revenues resulting for the support of existing and new state government activities—and ultimately an increase in taxation from this toehold of an income tax.

Even with the clear majorities supporting Measure 1053 and opposing Measure 1098, substantial variation was seen across the 39 counties of the state. The super majority measure received more than 75 percent support from voters in a number of counties in eastern Washington (e.g., Columbia, Douglas, Ferry, Garfield, Grant, Lewis, Lincoln, Pend Oreille and Stevens); in contrast, fewer than 60 percent of the citizens supported that anti-government measure in the Puget Sound area counties of King, Jefferson, San Juan, and Thurston. Likewise, the Robin Hood Tax measure received more than 40 percent support in the western Washington counties of Jefferson, King, San Juan, and Whatcom, and less than 25 percent support in the eastern Washington counties of Adams, Benton, Columbia, Douglas, Franklin, Grant, Lewis, and Yakima. On both measures, there are statistically significant differences between counties on the west side of the Cascades (mean = 66.8 percent on the supermajority measure and 35.5 percent on the tax measure) and those on the east side of the mountains (mean = 73.8 percent on the supermajority measure and 26.7 percent on the tax measures). Moreover, differences in county levels of support for those measures are clearly rooted in the social capital levels of the counties themselves. Counties with high social capital levels were significantly less likely to support the supermajority measure ($r = -.45$, $p = .002$), and were significantly more likely to support the "tax the rich" measure ($r = .38$, $p = .008$).

In addition to looking at economic and tax issues, it also is informative to look at potential cultural divisions over *social issues*. To do so, we examine voting on three statewide ballot initiatives: the 2012 referendum on marriage for same-sex couples (Initiative Measure 74), the 2012 initiative legalizing marijuana (Initiative Measure 502), and the 1998 vote relating to affirmative action (Initiative Measure 200). We also examine the 2012 vote for Supreme Court Justice Position 8 for which Justice Steven Gonzalez was a candidate. Justice Gonzalez was appointed to the bench by Governor Christine Gregoire in 2011 with considerable fanfare related to the promotion of diversity into the state's principal public institutions. Justice Gonzalez represented the first Latino-surnamed person to serve on Washington's highest court. He had served with distinction as a King County Superior Court Judge for ten years prior to his judicial appointment, was judged as exceptionally well qualified by all of the state's bar associations conducting judicial candidate assessments for the 2012 election, and virtually all of the state's major newspaper editorial boards endorsed his candidacy. Justice Gonzalez ran as an incumbent in a required retention election, and was challenged by a Kitsap County attorney named Bruce Danielson who had no prior judicial experience and whose involvement in public affairs up to that time was three failed attempts at election to local government office. While Justice Gonzalez was retained in the election, he was not the majority choice of citizens in 29 of the state's 39 counties where the unknown Danielson, who did no campaigning, won a majority of votes. The overwhelming majorities gained in the Puget Sound area placed Justice Gonzalez into office.

The county-level voting data in these four statewide contests were highly intercorrelated and were subjected to a cluster analysis, a statistical technique associated with factor analysis which can be used to identify which counties are most similar to each other across these four votes. The average intercorrelation across the 39 counties for the pairs of variables is r = .84 (p = .01), suggesting the presence of sets of counties very similar to each other, but with those sets themselves being quite different. Indeed, Table 8 shows that there are distinct groupings of counties falling into one of two clusters, one of which we can label the "Puget Sound Policy Cluster" and the second labeled "The Other Washington Policy Cluster" (Watkins 2008). As a reliability check on the current saliency of these two clusters, the 2016 election results for U.S. President are added to the four policy votes. Table 7 results show that only one county in the "Puget Sound" cluster (Snohomish) gave Donald Trump 50-plus percent support, and only six of the 29 "Other Washington" cluster counties gave him less than 50 percent of the vote. It is clear from examining the vote patterns in the two clusters that there are large and significant cultural differences between them. There are quite clearly "two Washingtons."

Table 7: Political Culture-Reflecting Policy Preference Clusters in Washington State

Counties in "Puget Sound" Cultural Policy Cluster (I)

	% Yes Marijuana Legislation	% Yes Same Sex Marriage	% Yes Gonzalez Election	% Yes Affirmative Action	% Yes Trump
Island	56%	52%	57%	39%	43%
Jefferson	65	64	63	44	30
King	63	67	77	48	22
Kitsap	56	54	56	40	39
Pierce	54	50	63	38	42
San Juan	68	71	64	48	25
Skagit	55	50	48	38	44
Snohomish	55	53	61	41	54
Thurston	56	56	60	44	36
Whatcom	57	55	57	42	37
MEAN %	**59%**	**57%**	**61%**	**42%**	**37%**

Counties in "The Other Washington" Cultural Policy Cluster (2)

	% Yes Marijuana Legislation	% Yes Same Sex Marriage	% Yes Gonzalez Election	% Yes Affirmative Action	% Yes Trump
Adams	39%	28%	32%	32%	66%
Asotin	49	37	34	35	59
Benton	44	37	44	32	59
Chelan	52	42	39	29	54
Clallam	55	48	51	36	48
Clark	50	47	46	30	46
Columbia	46	32	33	33	69
Cowlitz	46	42	39	31	53
Douglas	49	36	33	29	62
Ferry	51	35	39	29	61
Franklin	39	31	39	31	56
Garfield	37	28	34	33	68
Grant	45	31	33	29	65
Grays Harbor	54	46	43	38	50
Kittitas	48	46	42	35	53
Klickitat	50	42	41	29	54
Lewis	45	35	38	32	64
Lincoln	42	28	37	31	72
Mason	55	48	45	38	49
Okanogan	51	40	37	32	56
Pacific	54	47	44	44	50
Pend Oreille	49	33	40	27	64
Skamania	53	45	45	29	52
Spokane	52	44	49	35	50
Stevens	47	31	39	30	67
Wahkiakum	49	42	41	30	57
Walla Walla	45	40	42	57	54
Whitman	52	51	47	44	43
Yakima	42	36	36	28	54
MEAN	**47%**	**39%**	**38%**	**31%**	**57%**

Source: Authors.

What are the characteristics of these distinct clusters of Washington counties? Table 8 compares the Puget Sound cluster and the Other Washington cluster of counties on several dimensions, including important demographic characteristics, the types of organizational networks present in these two areas, and the religious composition of these clusters of counties.

Table 8: Differences between the Other Washington and Puget Sound County Clusters*

Variable	The Other Washington	Puget Sound	Statistical Significance
ORGANIZATIONAL & ASSOCIATIONAL NETWORKS			
Civic Groups Per Capita	2.26	2.19	ns
Religious Groups Per Capita	7.72	5.82	ns
Professional Groups Per Capita	.17	.36	.04
Business Groups Per Capita	.68	.75	ns
Labor Groups Per Capita	.52	.60	ns
RELIGIOUS AFFILIATIONS			
Evangelicals Per 1,000 (2010)	116	111	ns
Mainline Protestants Per 1,000 (2010)	51	49	ns
Catholics Per Capita (2010)	120	96	ns
Religious Diversity (2000)	.69	.71	ns
DEMOGRAPHIC CHARACTERISTICS			
% College Degree	20.2	32.1	.000
Median Income	$24,185	$30,985	.000
% Racial/Ethnic Diversity (Hero Index)	.32	.36	ns
% Democrat 2012	40.96	58.1	.000
Population Change, 2000 to 2010	+.12	+.14	ns
Average Age	38.2	39.1	ns
Sex ratio	1.0007	.9910	ns
% Poverty Households	16.6	10.8	.000

*Per capita measures are the ratio of individuals to the population multiplied by a constant for all counties.

The data in Table 9 indicate that there is much similarity between the two regions. The organizational and associational networks present in both do not differ greatly, with somewhat greater presence of professional groups in the Puget Sound area. Likewise, with respect to religious composition, racial and ethnic diversity, recent population change (both growing at virtually the same rate), gender, and age, the two areas are nearly identical. However, in terms of formal education, median family income, households living in poverty, and political party preferences, the differences are stark. The Puget Sound counties are populated by citizens who are significantly better educated, more prosperous, and living in communities where the presence of persistent poverty serves as a constant reminder of the need for active governmental action to address pressing social needs. It is this combination of higher formal education and considerably more advantaged income status within the social context of chronic need that may explain the socially and economically more liberal Democratic Party preferences found in the Puget Sound region.

To explore this supposition Table 9 compares the two clusters of counties in terms of their political orientations based on a 2015 (October 13–15) survey (*The Elway Poll*) of the Washington public, with respondents grouped into the Puget Sound and Other Washington areas of residence. Overall, there are consistent differences between the two clusters; while statistically significant, they are not particularly large in magnitude, indicating that substantial diversity is present throughout the state. The Puget Sound cluster is more likely than the Other Washington cluster to be Democratic in party identification (36 percent v. 28 percent) and less likely to be Republican (20 percent v. 28 percent). While Washingtonians in both clusters say they are frustrated or angry about the federal government (73 percent v. 86 percent), that posture is more prevalent in the Other Washington counties. Moreover, the citizens residing in the Puget Sound cluster counties are somewhat less likely to believe government is a threat to rights (40 percent v. 48 percent), less likely to self-identify as conservative (40 percent v. 50 percent), a little more likely to be liberal on social issues (49 percent v. 43 percent), less likely to be conservative on fiscal issues (53 percent v. 62 percent), and slightly less likely to agree that the government controls too much (34 percent v. 41 percent). Consistent with the moralistic political culture theme, the Puget Sound residents are more likely to agree that "government should guarantee every person enough to eat and a place to sleep" (53 percent v. 47 percent).

In the 2016 elections, the voting patterns of the counties also tended to cluster (Fisher 2016). Donald Trump carried 27 of the 39 counties, and received 38 percent of the vote. Patty Murray carried 15 counties and got 59 percent of the vote, and Jay Inslee carried 10 counties and received 54 percent of the vote. Thus, 28 of the 39 counties voted a majority Republican for at least two of the three offices of governor, senator, and president, and of those, 22 voted Republican for all three. No county gave Donald Trump a majority and at the same time failed to give a majority to at least one of the other two offices. Whitman County was the only one to vote Republican for governor and senate but not for president. On the other hand, nine counties voted for a Democrat majority for all three offices. All nine of those counties border on the Puget Sound.

Table 9: Political Orientations of the "Puget Sound" and "Other Washington" Clusters: 2015

	Puget Sound	Other Washington
Democrat	36%	28%
Angry/Frustrated about Federal Government	73%	86%
Say Government a Threat to Rights	40%	50%
Conservative Self-Label	40%	50%
Liberal on Social Issues	49%	43%
Conservative on Fiscal Issues	53%	62%
Strongly Agree that Government Controls Too Much	34%	41%
Agree that Government Should Ensure Food & Shelter	53%	47%
N=	(339)	(162)

Source: The Elway Poll (October 13-15, 2015). Sample derived from registered voter list. Data collected by telephone survey implemented by trained interviewers, and included both land lines and cell phones (28 percent). Demographic and geographic breakdowns indicate good representation statewide (King County=31 percent, Other Western Washington=49 percent, and Eastern Washington=20 percent) and in regard to gender (46 percent male, 54 percent female). 500 persons were interviewed, and the margin of sampling error for percents reported is +/-4.5 percent at the 95 percent confidence level.

The moralistic political culture characteristic of high social capital states (Putnam 2000; 346–47) and the social inclusiveness characteristic of areas with a major presence of creative class professions and businesses appear to lead to a distinctly moralistic political culture in the Puget Sound cluster of counties. In contrast, The Other Washington counties manifest a distinctly socially and economically conservative Republic Party preference and reflect much more of the individualistic political culture present in the political heritage of the Evergreen State. In some sense it might be said that Washington's MI classification by Elazar has, over recent decades, become bifurcated into two distinct subcultures, with the moralistic element predominating in the Puget Sound area and the individualistic element predominating in The Other Washington.

Conclusion

The state's moralistic political culture heritage, supplemented by an individualistic sub-strain favoring a heavy reliance upon voluntary compliance and free enterprise, invites high expectations. This predominantly moralistic political culture was brought to Washington by early settlers, and this social equity-promoting perspective on politics was reflected in—and received reinforcement from—the Populist and Progressive reform movements which swept across the American West at the turn of the century. This moralistic political culture finds clear expression in the Washington State Constitution and in amendments providing for direct legislation, and the popular election of executive offices and the judiciary. It clearly continues to exert a powerful contemporary influence in the Puget Sound region of the state. This is an area with a window on the Pacific Rim and global markets where there has been very strong population growth since the 1970s. That growth was occasioned by both in-state migration and out-of-state immigration to the world-class University of Washington and the high tech industries whose knowledge-based workforces are attracted to the prevailing "post-materialist values" (Inglehart 1990) and the active celebration of creativity in the greater Seattle area (Florida 2002). This region has come to dominate politically, winning statewide political contests and greatly influencing the operation of the executive, legislative, and judicial branches of state government.

The Other Washington has also grown robustly in population and ethnic diversity alike in recent decades, and the established and newly vibrant agriculture, viniculture, ranching, and forestry sectors therein reflect the individualistic political culture sub-strain of the state's historical legacy. The Other Washington finds its most forceful political representation in the state legislature. The moralistic-dominant and individualistic-secondary political culture in Washington is reflected in diverse ways in the politics of Washington, and many of these manifestations will be discussed in other chapters in this volume.

References

Andrews, Rhys. 2012. "Social Capital and Public Service Performance: A Review of the Evidence." *Public Policy and Administration* 27:49–67.

Bannerman, Sara, and Blayne Haggert. 2015. "Historical Institutionalism in Communication Studies." *Communication Theory* 25:1–22.

Campbell, Angus, Philip E. Converse, Warren E. Miller, and Donald E. Stokes. 1960. *The American Voter*. New York: John Wiley and Sons.

Coffee, Hilde, and Benny Geys. 2005. "Institutional Performance and Social Capital: An Application to the Local Government Level." *Journal of Urban Affairs* 27:485–501.

Coleman, James S. 1990. *Foundations of Social Theory*. Cambridge, MA: Belknap Press.

David, Paul A. 2007. "Path Dependence: A Foundational Concept for Historical Social Science." *Cliometrica* 1:91–114.

Elazar, Daniel J. 1984. *American Federalism: A View from the States*. New York: Harper and Row.

Elazar, Daniel J. 1994. *The American Mosaic: The Impact of Space, Time, and Culture on American Politics*. Boulder, CO: Westview Press.

Elway Poll. elwayresearch.com/elwaypoll.html.

Field, John. 2003. *Social Capital*. London: Routledge.

Fisher, Patrick I. 2016. "Definitely Not Moralistic: State Political Culture and Support for Donald Trump in the Race for the 2016 Republican Presidential Nomination." *PS: Political Science and Politics* 49:743–47.

Florida, Richard. 2002. *The Rise of the Creative Class*. New York: Basic Books.

Franko, William, Caroline J. Tolbert and Christopher Witko. 2013. "Inequality, Self-Interest and Public Support for "Robin Hood' Tax Policies." *Political Research Quarterly* 66:923–37.

Fukuyama, Francis. 1995. *Trust: The Social Virtues and the Creation of Prosperity*. New York: Free Press Paperbacks.

Greenwood, Daphne T. and Richard P. F. Holt. 2010. *Local Economic Development in the 21st Century: Quality of Life and Sustainability*. Armonk, NY: M.E. Sharpe.

Hendryx, Michael S., Melissa M. Ahern, Nicholas P. Lovrich and Arthur M. McCurdy. 2002. "Access to Health Care and Community Social Capital." *Health Services Research* 35:307–18.

Hetherington, Marc J. 2005. *Why Trust Matters: Declining Political Trust and the Demise of American Liberalism*. Princeton, NJ: Princeton University Press.

Inglehart, Ronald. 1990. *Culture Shift in Advanced Industrial Society*. Princeton, NJ: Princeton University Press.

Jeannotte, M. Sharon. 2003. "Singing Alone? The Contribution of Cultural Capital to Social Cohesion and Sustainable Communities." *International Journal of Cultural Policy* 9:35–49.

Kawachi, Ichiro, S.V. Subramenian, and Daniel Kim, editors. 2010. *Social Capital and Health*. New York: Springer.

Ladd, Everett Carll. 1999. *The Ladd Report*. New York: The Free Press.

Mead, Lawrence M. 2004. "State Political Culture and Welfare Reform." *The Policy Studies Journal* 32:271–96.

Nardulli, Peter F. 1990. "Political Subcultures in the American States: An Empirical Examination of Elazar's Formulation." *American Politics Quarterly* 18:287–315.

Northeast Regional Center for Rural Development. Department of Agricultural Economics, Sociology, and Education. Pennsylvania State University. aese.psu. edu/nercrd.

Paxton, Pamela. 1999. "Is Social Capital Declining in the United States? A Multiple Indicator Assessment." *American Journal of Sociology* 105:88–127.

Pierce, John C., Nicholas P. Lovrich, and C. David Moon. 2002. "Social Capital and Government Performance: An Analysis of 20 American Cities." *Public Performance and Management Review* 25:381–97.

Pierce, John C., Nicholas P. Lovrich, and William W. Budd. 2016. "Social Capital, Institutional Performance, and Sustainability in Italy's Regions: Still Evidence of Enduring Historical Effects?" *Social Science Journal* 53:271–81.

Putnam, Robert. 2000. *Bowling Alone: The Collapse and Revival of American Community*. New York: Simon and Schuster.

Rupasingha, Anil, Stephen J. Goetz, and David Freshwater. 2006. "The Production of Social Capital in U.S. Counties." *Journal of Socio-Economics* 35:83–101.

Sarigil, Zeki. 2015. "Showing the Path to Path Dependence: The Habitual Path." *European Political Science Review* 7:221–42.

Sharkansky, Ira. 1969. *The Politics of Taxing and Spending*. Indianapolis, IN: Bobbs-Merrill.

Uslaner, Eric M. 2002. *The Moral Foundations of Trust*. New York: Cambridge University Press.

Watkins, Marilyn P. 2008. *A Stimulus and Recovery Plan for Washington State: Blueprint for Change*. Seattle, WA: Economic Opportunity Institute.

Western States Arts Federation (WESTAF). Creative Vitality Index. cvi.westaf.org.

Williams, Dmitri. 2006. "On and Off the 'Net: Scales for Social Capital in an Online Era." *Journal of Computer-Mediated Communication* 11:593–628.

Woolcook, Michael. 2010. "The Rise and Routinization of Social Capital: 1988–2008." *Annual Review of Political Science* 13:469–89.

CHAPTER 2

Elections in Washington

Todd Donovan

Elections are a barometer that measures public sentiments on a regular basis. Most of all, elections are the primary method for holding government accountable. Given Washington State's populist and progressive roots, elections are conducted somewhat differently than in other states. How does this affect elections, and what do election results say about the partisan balance in Washington?

Unique Aspects of Washington Elections

The United States Supreme Court sets basic parameters for states to follow when conducting elections. Within these bounds, states determine who is allowed to vote and how voter registration is managed, establish criteria for drawing electoral districts, and set rules about who appears on the ballot. States also have some discretion in defining how (or if) campaign finances are regulated. Washington has adopted a number of election rules—some by direct democracy—that are rather unique. These rules have consequences for who participates in elections, and for who wins or loses.

Voter Registration and Turnout

One unique aspect of Washington's elections is voter registration. All states but North Dakota require that residents register prior to voting so the state may validate that a person is eligible to vote. States differ in terms of how far in advance of an election new voters must register, and in terms of how voters register.[1] Voter registration in Washington differs from other states on both of these features. Most states require registration at least three weeks before an election; however, fifteen states allow registration on election day.[2] Washington does not provide election day registration (EDR), but it does have one of the nation's more liberal rules for registration since it allows new voters to register within one week of an election.

Shorter advance registration requirements correspond with higher voter turnout (Rosenstone and Hansen 2003). One study suggests that EDR may have a modest effect on promoting turnout in some states (a 4 percent increase), but that the effect is absent in other states (Hanmer 2009). EDR has been proposed for Washington, but some county auditors fear they lack resources needed to process registrations on election day (Reed 2007). Nonetheless, voter turnout in Washington's elections was at least 5 percent higher than the national average from 2006 to 2016.

Registration without Parties

Registration in Washington also differs from many other states. Thirty-one states allow voters to declare a party affiliation when registering. Washington does not. This record of the voter's party affiliation can be used to determine how (or if) a person can participate in primary elections. Primaries determine which candidates appear on general election ballots in November. In most states, voters receive a primary ballot listing candidates from a single party. For example, voters registered as Republican receive a ballot that only lists Republican primary candidates. Partisan registration is one mechanism that insures a party's loyal voters pick the party's nominees in November. The Washington legislature adopted partisan registration in 1921, but voters repealed it by popular referendum in 1922. This means that primary elections are conducted without information about voters' partisan affiliations.

Primary Elections in Washington

Most states can be classified as having closed or open primaries. In 25 states, Republican primaries are closed to Democrats, and Democratic primaries are closed to Republicans. In some closed primary states, independent voters are allowed to pick one party's ballot and vote. Twenty-two other states open their primaries so any voter can pick one party's ballot, regardless of whether or not they are registered with a party (Donovan, Mooney, and Smith 2011, 158). In these 46 states "closed" or "open" primary ballots list candidates from just one party.

Washington, California, Louisiana, and Nebraska do not fit into these categories. In 1934, an initiative from the Washington Grange directed the legislature to adopt a primary where candidates from all parties appeared on a single ballot. With no record of voters' partisan affiliation, all voters received the same primary ballot. This meant a voter could support a Republican as the nominee for Governor and then cross over and support a Democrat as nominee for U.S. Representative, and so on. The Democratic candidate for each office with the most votes (regardless of their overall place of finish) would appear on the November ballot. Likewise, the top Republican would win a spot on the November ballot.

The Blanket Primary: 1935–2002

Washington used this "blanket primary" system from 1935 to 2002. Alaska used it briefly, and California did in one election (1998). In 2000, the U.S. Supreme Court ruled that the blanket primary unconstitutionally forced the Democratic Party to let independents and Republicans pick their nominees, and forced Republicans to let non-Republicans pick Republican nominees (*California Democratic Party et al. v. Jones* 530 U.S. 567, 2000). The court nullified Washington's blanket primary when ruling a political party had a First Amendment right to determine who nominated its candidates.

The Pick-a-Party Primary: 2004–2006

Since 2002 the state has used two different primary election systems. In 2004 the legislature passed a "pick-a-party" open primary law. This system allowed any voter to select a party's ballot, and participate only in that party's primary. Under this system, a voter could not select nominees from different parties for different offices. The pick-a-party system was used again in 2006, but it was short-lived.

The Top-Two Primary: 2008–Present

Voters approved another Grange initiative in November 2004 that established a "top-two" primary. This sent the first and second place candidates for each office to the November ballot regardless of their party. The top-two ballot places all candidates on one ballot and allows any voter to participate. Candidates can list a party they "prefer," but the ballot states that a candidate's party preference does not imply that a party nominated, endorsed, or approved the candidate. In addition to stating they prefer "Democrat" and "Republican," candidates have said they prefer the "Lower Taxes Party," the "Reluctant Republican Party," the "Constitution Party," and the "Independent Democratic Party." The "top-two" aspect means that two Democrats (or two Republicans) can end up facing each other in the general election if they placed first and second in a primary.

As of 2016, all but one top-two primary for statewide offices produced general election contests between candidates who said they preferred the Democratic Party and candidates who said they preferred the Republican party. The exception was the 2016 primary for Treasure, when three Democrats divide 51 percent of the vote but placed behind two Republicans. Most state legislative contests have also been between a Democrat and a Republican. However, some legislative primaries in eastern Washington produce general election contests between two Republicans, and some primaries in western Washington produced contests in November between two Democrats.

Table 1: Percent WA State House Seats Contested in General Elections

	% seats D vs. R	% Seats Two Major Party Candidates		% seats D vs. R	% Seats Two Major Party Candidates
1968–1995	87%*	87	2006	73+	73
1996	83*	83	2008	66^	73
1998	70*	70	2010	66^	73
2000	77*	77	2012	60^	72
2002	66*	66	2014	60^	66
2004	84+	84	2016	61^	67

*Blanket Primary
+Pick a Party Primary
^Top-Two Primary

Some argue that electoral competition between two parties is important because it may increase the likelihood that elected officials will be responsive to the public (e.g., Key 1949). Others note that electoral competition can dampen public corruption (Meier and Holbrook 1992; Hill

2003), increase public attention to local campaign news (Bowler and Donovan 2011), and increase voter turnout (Cox and Munger 1989).

Electoral competition in state elections has been declining for decades (Ansolabehere et al. 2007; Neimi et al. 2006). Reduced competition may reflect higher costs of campaigns, increased incumbent advantages, types of primaries used, or the way districts are drawn. Under the blanket primary, Washington's legislative elections were among the most competitive in the nation (Hamm and Moncrief 1999). Washington still ranks among the states with more contested elections (McGlennon 2009), but as Table 1 illustrates, electoral competition declined in Washington while the blanket primary was still in use, and has continued to decline. Under the top-two system some of the remaining competition reflects intra-party contests (D vs. D or R vs. R), rather than Democrats running against Republicans.

The Effects of Primary Election Rules

Washington has a long tradition of primary rules that open participation to all voters. This conflicts with efforts by parties to assert more control over who participates. But what difference does it make if participation in primaries is open to everyone?

Proponents of open and top-two systems suggest that if primaries shut out independent voters, "hard core" partisans may elect candidates who appeal to only a narrow portion of the electorate. Closed partisan primaries could leave general election voters facing choices between Democrats from the far left competing against Republicans from the far right. Washington-style primaries, by encouraging independent and moderate voters to participate, may help "moderate" candidates win elections (Fiorina et al. 2005, 107; also see Cain and Gerber 2002).

Moderates, Mavericks, and the Median Voter

The state's primary rules are cited as one reason Washington occasionally elects people who do not fit standard partisan categories. The Democrats' 1976 gubernatorial candidate, Dixie Lee Ray, is one example. Ray had limited formal interaction with the party prior to the primary, but she defeated three other Democrats in a close race with just 24 percent of the vote.[3] There is no survey data to test who supported Ray in the primary, but the fact that she was elected Governor by a large margin in November suggests she had wide appeal among voters in both parties. Observers also point out other moderates elected in Washington, such as former Republican Governor Daniel Evans (1965–1977) and former Democratic Senator Henry "Scoop" Jackson. Jackson is cited as a classic "maverick" who was not easy to pigeon-hole as a partisan (Borger 2002). Yet the blanket primary system also produced many candidates who might be seen as highly predictable partisans (e.g. former Democratic Governor Mike Lowry or former U.S. Representative Jim McDermott).

One study of the effect of different primary rules found that members of Congress from states with closed primaries cast votes that were further from the policy preferences of the median voter in their district. Representatives from Washington and other states with more open rules cast votes more in line with the typical voter (Gerber and Morton 1998, 321). This suggests that open primaries and top-two systems do produce different candidates than closed primaries. It also suggests that candidates who win in closed primaries have a greater incentive to cast votes that appeal to their narrow partisan base. But as noted below, political parties in Washington state are among the most polarized in the United States.

Presidential Primaries and Caucuses

Presidential primaries are governed by different rules. The state and national committees from each party determine when and how delegates are selected for their party's national convention. Candidates who win the most delegates nationally win their party's presidential nomination. Most states use primaries to award these delegates. Washington has used a mix of precinct caucuses and primary elections. A citizen initiative led to the use of presidential primaries from 1992 to 2008. The parties have been reluctant to award many of Washington's delegates based on primaries that were open to all voters, and the state's major parties have long relied on using precinct caucuses to selecting most delegates. As a result, Washington's presidential primary, particularly for Democrats, has been little more than a beauty contest. The presidential primary was suspended in 2012 in order to save money then resumed in 2016, although only Republicans used it to allocate delegates. In 2016, Democrats had the awkward experience of having Bernie Sanders win 73 percent support in low-turnout caucuses, and then having Hillary Clinton win a meaningless primary that far more people voted in.

Voting by Mail: "Election Day" Can Go for Weeks

Nationally, a growing proportion of votes are now cast in advance of election day. It is estimated that one-third voted early in the 2016 presidential election, either through the mail or at early voting stations (Donovan 2018).

However, Oregon and Washington are the only states where elections are conducted almost exclusively by mail. Oregon conducted the nation's first statewide all-mail election in 1996 (Southwell 2004). The transition to elections by mail in Washington was gradual. In 2000, just over 50 percent of votes were cast by mail, yet most counties continued to staff polling places on election day. A bill passed in 2011 ended Pierce County's status as Washington's last county with voting at polling places.

Ballots are mailed two weeks prior to an election. Unlike Oregon, where votes are counted only if they arrive back by election day, Washington will count a ballot that bears an election day postmark. Ballots dropped in the mail on election day (or just before election day) can take days to meander through the postal system. This, combined with the fact that a substantial proportion of voters wait until election day to vote, means that it can take several days (or longer) to know the winner of close elections.

In 2016, officials were able to count just 87 percent of votes a week after election night. It is not uncommon for candidates who had a lead on election night to end up losing after several days of counting. Given King County's large population and the heavy concentration of Democratic voters there, late arriving ballots in statewide races can tilt toward liberal and Democratic candidates. Unfortunately, legitimate ballots counted after election day from Washington, California, and other states fueled false narratives about election fraud, which were propagated by Donald Trump and others with no empirical evidence to support the claims.

The Effects of Voting by Mail

What are the effects of voting by mail? Regardless of when votes are finally totaled, mail elections change campaigns. Early voting requires campaigns to target events and advertising differently. Mail elections may also increase turnout while not necessarily changing who participates. Turnout increases because mail ballots make voting more convenient. Studies suggest that participation increases among older, wealthier, well-educated, white people—people who already vote at the highest rates (Karp and Banducci 2000; Berinsky 2005). In Oregon, the increase in turnout appeared to be most pronounced in local races that generated limited interest. Turnout in vote by mail presidential elections, in contrast, was just 2 percent greater than in presidential elections conducted at polling places (Karp and Banducci 2000, 228). After five years of use in Oregon, voting by mail was widely popular— over 75 percent of voters approved of it (Southwell 2004). Attitudes may still be crystallizing in Washington. Surveys conducted in King County in 2006 (before the change to vote by mail) found voters were split when asked if they supported the change. Republicans were less supportive than Democrats, in part because of lingering suspicions about the contentious recount of the 2004 governor's race.

Campaign Finance

Campaign finance regulations also affect how elections are conducted. Washington has some of the nation's most detailed rules for disclosure of campaign revenue and spending. Another voter-approved initiative, I-276 in 1972, established the state's Public Disclosure Commission (PDC). Candidates for state and local contests must file detailed weekly reports to the PDC of contributions received and monthly reports of how money is spent. Reports must be filed more frequently immediately prior to the general election. Yet another initiative (I-134 of 1992) established a rather porous set of contribution limits for partisan races. As of 2016, contributions to judicial candidates and candidates for state office from individuals, interest groups, unions, and corporations were limited to $2,000 per primary and general election. Contributions to legislative candidates and local candidates were limited to $1,000 per election. But Washington's limits do not really constrain what can be given to parties, nor what parties can spend. Any party committee (state, county, legislative district) can collect "exempt" funds without limit and direct unlimited funds to any of their other party committees.

Effects of Campaign Finance Rules

One effect of these rules is that parties play a more significant role in financing elections in Washington than they do in many other states. Another is that citizens and media have more access to information about the sources and uses of campaign money. But it is not always easy to track campaign cash. Millions of dollars of Political Action

Committee (PAC) funding ends up in a few legislative races after first being donated to party and candidate accounts. That money can be transferred again to a different party fund, before finally being bundled into large gifts to a candidate in a close race. Interest groups can also target these rare races directly, spending as much or more than they do through parties independently, with their spending even harder to track as the create shell groups to spend money through.

Figure 1: Campaign Spending in Washington Elections

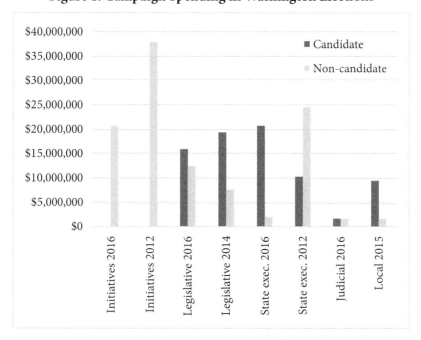

Sources: Washington Public Disclosure Commission (PDC).

U.S. Supreme Court decisions such as *Citizens United* make it nearly impossible to limit how much additional money interest groups may spend on elections as long as these "independent expenditures" are not formally coordinated with a campaign.[4] Big spending groups sympathetic to the major parties often use generic names to mask their identity while running ads. In the most recent open seat gubernatorial race at the time of this writing, "Our Washington" used over $8 million independent expenditures to attack Republican candidate Rob McKenna. The vast majority of "Our Washington" money came from unions and Democratic party organizations with Washington, DC, zip codes. Likewise, over $9 million in independent expenditures were directed against the Democratic candidate, Jay Inslee, from the Washington, DC-based Republican Governors Association.

Figure 2: Trends in Spending per Legislative Candidate 1992–2016, inflation adjusted dollars.

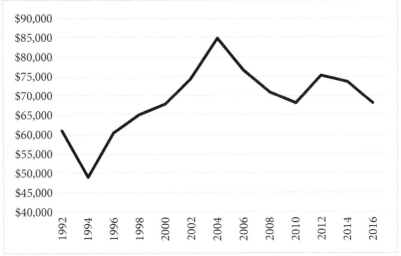

Source: Washington Public Disclosure Commission (PDC).

Washington's state disclosure rules have generally made the sources of campaign spending more transparent, but regulations do not limit total spending. In 2016 over $144 million was spent on state and local elections in Washington, with most of this money coming from businesses, PACs, political parties, and unions. This is down from $166 million in 2012. Figure 1 illustrates that much of this spending went to initiative campaigns and gubernatorial races. Figure 1 also illustrates money spent by candidates' campaigns and by non-candidate groups. Non-candidate groups such as political parties and independent interest groups are not subject to contribution limits. As such, it is not uncommon for initiative campaigns and gubernatorial contests to have a single donor (or party committee) providing millions of dollars. Non-candidate spending can match or exceed candidate spending in some contests. Total spending on state legislative contests was fairly constant between 2010 and 2016, with roughly $28 million raised for the 2016 races. Figure 2 illustrates trends in spending per legislative candidate. On average, about $70,000 has been spent, per candidate, in state legislative races. This figure masks the fact that a disproportional amount of spending is concentrated on a handful of legislative contests in the rare competitive district. Spending in some competitive senate contests has topped the $1 million level.

Redistricting

Within bounds set by federal courts, states determine how state legislative and U.S. Congressional districts are drawn. In most states, maps that define districts must be approved by the legislature then signed by the governor.

As a result of population growth and mobility, the number of people in existing districts changes. Washington added more than 800,000 residents over the decade ending in 2010. State legislative districts in the state's fastest growing areas such as Benton, Clark, Cowlitz, and Walla Walla Counties and east King County ended up with as many as 30,000 to 45,000 more people than districts in slower growing places like Pacific County and Spokane. The population of congressional districts also became unbalanced. Without redistricting, people in heavily populated districts would end up with less representation per person than people in sparsely populated areas.

This is why states redraw district maps at least once every ten years after new Census data are available. The last redistricting was done in 2011; the next will be done in 2021. Much was at stake in 2011. For example, some of the fastest growth in Washington has been in eastern and southern King County districts with competitive elections (e.g., the 41st, 45th, and 47th legislative districts circa 2010) and in safe Republican areas (e.g., the 5th legislative district) by 2010. Some neighboring districts that were heavily Democratic grew much slower (e.g., Seattle-area 11th, 37th, and 46th legislative districts and the 32nd legislative district in Shoreline). If "surplus" Republican voters from the over-populated, safely Republican 5th legislative district were transferred to neighboring, competitive districts, Republicans could win more seats. Conversely, if new districts placed parts of fast growing Republican strongholds into solidly Democratic Seattle districts,

Democrats would have the advantage. The stakes were even greater in 2011 because Washington gained a new 10th congressional district.

Given such stakes, redistricting tends to be a highly politicized process. But redistricting in Washington differs from the national norm. In most states, laws that define district maps are adopted through the normal legislative process. A party with majorities in both houses that also controls the governor's office can take advantage of the minority party by gerrymandering districts to maximize the number of safe seats for themselves. The U.S. Supreme Court simply requires that districts must be drawn such that they are "contiguous" and equal in population. This leaves room for a good deal of strategic cartography.

Washington is one of a dozen states where redistricting is largely out of the legislature's hands. Voters approved a constitutional amendment in 1983 to have districts drawn by a five member commission composed of two members appointed by Democrats, two appointed by Republicans, and a fifth member chosen by the other four. After the commission agrees on a plan for congressional and state legislative district boundaries, it can only be amended by a 2/3 vote by both houses of the legislature, and it cannot be vetoed by the governor. If the commission fails to produce a plan, the State Supreme Court does so. The plan adopted in 2012 created a new 10th Congressional District that leans safely Democratic, and a newly drawn 1st District that leans Democratic. Four districts remained safely Republican, and four others remained safely Democratic. State legislative elections in 2012, after redistricting, produced nearly identical results as elections in 2010, albeit with slight gains for Republicans in the state senate.

Effects of Redistricting Practices

Given incentives to gerrymander, and given the larger issue that people tend to move to places where they are around people like themselves, it is difficult to produce many districts that have the same number of Democratic and Republican voters. However, states with bipartisan redistricting commissions (such as Washington) may be slightly more likely to adopt plans that produce districts that are two-party competitive than states that rely on redistricting by the state legislature. Districting done by legislators tends to produces more districts that are safe for incumbents (Krebs and Winburn 2011).

The Electoral Landscape

The previous section detailed how Washington's electoral practices are unique when compared to other states. But what do election results in Washington tell us about the state?

Well before the 2016 presidential election, Washington was seen as a safe Democratic state. It remained solidly Democratic in 2016, and many expect it to remain so for years to come. Consider the evidence that Washington voters have made this a solidly "blue" state. Democratic presidential candidate Hillary Clinton carried Washington by 15 percent over Donald Trump in 2016, yet Clinton only edged Trump by 2 percent in the national popular vote. Barack Obama beat Republican Mitt Romney by nearly the same margin in Washington in 2012, and Obama had a 17 percent margin over Republican John McCain in Washington in 2008. Democratic presidential candidates regularly run much stronger in Washington than they do nationally, and the last Republican presidential candidate to win Washington was Ronald Reagan in 1984. Obama won Washington with 57 percent in 2008—posting the largest victory margin for a Democratic presidential candidate in the state since 1940 (when Franklin D. Roosevelt defeated Wendell Willkie).

More daunting for Republicans is the fact that state-level support for Democrats in Washington appears to be deep and enduring. Democrats won every gubernatorial election from 1984 through 2016. At every state election since 1992, Democrats won at least five, and usually six, of the eight statewide partisan executive offices. Democrats won every U.S. Senate contest since 1998, and controlled majorities of the state's U.S. House delegation in every election since 1994. While the 2010 midterm election produced massive gains for Republicans in other states, in Washington Democrats reelected a U.S. Senator and maintained their majorities in both chambers of the state legislature. Republicans did pick up one U.S. House seat in 2010 after retiring Democrat Brian Baird was replaced by Republican Jamie Herrera in the 3rd Congressional District.

Given all of this, we might categorize Washington as one of the nation's most solidly Democratic states. Indeed, scholars have categorized Washington as one of the nation's twelve most Democratic-dominant states. Indeed, among the twelve states where Democrats were dominant from 2003 to 2006, only Illinois, New Jersey, and New Mexico had gains for Democrats during this period that exceeded those in Washington (Holbrook and La Raja 2008).

Blue State, Purple State, or Polarized State?

However, categorizing Washington as safe for the Democrats is problematic. By several measures that account for legislative and even gubernatorial races, Washington ranks near the top in measures of two-party competition, along with Colorado, Wisconsin, Pennsylvania, and North Carolina (Hinchliffe and Lee 2015).

There is a puzzle as to how Washington can be so overwhelmingly Democratic in presidential contests, while having such razor-close two-party competition in the state legislature. Just as Democrats win more votes nationally in presidential contests while failing to win congressional or electoral college majorities, Democrats for statewide offices in Washington can win by large margins while Republicans control part of the state legislature. The geography and demography that causes this in Washington mirrors what is often seen nationally. Republicans dominate elections in Washington's rural areas and are competitive in the state's suburban regions—just as they are nationally. Likewise, just as Democrats run well in larger cities and on the coasts nationally, voters west of the Cascades provide large margins for Democratic candidates in Washington.

As in national elections, many of Washington's Democratic voters tend to be concentrated in urban areas. Single-member districts work better for a party that has voters efficiently distributed across many districts, something that may advantage Republicans in Washington's legislative elections. This may explain, in part, how Obama or Clinton can win huge margins in Washington while Republicans are close to parity in the legislature. One possible side-effect of this close competition in the legislature is that Washington's legislature ranks as one of the five most polarized in the country (Shor 2014). This may be because the stakes are high for rival legislative parties in close competition. They may have stronger incentives to organize electorally and to work to discredit their opponents (Hinchliffe and Lee 2015).

Districting and geography, however, cannot fully explain the puzzle of why the party that runs so strong statewide has no corresponding dominance in the legislature. Other states with similarly close two-party legislative competition may also be equally competitive in presidential and statewide races. But not Washington. The answer is probably not simply differential turnout rates between presidential and non-presidential years, because legislative races also occur in presidential years. This leaves candidate effects as a potential, but not completely satisfying, explanation. Indeed, Dino Rossi's nearly successful 2004 gubernatorial campaign, and the success of other Republicans elected as Secretary of State, demonstrates that "mainstream" Republicans are competitive statewide. Moreover, Republican candidates for U.S. Congress and state legislature are elected in districts that Obama and Clinton had carried.

These cases and other elections illustrate that, even in statewide races, Washington can be competitive. Democrat Maria Cantwell won her first Senate race in 2000 by a narrow 0.09 percent margin. The 2004 governor's race between Rossi and Democrat Christine Gregoire was decided by just 133 votes. Republicans Sam Reed and Rob McKenna were reelected to statewide executive offices with large margins in 2008. Patty Murray's reelection for a fourth term in 2010 (against Rossi) was one of the most competitive and expensive U.S. Senate contests of 2010. Kim Wyman was elected to an open Secretary of State seat in 2012, and reelected in 2016. Republicans who appeal to independent voters west of the Cascades do win state races. Nonetheless, it is striking that a range of recent Republican presidential candidates, from maverick (McCain, 40 percent) to mainstream conservative (Romney, 41 percent) to nationalist-populist (Trump, 37 percent), failed to gain any real traction in Washington.

Trends in Voting and Attitudes

There are a number of ways we can illustrate trends in Washington elections over time. Figure 3 uses decades of election results to illustrate the balance of power in the legislature. Since 1994, Democrats made steady gains in winning state legislative seats and flirted with supermajority status in 2008. But Washington's statewide electoral competitiveness is also reflected here. Since 1980, partisan control of at least one chamber has often been narrow, and every election from 1992 to 2002 altered party control of at least one chamber. However, Democrats won legislative majorities in both chambers—albeit some narrowly—from 2004 to 2012. Republicans effectively had control of the senate from 2014 through the time of this writing.

**Figure 3: Democratic Seat Shares in Washington State
Legislature After Elections: 1974–2016.**

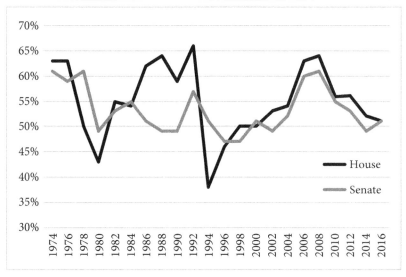

Source: Washington Secretary of State, election returns various years.

**Figure 4: Trends in Statewide Popular Vote for
U.S. House candidates: 1990–2016.**

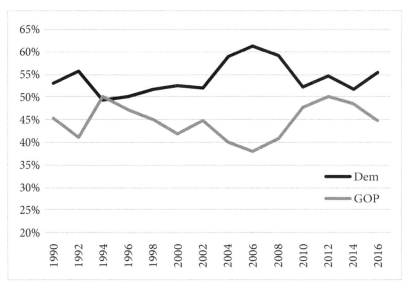

Source: Washington Secretary of State.

Figure 5: Partisan Identification, Washington Voters 1999–2016

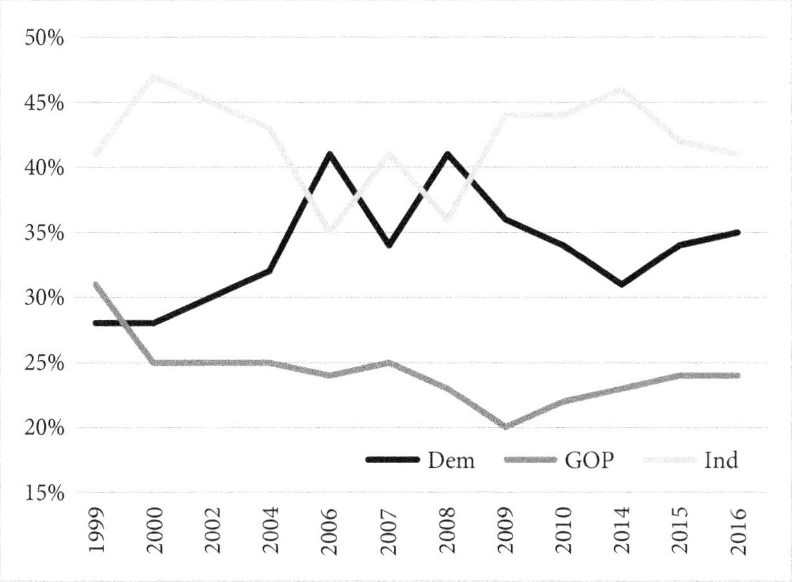

Sources: Washington Poll (2006–2010); Author's polls (1999–2002); Elway Poll (2015).

Figure 4 illustrates trends in electoral competition using popular vote totals from U.S. House elections. Again, we see high points for Republicans in 1994 and 2012 but an overall trend that has advantaged Democrats. Since 1990 the combined statewide vote for Republican House candidates reached a majority just once (1994).

A voters' partisan identification is usually a good predictor of their voting behavior (e.g., Campbell et al. 1960; Bartels 2000). Overall levels of party identification may thus describe each party's long-term electoral base. Figure 5 shows trends in response to the question, "generally speaking, do you consider yourself a Democrat, Republican, independent, or what?" From 2000 to 2016, more Washingtonians identified themselves as Democrats than Republicans. However, in most years a plurality of Washingtonians did not claim to consider themselves as a Democrat or Republican. As Table 2 illustrates, a large plurality of "independents" said they leaned toward Democrats from 2006 to 2008.[5] Yet by 2010 independents split rather evenly between Democrats and Republicans, and this persisted in 2014. If party identification remains stable as a person ages, as some suspect (Flanigan and

Zingale 2010, 105; Jennings and Neimi 1984) this may give Washington Democrats an advantage in future elections. That said, more voters identified themselves as Republican in 2010 than in 2009.

Table 2: Washington Independent Voters' Party Preferences

	2006	2007	2008	2009	2010	2014
Democrat	47%	42%	42%	33%	36%	35%
Republican	29%	35%	30%	44%	37%	37%
other	6	7	11	11	10	8
none/neither	11	11	11	8	13	15
don't know	2	3	3	1	3	3
refused	5	2	3	2	1	2
(total other)	31%	33%	31%	40%	44%	37%

Source: Washington Poll, various years.

Conclusion

This chapter illustrates that elections in Washington are somewhat unique when compared to other states. Washington's unique election rules reflect popular preferences for elections that are transparent and open to full voter participation. Surveys asking about the voter's role in elections find enduring strands of populism in Washington. Polls show Washington voters think they are just as good at making important policy decisions—or more capable—as elected representatives. Very few voters think their representatives are better qualified than they are. Polls also find that Washingtonians want the ability to use elections as a check on their representatives and judges. Large majorities of Washingtonians oppose proposals that would limit their ability to hold the state's judges accountable via elections (Bowler, Donovan, and Parry 2009). Year after year, Washington voters express high levels of support for the citizens' initiative process, and they resist proposals to limit it (Bowler et al. 2001). Indeed, many of the election rules discussed in this chapter—nonpartisan voter registration, wide-open primary elections, campaign finance disclosure rules, and contribution limits—were adopted through direct democracy.

Notes

1. Federal law (the Help America Vote Act) has created some national standards for these practices.
2. "Same Day Voter Registration." National Congress of State Legislators, last updated July 27, 2017, www.ncsl.org/research/elections-and-campaigns/same-day-registration.aspx.
3. The second place Democrat had 23 percent. The first place Republican had 22 percent.
4. See *Buckley v. Valeo,* 424 U.S. 1 (1976) and *Citizen's United v. Federal Communications Commission,* 558 U.S. 08-205 (2010).
5. From 2006 to 2008, more independents said they felt closer to the Democrats than Republicans. In 2009, more independents said they felt closer to Republicans.

References

Ansolabehere, Stephen, John Mark Hansen, Shigeo Hirano, and James M. Snyder Jr. 2007. "The Incumbency Advantage in U.S. Primary Elections." *Electoral Studies* 26(3):660–68.

Bartels, Larry. 2000. "Partisanship and Voting Behavior: 1952–1996." *American Journal of Political Science* 44(1):35–50.

Berinsky, Adam. 2005. "The Perverse Consequences of Electoral Reform in the United States." *American Politics Research* 33(4):471-91.

Borger, Julian. 2002. "Democrat Hawk Whose Ghost Guides Bush." *The Guardian,* December 6, 2002. guardian.co.uk/world/2002/dec/06/usa.julianborger.

Bowler, Shaun, and Todd Donovan. 2011. "Electoral Competition and the Voter." *Public Opinion Quarterly* 75(1):151–64.

Bowler, Shaun, Todd Donovan, and Janine Parry. 2009. "Public Reasoning about Judicial Selection Methods." Paper presented at the Western Political Science Association meeting. Vancouver, BC.

Bowler, Shaun, Todd Donovan, Max Neiman, and Johnny Peel. 2001. "Institutional Threat and Partisan Outcomes: Legislative Candidates' Attitudes toward Direct Democracy." *State Politics and Policy Quarterly* 1(4):364–79.

Cain, Bruce E., and Elisabeth R. Gerber. 2002. *Voting at the Political Fault Line: California's Experiment with the Blanket Primary.* Berkeley: University of California Press.

Campbell, Angus, Philip E. Converse, Warren E. Miller, and Donald E. Stokes. 1960. *The American Voter.* Chicago: University of Chicago Press.

Cox, Gary W., and Michael C. Munger. 1989. "Closeness, Expenditures and Turnout in the 1982 U.S. House Elections." *American Political Science Review* 83(1):217–31.

Donovan, Todd. 2018. *Changing How America Votes.* Rowman and Littlefield.

Donovan, Todd, Christopher Z. Mooney, and Daniel A. Smith. 2011. *State and Local Politics: Institutions and Reforms.* Boston: Wadsworth Cengage Learning.

Elway Poll, The. 2015. elwayresearch.com/elwaypoll.html.

Fiorina, Morris P., Samuel J. Abrams, and Jeremy C. Pope. 2005. *Culture War? The Myth of a Polarized America*. New York: Pearson Longman.

Flanigan, William H., and Nancy H. Zingale. 2010. *Political Behavior of the American Electorate*. 12th edition, Washington, DC: CQ Press.

Gerber, Elisabeth R., and Rebecca B. Morton. 1998. "Primary Election Systems and Representation." *Journal of Law, Economics and Organizations* 14(2):304–24.

Hamm, Keith E., and Gary F. Moncrief. 1999. "Legislative Politics in the States." In *Politics in the American States: A Comparative Analysis* 7th edition, edited by Virginia Gray, Russell L. Hanson, and Herbert Jacob. Washington, DC: CQ Press.

Hinchliffe, Kelsey L., Frances E. Lee. 2015. "Party Competition and Conflict in State Legislatures." *State Politics and Policy Quarterly* 16 (July 2015).

Hanmer, Michael J. 2009. *Discount Voting: Voter Registration Reforms and Their Effects*. Cambridge: Cambridge University Press.

Hill, Kim Quaile. 2003. "Democratization and Corruption." *American Politics Research* 31(6):613–31.

Holbrook, Thomas M., and Raymond J. La Raja. 2008. "Parties and Elections." In *Politics in the American States: A Comparative Analysis* 9th edition, edited by Virginia Gray, Russell L. Hanson, and Herbert Jacob. Washington, DC: CQ Press.

Jennings, M. Kent, and Richard G. Neimi. 1984. *Youth Parent Socialization Panel Study 1965–1973*. Ann Arbor, MI: Inter-university Consortium for Political and Social Research.

Karp, Jeffrey A., and Susan A. Banducci. 2000. "Going Postal: How All-Mail Elections Influence Turnout." *Political Behavior* 22(3):223–39.

Key, V.O. [1949] 1984. *Southern Politics in State and Nation*. Knoxville: University of Tennessee Press.

Krebs, Timothy B., and Jonathan Winburn. 2011. "State and Local Elections: The Unique Character of Sub-National Contests." In *New Directions in Campaigns and Elections*, edited by Stephen K. Medvic. New York: Routledge.

McGlennon, John. 2009. "The Competition Gap: How Candidate Recruitment in State Legislative Elections Foreshadows Party Change." Report for the Thomas Jefferson Program in Public Policy. College of William and Mary.

Meier, Kenneth J., and Thomas M. Holbrook. 1992. "'I Seen My Opportunities and I Took 'Em': Political Corruption in the American States." *Journal of Politics* 54(1):135–55.

Neimi, Richard G., Lydia W. Powell, William D. Berry, Thomas M. Carsey, and James M. Snyder Jr. 2006. "Competition in State Legislative Elections: 1992–2002." In *The Marketplace of Democracy: Electoral Competition and American Politics*, edited by Michael McDonald and John Curtis Samples. Washington, DC: Brookings Institution Press.

Reed, Sam. 2007. "Voter Registration Change Would be a Costly Step Backward." *Tacoma News Tribune*, April 10, 2007.

Rosenstone, Steven J., and John Mark Hansen. 2003. *Mobilization, Participation, and Democracy in America*. New York: Longman.

Shor, Boris. 2014. Update: Aggregate Data for Ideological Mapping of American Legislatures [computer file]. V1. Cambridge, MA Harvard Dataverse.

Southwell, Priscilla. 2004. "Five Years Later, A Re-Assessment of Oregon's Vote by Mail Electoral Process." *PS: Political Science and Politics* 37(1):89–93.

Washington Poll, The. University of Washington Department of Political Science. www.washingtonpoll.org/archives.html

Washington Public Disclosure Commission (PDC). www.pdc.wa.gov

Washington Secretary of State. www.sos.wa.gov

CHAPTER 3

Political Parties in the Evergreen State

Kevin Pirch

In the United States ideas about what political parties do, or should do, are as varied as the activists who work with them and the scholars who study them. While these debates appear endless, there are a few generally accepted assumptions about the function of political parties. In his 1942 work, E. E. Schattschneider described political parties as an "organized attempt to get control of the government." Similarly, famed political scientist V. O. Key argued (1964) that political parties take a multitude of roles, shapes, and identities, but two of their major roles were to connect the electorate to the government (the party in the electorate) and to recruit and train people to run for office and govern (the party as an organization).

It would then appear that, even though there is vast diversity in their ideologies and structures, a reasonable definition of a political party could be "groups of like-minded individuals who use elections to connect voters to their government and enact specific policies." Moreover, given that both the state and national governments are based on separate branches with distinct and diffuse powers, Washington's governmental structure almost demands that political parties are formed in order to control the institutions of government effectively.

However, the idea that the unifying force of political parties is necessary for government to operate effectively is challenged in Washington State, and many other western states. Populist attitudes and a corresponding distrust of parties, elected officials, and elites are enshrined in the state's constitution and in the laws that regulate how parties and other political institutions operate. This distrust of parties and elites can be witnessed in laws the Evergreen State has enacted such as the initiative, referendum, and recall—all of which are seen as popular checks on parties, the institutions of government, and interest groups that might seek to use outsized influence to control the state government. Washington State government then operates in a disjointed environment where it needs healthy political parties to operate, but where laws demonstrate an inherent skepticism of those parties and elites. This chapter will explore two of those issues: the system by which major party candidates are nominated in Washington State, and the way the political parties financially assist candidates in campaigning for office.

Nominating Party Candidates in Washington State

Since almost the beginning of the republic, political parties have had the responsibility of selecting individuals to be their representatives in general elections. From the clichéd smoke-filled backrooms of party conventions to modern democratic election processes, the way these parties have selected their nominees have evolved both with the culture of the state and the changing norms of society.

Populist and progressive reforms have shaped how parties operate in Washington. Early in the twentieth century, Washington had a primary system with separate ballots printed for each major party, and voters declared a party affiliation when they voted on one of those ballots. In 1921, the legislature adopted laws to give parties more control of who participated in their affairs. The laws required that voters register with a party affiliation in advance of elections, restricting primary voting and participation in party affairs (including caucuses) to those registered with the party. Voters repealed these laws by popular referendums (R-14 and R-15) in 1922.

Beginning in 1936 Washington State began using a blanket primary as a means of selecting all of its partisan nominees for general elections except for the president. The blanket primary was proposed as an initiative to the legislature (Initiative 2, 1934) by the Washington State Grange and the American Federation of Labor (AFL).[1] Its purpose was to minimize the power of the political parties and their interests, while allowing all members of the electorate to select the candidates of their choosing regardless of their political affiliation.

The blanket primary was a relatively straightforward process. The state printed one primary election ballot that every voter received. The ballot listed every office and included every candidate seeking each party's nomination for each office. These primary ballots could be quite long, given that multiple candidates from multiple parties were seeking nomination for several offices. Several Democrats could be listed as running for governor, along with several Republicans, third-party candidates, and independent candidates, and so on, for each office. Voters would then choose their favorite candidate for each office regardless of their party affiliation, and, because all candidates were on the ballot, voters could select candidates from different parties for different offices. For example, a voter could select a Republican for governor and a Democrat for United States Senate. The top vote getter from each major party—regardless of their overall place of finish—then advanced to the general election.

Voters in Washington State liked the blanket primary and viewed it as a mechanism both to reduce the power of the political parties and to encourage more moderate, centrist candidates. Unlike closed party primaries or caucuses, where generally only truly committed partisans vote for what tend to be the most ideologically committed partisans, it was believed that candidates would reap more electoral rewards by positioning themselves as more centrist candidates in blanket primaries. These centrists would be able to capture the independent, moderate voters, moderate partisans, and, perhaps, even some of the other party's voters. Ideologically moderate candidates would then have an easier time competing in the general election, without having to worry about credibly moving from a position on the ideological fringe to a more centrist position for the general election.

Moreover, it was believed that by promoting more moderate, centrist candidates in primaries, the elected officials would be less partisan and more willing to work across the aisle with the opposition once elected. In essence, the blanket primary was designed to allow parties to continue to serve their purpose of nominating candidates and creating unified policy positions, while encouraging moderation in the positions by allowing nonpartisans to vote for specific candidates. Not surprisingly, in a state like Washington where citizens pride themselves on independence and good governance—and where the public maintains a distinct populist streak of distrusting institutional elites—the blanket primary was well regarded.

In fact, a report by Secretary of State Sam Reed in the early 2000s found that the majority of Washingtonians supported the blanket primary (Ebel 2004). Voters in Washington, whom the study described as mostly independent, wanted to be able to participate in the primary system without publicly declaring a partisan affiliation. However, the very reasons that caused voters to support the blanket primary were, in large part, the same things that caused the political parties to oppose it. Political parties in Washington argued that the blanket primary fundamentally violated the parties' First Amendment rights to freedom of association, and that it constrained a party's ability to pick their own nominees. Political parties, as private organizations, chafed at the prospect of non-members being able to have input on who their nominees should be.

While initially a unique creation of Washington State, the blanket primary was adopted in Louisiana and Alaska, and in 1996 California voters passed Proposition 198, which instituted the blanket primary in that state in 1998. The California Democratic Party, the California Republican Party, and two minor parties sued the state in federal court arguing that the blanket primary violated a party's First Amendment right to freedom of association (*California Democratic Party et al. v. Jones et al.*). While the District Court and Ninth Circuit Court of Appeals rejected the parties' arguments that their association rights were harmed, in 2000, the U.S. Supreme Court agreed with the political parties that California's blanket primary violated their First Amendment rights. Declared unconstitutional in California, the blanket primary faced an uncertain future in Washington State.

Despite a similar system in California being declared unconstitutional, Washington State continued to use the blanket primary in 2000, and in 2002 the Federal District Court of Western Washington upheld the constitutionality of the blanket primary in the Evergreen State. Washington's Democratic, Republican, and Libertarian parties immediately appealed the decision, and in 2003 the Ninth Circuit Court of Appeals found Washington's blanket primary was indistinguishable from the California system. The Court of Appeals ruled that Washington's blanket primary violated the parties' right to freedom of association and was therefore unconstitutional (*Democratic Party of Washington v. Reed*). The Washington State Grange and the State of Washington appealed to the U.S. Supreme Court, which declined to review the case, thereby ending the state's 70-year use of the blanket primary. What followed was nearly a decade during which the state attempted to find a system to nominate candidates that appealed to the independent, centrist desires of the voters while still respecting the parties' constitutional rights of association.

With the 2004 election months away, the state needed to find an alternative primary system quickly and two choices appeared viable. The first option was the "pick-a-party" primary, also known as the Montana primary. The second option was a "top-two" primary. In essence, the pick-a-party system is a closed primary where voters must declare an affiliation with a party and then select candidates from a primary ballot that only listed that party's candidates. Separate primary ballots were printed for Republicans, Democrats, Libertarians, and for nonpartisan races—the latter for voters who did not want to participate in any party's primary. Voters received all four ballots. Unlike other closed party primaries, the Washington pick-a-party system asked voters to identify with a party only when they picked which ballot to vote, and that selection would not be a part of the public record.

Top-Two Primary and Political Parties

The top-two system in many ways appeared similar to the blanket primary. A single ballot went to all eligible voters in the state with a list of all possible candidates for all offices. Like the blanket primary, voters could choose among candidates with different partisan affiliations for different offices. However, there were two crucial differences between top-two and blanket primaries. First, unlike the blanket primary where the top vote getter for each party advances, in a top-two primary, only the top two candidates advance to the general election—regardless of their partisanship. This created the possibility of having two candidates from the same party face each other in the general election.

Second, in a top-two primary the ballot makes no claims about candidates being supported by or endorsed by any political party. Rather, the idea of partisan association only goes one way—from the candidate to the party. In each partisan race in a top-two primary, candidates are asked declare the party they prefer. The candidate's party preference is placed in parentheses next to their name—for example: Jay Inslee (prefers Democratic Party). Top-two ballots contain a disclaimer noting that a candidate's party preference does not mean the candidate is nominated or endorsed by the party, or that the party approves of or associates with the candidate. The net effect of these two differences allows the top-two primary to be cast as "nonpartisan" because the process, even applied to partisan offices, does not determine any party's nominations.

With a decision needed quickly in the spring of 2004 between top-two or pick-a-party, Governor Gary Locke vetoed portions of the legislation that would have allowed the state to use the top-two primary, over the objections of Secretary of State Reed. The state was therefore obligated to use the pick-a-party system for the September 2004 primaries. Although satisfying the parties' constitutional rights, the pick-a-party system was highly unpopular with the general public, with only 21 percent of voters saying they approved of the modified closed primary system (Appleton 2011). Because of this strong dissatisfaction with the pick-a-party system and a desire for a less partisan system, Washington voters approved a ballot initiative from the Washington State Grange (I-872) in November 2004 with more than 60 percent support. Initiative 872 would have replaced the pick-a-party system with a top-two primary. However, the change would not be quick or easy. Almost immediately, the Republican Party of Washington State sued, and was joined by the Washington State Democratic Central Committee and the Libertarian Party of Washington. The parties argued that the top-two primary was an unconstitutional infringement on their association rights (*Washington State Republican Party v. Washington State Grange*).

At issue was the parties' claim that the top-two system violated the party's freedom of association. The parties argued that the First Amendment's phrase that states "Congress shall make no law respecting…the right of the people peaceably to assemble" was violated by not allowing the parties any measure of control over who ran under their party's banner. Simply put, the parties argued they would be forced to associate with anyone who claimed to be affiliated with their party for the purposes of the primary regardless of the party's desires.[2] Accepting the parties' arguments, the 9th Circuit Court of Appeals struck down I-872, declaring it unconstitutional in August 2006. This meant that a pick-a-party primary was held again in 2006. However, the Grange and the State of Washington appealed to the United States Supreme

Court and, in March 2008, the Court decided 7–2 that the top-two system did not place a severe burden on the parties. The Court ruled there was no evidence that voters could confuse a candidate's party preference listed on the ballot with an endorsement by or any formal affiliation with a political party. So, since 2008, the state of Washington has continued to use the top-two primary with surveys showing that 76 percent of the public approve of the system.

Beside the legal challenges from political parties, the top-two primary is not without some criticisms. One of the primary concerns come from minor parties and their supporters which now face an even larger challenge in accessing the general election ballot—especially for statewide offices. While weaker in specific regions, both major parties are supported enough to generally assure that they will make it past the primary election and appear on the ballot (if they have a candidate running in the primary).

However this is not necessarily true for legislative races, where one of the major parties tends to dominate. For example, Democrats have disproportionate support in Seattle, while Republicans dominate some districts in eastern Washington. In 2016, out of the 122 legislative races in the general election, there were 63 "non-traditional legislative races," which did not include both a Democrat and Republican candidate. Among these races were 27 uncontested races where only one name appeared on the ballot, including two districts—the 20th (Republicans in southwest Washington) and the 36th (Democrats in Seattle)—where all three legislators running for office faced no opposition. Additionally, there were eight races where both candidates were from the same party and ten races with Libertarians. The other 18 non-traditional races had other minor parties or parties that do not formally exist—such as the "Independent GOP Party" or the "Non-Partisan Party."

There are valid concerns that if candidates are facing only opposition from their own parties, then they will have incentives to become more ideologically pure and "extreme" in order to win the primary. These candidates will then go to Olympia as more extreme partisans and might be less willing to compromise with the other party for fear of appearing ideologically weak when they return home. Likewise, it might be possible that candidates who face no competition whatsoever have the potential to become less responsive to the voters back home if they lack the threat of a credible opponent challenging them. Additionally, if there is only one choice for office in an election, or if only one party is on the ballot in the general election, there becomes less incentive for voters to participate in the election given that the outcome is largely already decided. In either of these two instances, some of the goals of the top-two primary—decreasing partisanship and increasing citizen involvement—might not be met.

Despite the inherent logic in the idea that more open primaries would create less ideologically extreme candidates, evidence from political science research—while somewhat divided—seems to indicate that the type of primary might not influence the political extremity of candidates as much as the public imagines. While there have been some studies indicating that more open primaries produce less extreme candidates (Gerber and Morton 1998),other studies have found that people rarely strategically vote for the oppositions' least-electable candidate and that states with different primary types do not select different presidential candidates in primaries (Southwell 1991). Other studies have found that only in less partisan districts in California do the effects of blanket primaries produce more moderate candidates (Bullock and Clinton 2011). Newer studies looking at all of the states, rather than just California, also indicate that partisan extremism is not a result of the primary type (McGhee et al. 2014). Simply put, while the debate is not settled, the preponderance of the evidence seems to indicate that the type of primary has little, if any, impact on the candidates people elect.

Nominating Presidential Candidates

Different nomination rules are in place for presidential elections. While the top-two primary is used for all statewide, legislative, and Congressional races, the state of Washington offers the political parties two options for selecting delegates to the national conventions to nominate the president—a primary and caucus. Originally, the state's nominating process was exclusively done through a caucus system, in which partisans meet in their communities and debate the merits of the candidates before coming to a general consensus on a favorite candidate. People at these neighborhood caucuses pick representatives to attend a county caucus to express their views. Those county meetings select representatives to attend congressional district caucus meetings and, eventually, they convene at a statewide convention to formally select delegates to attend the national party convention and vote for the party's presidential nominee.

However, various issues compelled the state legislature to pass legislation creating a presidential primary. First, in 1989, more than 200,000 voters signed an initiative to the legislature proposing a presidential primary (Initiative 99). Second, caucuses are often criticized because the time commitment and other demands of participation often encourage only the strongest partisans and members of specific socioeconomic groups to participate. Caucuses have far lower levels of participation than primary elections. This issue is expressed in the citizen-initiated law RCW 29A.56, which states: "The presidential nominating system in Washington State is unnecessarily restrictive of voter participation in that it discriminates against the elderly, the infirm, women, the disabled, evening workers, and others who are unable to attend caucuses and therefore unable to fully participate in the most important quadrennial event that occurs in our democratic system of government."

In addition, in 1988 the Republican establishment was embarrassed when the Republican caucus process nominated conservative Christian minister Pat Robertson against the wishes of the party elite, who supported George H.W. Bush (Brunner 2016). Pressured by the initiative, by concerns of partisan elites losing control to a specific faction, and by worries that many segments of the electorate were effectively disenfranchised from the caucus system, the legislature adopted a new system of presidential primary elections in 1989. However, as private associations, political parties cannot be forced to use results from the primaries to allocate delegates to their conventions.

As a result, political parties in Washington have two mechanisms for allocating their delegates for the national conventions, either the caucuses or a primary. Or in some years, both. Since the presidential primary bill was passed, primaries have been used in bewildering combinations with caucuses, or simply canceled. The 2016 presidential primary was essentially the pick-a-party system. All registered voters received a primary ballot that forced the voter to choose either the Democratic Party or the Republican Party, and vote only for a candidate of that party. The voter was also required to declare a party affiliation on the return envelope. Democrats and Republicans also held caucuses in 2016. To prevent people from participating in both parties' selection process by voting with one party in the primary and caucusing with the other party, each political party received a list of voters who voted in the other primary. Those voters were prohibited from participating in the other party's caucus.

Presidential primaries in Washington have also mirrored the blanket primary and listed all candidates together, regardless of party. In the 2000 primary, voters could declare a party, or vote without declaring any party affiliation. A plurality of votes was cast that year by "unaffiliated" voters. Other years the presidential primary was cancelled because parties had no interest in using the results to allocate delegates (1996, 2004, 2012). Indeed, as of this writing Washington State Democrats have never used results from the presidential primary to allocate delegates, relying instead on caucuses. Washington Republicans allocated part of their delegates by caucus and part by primary in 1992, 2000, and 2008.

In 2016, citing a desire to expand their base and get more of the electorate involved in their nominating process, the Washington State Republican Party chose to allocate all of their delegates to the national convention based upon the results of the primary rather than the caucus. Democrats, on the other hand, chose the opposite tact and continued to allocate all of their delegates based upon the results of the caucuses.

Party primaries are generally low-turnout affairs in Washington State with only 35 percent of registered voters returning their ballots in 2016, compared to 79 percent in the general election that year. This was probably due in part to the Democratic Party's decision not to use the primary results in national convention delegate allocation. However, turnout was low for other presidential primaries in Washington, with only 42 percent of the voters returning their ballots in 2008. Because of the expense of the election that the state government must incur, and the low turnout, Democrats have pushed for the cancelation of the presidential primary and succeeded at canceling it in 2004 and 2012.

Financing Campaigns

Like many states, Washington did not have many laws restricting the use of campaign funds until the 1970s. Until then, the only state law governing campaign finance required candidates to disclose all expenditures made during party primaries. However, there were no requirements for disclosing any activities during the general election nor any campaign contributions received (Kramer 1972). After failing to get a bill regulating campaign finance reform passed through the state legislature in the early 1970s, voters passed Initiative 276 with 72 percent of the vote in 1972. In some regards similar to the Federal Election Campaign Act passed earlier that year, I-276 was the first broad attempt to regulate money in Washington's elections. First, the law created a government agency, the Public Disclosure Commission (PDC) tasked with monitoring campaign finances and lobbying activity. The law also required the disclosure of all contributions and expenditures, and placed caps on individual expenditures in statewide and state legislative races. Noticeably missing from the 1972 law were limits on how much money could be contributed to individual campaigns, thereby allowing businesses, unions, individuals, and special interest groups to donate large sums to campaigns.

These issues were addressed twenty years later by Initiative 134, which, again, passed with 73 percent of the vote. The prime advocate of Initiative 134 was Linda Smith, then a Republican state senator. This law placed limits on donations by individuals, businesses, unions, and special interest groups to individual candidates, and required those donations to be disclosed to the public through the PDC. It placed only nominal limits on contributions to parties and party spending. Initially, donations to candidates were limited to $500 for a legislative race and $1,000 for a statewide race per election (given that there is both a primary election and a general election, it is useful to double the limits to discover the actual contributions allowed). The law allowed the limits to be increased for inflation and have doubled in the intervening twenty years. It also required independent campaigns to disclose the identities of their top five contributors.

The initiative was supported by conservative-leaning groups such as the National Federation of Independent Business and the Washington State Dairy Federation, and opposed by such liberal-leaning groups as the Washington State Labor Council, the Washington Environmental Council, and the Washington Public Interest Research Group (WashPIRG). The League of Women Voters opposed the initiative. These groups opposed it either for political reasons—unions could

Table 1: Washington State Political Finance Limits

RECIPIENTS	CONTRIBUTORS					
	State Party	County and Legislative District Party Committees (Jointly)	Caucus Political Committee	Candidate Committees	Pacs, Unions, Corps and other entities	Individuals
State Party	Not Applicable	No Limit	No Limit	Only from Surplus Funds No Limit	$5,500 per calendar year / No Limit (exempt)	No Limit
County and Legislative District Party Committees (Jointly)	No Limit	No Limit	No Limit	Only from Surplus Funds No Limit	$5,500 per calendar year / No Limit (exempt)	No Limit
Caucus Political Committee	No Limit	No Limit	No Limit	Only from Surplus Funds No Limit	$1,000 per calendar year	No Limit
State Executive Candidate	$1.00 per Reg. Voter per cycle	$0.50 per Reg. Voter per cycle	$1.00 per Reg. Voter per cycle	Prohibited	$2,000 per calendar year	$2,000 per calendar year

Legislative Candidate	$1.00 per Reg. Voter per cycle	$0.50 per Reg. Voter per cycle	$1.00 per Reg. Voter per cycle	Prohibited	$1,000 per calendar year	$1,000 per calendar year
Judicial Candidate	$2,000 per election	$2,000 per election	$2,000 per election	Prohibited	$2,000 per calendar year	$2,000 per calendar year
LOCAL OFFICES: • **County Office** • **Mayor** • **City Council** • **School Board**	$1.00 per Reg. Voter per cycle	$0.50 per Reg. Voter per cycle	$1.00 per Reg. Voter per cycle	Prohibited	$1,000 per calendar year	$1,000 per calendar year
King Co Hospital Dists 1 & 2 and Snohomish Co Hosp Dist 2	$0.95 per Reg. Voter per cycle	$0.50 per Reg. Voter per cycle	$1.00 per Reg. Voter per cycle	Prohibited	$1,000 per calendar year	$1,000 per calendar year
Port of Seattle and Port of Tacoma Commissioner Candidates	$1.00 per Reg. Voter per cycle	$0.50 per Reg. Voter per cycle	$1.00 per Reg. Voter per cycle	Prohibited	$2,000 per calendar year	$2,000 per calendar year
PACS	No Limit	No Limit	No Limit	Prohibited	No Limit	No Limit

Source: Public Disclosure Commission, Olympia, WA (2016)

no longer give unlimited funds to candidates or PACs—or because it did not cap expenditures and repealed local laws in Seattle and King County that were much more stringent and considered more effective by good government groups (Munro 1992).

As a result of the law, in 2016 corporations, unions, PACS, and individuals were allowed to contribute up to $2,000 to legislative candidates per election ($1,000 in each of the primary and general elections), and $4,000 to candidates for statewide office, judicial campaigns, or commissioners for the ports of Seattle and Tacoma (again, $2,000 per election). Initiative 134, combined with subsequent court decisions, effectively allows unlimited contributions to (and unlimited spending by) party organizations.

One of the consequences of capping limits on contributions to candidates' campaigns is that those groups and individuals who want to donate more money than the law allows must find a new vehicle for those funds. Large-scale political influencers—whether they are unions, corporations, political action committees, or individuals— might not feel satisfied contributing only $2,000 per year to favorite legislative candidates. For these groups, political parties become a convenient way to continue to fund candidates while still respecting the letter of the law.

State law has created numerous avenues for supporting candidates and issues, not the least of which is campaign donations. There are several different types of political party organizations that can accept large contributions that must be reported to the PDC: the state parties, county parties, legislative district parties, and affiliated political clubs such as the Republican Women of Clark County or the Young Democrats of Spokane, which are arms of the county party. In addition, the party caucuses in both houses of the legislature have created multiple campaign accounts that can solicit donations in support of both House and Senate campaigns.

As with the national political parties under the Federal Election Campaign Act, the political parties must divide their funds into two seemingly distinct accounts: exempt and non-exempt funds. Exempt funds (soft money) are exempt from contribution limits. Originally, under Initiative 134, non-exempt funds could be used only for specific purposes such as "party building activities." These excluded spending on campaign ads, and were limited to activities such as get-out-the-vote campaigns, voter registration programs, poll watchers, and internal party expenses, such as rent and office supplies not used for campaigns. However, in 2000 the Washington Supreme Court ruled that Initiative 134's ban on using exempt party funds for "issue-oriented" campaign advertising was unconstitutional (*Washington State Republican Party v. State Public Disclosure Commission*). This allowed parties to raise and spend unlimited exempt funds for political advertising. As a result, and due to Initiative 134's initially loose limits on contributions to parties, party committees are the dominant source of funds in key races in Washington.

Figure 1: Flow of Money Into and Out of Political Parties

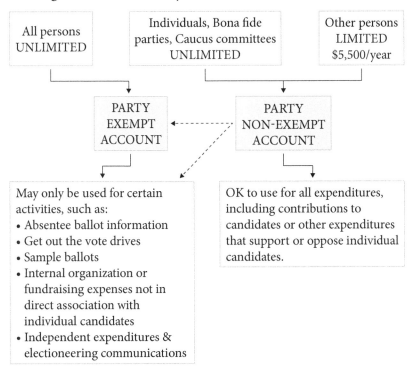

The creation of multiple political party campaign arms allows groups who want to contribute more money a readily accessible way to donate more funds to political campaigns. Individuals may give limitless amounts of money to political parties at all levels of the state, and

PACs, unions, and corporations may give unlimited money to parties' exempt funds. The parties then have choices about what to do with these funds: if they desire, parties can give that money directly to individual campaigns. These contributions are generally capped at $1.00 per registered voter, per election cycle, for the state party and $0.50 per registered voter, per cycle, for the legislative and county parties. For perspective, in December 2016, there were approximately 4,270,500 registered voters in the state, and anywhere from approximately 63,400 registered voters in the 29th legislative district around Tacoma to 103,700 registered voters in the 36th legislative district in Seattle. If the parties do not want to donate this money directly to the candidate, they can use this money to run separate, independent campaigns on behalf of, or against, any particular candidates.

Parties in Washington also have additional sources of funds for campaigns. Other candidates may, if they desire, transfer money from their campaigns to a political party fund. Thorough the use of an account called a "Surplus Funds Account," candidates may make unlimited transfers to any party fund in the state. This creates an opportunity for candidates in relatively safe districts to solicit more money than they will need for their individual campaigns and then transfer that money to their party. The party can then use it to help other party members in more competitive races. This transfer is beneficial to all actors involved in the transaction—donors can contribute more money to candidates, the candidates who transfer the money are seen as "team players" and gain influence in the party, and the candidate in competitive races gets additional campaign help.

In election years with statewide races (2008, 2012, 2016), state party committees have spent about $10 million per year. County party committees and legislative district committees have spent another $4 to $5 million per election year, primarily on state legislative races. However, the largest category of party spending flows through the caucus committees. These include the Democrats' largely union-funded Harry Truman Fund, the Republicans business-funded Reagan Fund, and House and Senate caucus funds that collect millions raised by incumbents in safe seats and redirect those funds to the rare competitive races. These caucus committees spent $16 million in 2016 on state legislative races, and over $12 million in 2014.

Follow the Money?

Much of this party caucus money is not easy to track. As an example, Republicans spent millions on state legislative races through their Olympia-based Leadership Council. Top donors to that party committee have been the Washington, DC-based Republican Leadership Council. The top contributors to that group include some of America's largest corporations (Reynolds America, Wal-Mart, Koch Industries, Exxon, Philip Morris, Comcast, and a number of pharmaceutical companies), the Las Vegas Sands casino, and the U.S. Chamber of Commerce, which is funded by a few multi-million dollar contributions that are difficult to track (Public Citizen 2014).

The Republicans' Olympia-based Leadership Council then funnels that money to groups called the Good Government Leadership Council and Working Families, and then uses those groups to fund millions of dollars of negative ads against Democratic legislative candidates. Some of the Leadership Council money also flows to Republican Party county organizations. Democrats, likewise, have funneled millions from state labor unions through their Truman Fund into the New Direction PAC and Mainstream Voters of WA PAC to attack Republican legislative candidates.

In the 2016 election cycle, both political parties amassed impressive sums of money for the campaigns. The Republican party organizations (state, county, and legislative parties but not the caucuses) raised almost $6,870,000 and spent $5,270,000 in the election cycle. Of this, more than $3.8 million went to the state party, $2.8 million went to the county parties, and the remainder—only $126,500—went to the legislative district parties. Democrat party organizations raised a combined total of about $8.3 million and spent about $7.1 million. Like the Republicans, the majority of money flowed through the state party (about $5.9 million raised and $5.3 spent, including debts). Unlike the Republicans, Democrats used legislative district parties more, raising $1.08 million and spending about $900,000. In total, the two major parties raised $17.8 million in the 2016 election cycle and spent $16.1 million through state, district, and county party organizations. When caucus spending in legislative races is accounted for, the major parties spent $32 million in 2016.[3] For perspective, the minor parties (parties that do not get 5 percent of the vote in a presidential election) in the state raised $16,115 and spent $14,071.

Table 2: Washington State Campaign Funding 2010-2016

	Party		Legislative Candidates		Statewide Offices		Judicial Candidates	
	Raised	Spent	Raised	Spent	Raised	Spent	Raised	Spent
2016	$33,092,038	$29,340,437	$28,870,948	$25,184,821	$22,591,581	$20,949,127	$3,624,229	$3,375,923
			Total Raised = $88,178,796		Total Spent = $78,850,308			
2014	$22,072,757	$18,782,608	$26,829,285	$25,089,688	$0 (Statewide Offices*)	$0	$2,300,831	$2,046,177
			Total Raised = $51,202,873		Total Spent = $45,918,473			
2012	$26,926,927	$24,974,900	$26,077,891	$24,982,905	$34,763,007	$34,706,959	$3,884,294	$3,782,855
			Total Raised = $91,652,119		Total Spent = $88,447,619			
2010	$14,223,996	$12,314,309	$24,625,145	$23,505,709	$0 (Statewide Offices*)	$0	$2,569,878	$2,463,326
			Total Raised = $41,419,019		Total Spent = $38,283,344			

*No major statewide elections held in 2010 and 2014.
Source: Author

All of the 11 most well-funded legislative parties were Democratic, with the 34th, 46th, and 28th legislative district parties all raising more than $80,000—with the Democrats winning all but two of those seven races. In these parties, generally speaking, the largest donations came from either individual campaigns or unions. Among the county parties, the most well-funded parties were generally Republican with King, Pierce, Snohomish, Clark, and Spokane County Republicans— along with the Thurston County Democrats—raising the most money.

As seen in Table 1, with the exception of the exceptionally expensive statewide races in 2012, the amount of money going into all facets of campaigns in Washington State is generally increasing. However, what is most striking is the amount of money going into the caucus campaign committees and their ancillary groups. Starting in 2010, those campaign committees raised a combined total of about $7,864,000 and spent $6,916,00; by the 2016 campaign those groups had raised more than $17,700,000 and spent about $15,900,000 while leaving some money for the next campaign. In many regards, it appears that these legislative caucus drive funds will become the future of campaign financing in the state of Washington. Controlled by the leadership of each party in the legislative chambers, they allow another way for those people to exercise control by rewarding those who raise large sums of money and using that money in close campaigns, thereby insuring a level of loyalty and appreciation from those winning candidates. Relatively unknown to the public, they afford the parties an excellent way to increase contributions with minimal scrutiny.

In summary, Washington State has stricter campaign finance laws than many states. It requires disclosure of both contributions and expenditures and has strict laws governing the amount of money individuals and groups many donate to candidates. However, it is also true that money is attracted to political power—or more accurately, those with financial resources like to use those resources to influence political policy making—and those with money will find ways to get that money to political elites. Because of those campaign laws, political parties are becoming an increasingly important tool in Washington for financing campaigns and attempting to curry favor with elected officials. Simply, there are two main ways parties help facilitate this: First, interested actors may give money to political parties directly; parties then either donate that money to candidates or run their own independent campaigns in support of those candidates. Second, groups may give money to candidates in safe seats, who will then give that money to the political parties or caucuses, who will in turn run independent campaigns in competitive districts. In either case, additional money continues to flow to the political parties in support of campaigns in the Evergreen State.

Parties in a Comparative Context

Like other institutions in a federal system, political parties are dynamic and evolve to meet the needs of the issues and individuals in their particular states. While there are similarities between the political parties at the state level across the nation, they also are different. In one peculiarly interesting way, Washington State has bucked a national trend in the twenty-first century with the amount of party competition in state government.

One way of measuring this party competition was developed by Austin Ranney, who used three variables to measure the strength of the Democratic Party (and, in turn, Republican strength): the percent of the gubernatorial race the party won, the portion of the state House and Senate the party won, and the amount of time the party controlled these institutions (Ranney 1965). On this scale, 0.0 indicates perfect Republican dominance of the state, 100 is perfect dominance by the Democrats, and 50 means the state is competitive. In the time between 1980 and 2000 Washington State scored a 59.4 on the Ranney Index, indicating a Democratic lean in the state, but still relatively competitive. However, between 2007 and 2011 the state became more Democratic with a score of 64.4. At the same time, the nation as a whole has become more Republican, with an average score shifting from 55.6 to 48.6 (Donovan et al. 2015). Simply put, the state of Washington has become more Democratic over the past generation, while the 50 states as a whole have become more Republican. While nationally much of the shift in partisan predisposition in the states can be attributed to the partisan realignment of the South over the past 40 years, Washington State was only one of 15 states that became more Democratic in its state government between 1980 and 2011.

Conclusions

Since its inception, the State of Washington has remained in a constant battle between its citizens' populist instincts to distrust political institutions—especially political parties and the influence they exert—and the apparent need for political parties to serve as an intermediary in the Madisonian system and those parties' First Amendment rights. Using the democratic mechanisms the state constitution provides, such as the initiative system, people have repeatedly attempted to impose limits on many of the critical aspects of the political parties including nominating candidates (with I-2, I-99, and I-872) and funding campaigns (I-276 and I-134). However, despite these desires to limit the role and influence of political parties, these organizations continue to innovate new ways to participate in the governance of Washington State.

Notes

1. The Washington State Grange is part of a national, grassroots organization. Granges tend to support populist and democratic policies—such as initiatives, referendums, and campaign finance reforms—and other policies that benefit small farmers and rural communities.
2. Examples of candidates whom the political parties might not have wanted to associate themselves with could include people such as Goodspaceguy, a perennial candidate for various offices, who ran as a Republican for governor in 2016, or Mike the Mover, who ran for U.S. Senate as a Republican in 2012 and for Congress in 2014 as a minor party candidate.
3. Accounting for party totals is complicated by transfers across party funds inside each party.

References

Appleton, Andrew, and Renee Edwards. 2011. "Political Parties." In *Governing Washington: Politics and Government in the Evergreen State*, edited by Cornell W. Clayton and Nicholas P. Lovrich. Pullman: Washington State University Press.

Brunner, Jim. 2016. "Washington GOP to Caucus Saturday, But It Won't Count for Presidential Race." *Seattle Times*, February 19, 2016.

Bullock, Will, and Joshua D. Clinton. 2011. "More a Molehill than a Mountain: The Effects of the Blanket Primary on Elected Officials' Behavior for California." *The Journal of Politics* 73:3(915-930).

California Democratic Party et al. v. Jones et al. 530 U.S. 567 (2000).

Donovan, Todd, et al. 2015. *State and Local Politics: Institutions and Reform*. Boston: Cengage Learning.

Ebel, Erich. 2004. "Polls favor modified blanket primary." Washington State Secretary of State. www.sos.wa.gov/office/news-releases.aspx#/news/231.

Gerber, Elisabeth R., and Rebecca B. Morton. 1998. "Primary Election Systems and Representation." *Journal of Law, Economics, and Organization* 14:2(304–324).

Key, V. O. 1964. *Politics, Parties, and Pressure Groups.* New York: Thomas Y. Crowell Company.

Kramer, A. Ludlow. 1972. *Official Voters Pamphlet.* Washington State Secretary of State. www.sos.wa.gov/_assets/elections/Voters'%20Pamphlet%201972.pdf.

McGhee, Eric, et al. 2014. "A Primary Cause of Partisanship? Nomination Systems and Legislator Ideology." *American Journal of Political Science* 58:2(337–51).

Munro, Ralph. 1992. *Voters Pamphlet.* Washington State Secretary of State. www.sos.wa.gov/_assets/elections/Voters'%20Pamphlet%201992.pdf.

PDC (Public Disclosure Commission). 2016. "Contribution Limits." www.pdc.wa.gov/learn/contribution-limits.

———. 2016. "Exempt & Non-Exempt Accounts." www.pdc.wa.gov/learn/publications/political-committee-instructions/prohibitions-and-restrictions/contributions-7.

———. 2016. "Party Committee Search." web.pdc.wa.gov/MvcQuerySystem/Committee/party_state_committees.

Public Citizen. 2014. "The Dark Side of Citizens United." www.citizen.org/sites/default/files/us-chamber-of-commerce-dark-money-spending-report.pdf

Ranney, Austin. 1965. "Parties in State Politics." In *Politics in the American States,* edited by Herbert Jacobs and Kenneth N. Vines. Boston: Little, Brown.

Schattschneider, E. E. 1942. *Party Government: American Government in Action.* Transaction Publishers.

Southwell, Priscilla L. 1991. "Open Versus Closed Primaries: The Effect on Strategic Voting and Candidate Fortunes." *Social Science Quarterly* 72:4(789–96).

Washington State Democratic Party et al. v. Sam Reed, W.D. Wash. 2002.

Washington State Grange v. Washington State Republican Party. 552 U.S. 442. 2008.

Washington State Republican Party v. State Public Disclosure Commission. No. 67442-6. 2000.

Washington State Secretary of State. "Election Results Search." www.sos.wa.gov/elections/results_search.aspx.

Washington State Secretary of State. 2014. "History of Washington State Primary Systems." www.sos.wa.gov/_assets/elections/history%20of%20washington%20state%20primary%20systems.pdf.

Washington State Secretary of State. ND. "History of the Blanket Primary in Washington." www.sos.wa.gov/elections/bp_history.aspx.

Washington State Secretary of State. ND. "The Blanket Primary in California." www.sos.wa.gov/elections/bp_california.aspx.

Washington State Secretary of State. ND. "1971–Now: Changes in Voting." www.sos.wa.gov/elections/timeline/time5.htm.

Washington State Secretary of State. 2002. "Washington State Wins Blanket Primary Case." News Release. March 27, 2002.

Washington State Secretary of State. 2003. "9th Circuit Court of Appeals reverses blanket primary decision." News Release. September 15, 2003.

CHAPTER 4

Interest Groups in Washington

Clive S. Thomas and Richard Elgar

Introduction

Interest groups and lobbyists are a natural product of the particular needs of various segments of society that often clash with each other when promoting their interests to government. Although they can be considered essential to the functioning of democracy, few aspects of American and Washington State politics generate a more negative reaction from the public than do special interest groups and the lobbyists who represent them. Most members of interest groups, however, do not see themselves as "special interests" but as "stakeholders" protecting and promoting public policy in areas that affect them such as business, education, and environmental concerns, among other interests. In this chapter we ask to what extent do interest groups promote or undermine democracy in the Evergreen State?

The Parlance of Washington State Interest Groups, and the Essence of Democracy

Interests and *interest groups* operate in a democracy by lobbying— conveying their views through a process of advocacy to elected and appointed officials for the purpose of influencing public policy. Lobbying involves four stages that often overlap in practice:

1. Gaining access to policy makers;
2. building a relationship with them;
3. providing them with information on an issue or cause; and,
4. influencing their actions.

Although interest groups are usually defined narrowly to include only those groups required to register under state laws, many groups and organizations engage in lobbying that are not required to register, including those representing various levels and agencies of government. Washington State does not require public officials at any level of government to register as lobbyists. Therefore, in this chapter we use the following definition:

An *interest group* is an association of individuals or organizations, or a public or private institution, which, on the basis of one or more shared concerns, attempts to influence public policy in its favor.

Interest groups in Washington State comprise of:

1. **Membership groups**—individuals promoting a host of economic, social, and political concerns, such as senior citizens, environmentalists, schoolteachers, nurses, and anti-tax advocates.
2. **Organizational interests**—entities such as business associations or trade unions—in effect, organizations of organizations.
3. **Institutional interests**—private and public organizations, such as businesses, think tanks, universities, state and federal agencies, and local governments. They are the largest category of organized interests operating in state politics (Gray and Lowery 2001).

A *lobby* is a collection of interests concerned with a similar area of public policy. For example, the higher education lobby in Washington is comprised of student and faculty groups, as well as institutions such as Washington State University and the University of Washington. Lobbying takes place throughout the government, including the legislature and executive branch agencies (Nownes and Freeman 1998).

A *lobbyist* is a person who represents an interest or interest group in an effort to influence government decisions in that group's favor. Lobbyists include not only those required to register by law but also those representing non-registered groups and organizations, particularly government organizations.

The *state interest group system* is the array of groups and organizations, both formal and informal, and their lobbyists working to affect public policy in a state. It is the characteristics of the interest group system—its size, development, composition, methods of operating, and so on—that shape much of the politics in a state. Three core issues relate to the relationship of interest groups with democracy:

1. the extent to which these organizations are representative of society as a whole or biased in favor of one or more segments of society;

2. the degree to which their political activities promote or undermine the democratic process;
3. balancing the right of groups to represent their causes with the
need to regulate their potential abuse of power.

Public Ambivalence

Both interest groups and political parties facilitate the essential democratic function of representation—linking the citizenry with their government. Unlike political parties, which are, in essence, umbrella organizations for a collection of like-minded political perspectives seeking
to win control of government, the majority of interest groups exist for
the economic, personal, recreational, or other non-political benefit
of their members. For instance, the primary function of the Building
Industry Association of Washington (BIAW) is to aid its members in
their business of construction, such as providing information about
new developments in the industry. But many groups, including the
BIAW, become involved in politics because of the government affecting their activities, or their need for government aid.

When interest groups get involved in politics they have one overriding goal—to influence the political process and public policy in their
favor. In their political role, interest groups perform several essential
functions that enhance democracy. They make representation more
efficient and potentially more effective than if each person lobbied
individually. They provide policymakers with needed information and
alternative perspectives, as well as aiding in the process of compromise and bargaining. Interest groups also provide education on issues
to their members, recruit candidates for public office, and some groups
help to fund election campaigns.

Yet these public roles of interest groups are purely incidental. In their
private capacity the vast majority of interest groups do not exist to either
facilitate or improve the democratic process, and many groups work to
undermine the access and influence of their opponents. Furthermore,
as vehicles of representation, interest groups are far from the ideal
link between the governed and the government. The major problem
is that they do not represent all segments of the population equally.
Their bias is toward better-educated, higher income, white, and male
segments of the population. The interests of women, minorities, the

less well educated, and lower income segments are underrepresented in the political process by interest groups. As umbrella organizations embracing a host of groups and interests, political parties are far more representative political organizations.

In the past, the public's negative view of interest groups came from a combination of two factors. One was that interest groups sometimes engaged in unethical and illegal activities such as bribery. The second was that powerful interests often dominated a state or town, as with the railroad, lumber, and fishing industries in Washington during territorial and early statehood days. In 2015, a national Gallup Poll found the public rated lobbyists' ethics lower than any other profession (Gallup Poll 2015).

However, while the media often reinforce these attitudes, the vast majority of groups work within the law. Very few lobbyists make huge salaries and many advocacy groups are not very influential but plod away diligently, working with public officials. Moreover, most public officials, especially elected officials, have a more positive attitude toward interest groups and lobbyists than the general public. This is because they need the technical information groups can provide as an efficient means for gauging the views of particular political constituencies and or making policy.

The Relationship between Interest Groups and Democracy

Washington was dominated in its early years by a few powerful interests, primarily railroads and natural resource extraction industries, such as the Weyerhaeuser Corporation (Clark 1976). Over time the dominance of these interests was challenged. From the early years of statehood, regulating the powers of railroads and major corporations was a primary target of the populist reformers who drafted Washington's constitution. Reforms in this period included public ownership of utilities (Bone 1969) and the adoption of voter initiatives and referenda (Long 2004). These developments and the challenge to the power of business by the rise of organized labor set the political stage for the evolution of Washington's interest group system.

Three developments between the 1930s and 1960s were important. First, besides business and agriculture, other interests established a permanent presence in Olympia, particularly labor unions, education interests, and local governments. Second, the initiative process was used increasingly by interest groups (Bone 1969). And third, public suspicion about the role of interest groups in campaign financing and providing other perks to legislators led to pressure for more regulation of interest group activity (Gissberg and Boswell 1996; Petersen 2013).

By the 1960s Washington State's interest group system was still underdeveloped by today's standards. The range of groups was narrow, and insider groups (those with long-standing, close ties to policy-makers) dominated the Olympia scene. Lobbying techniques primarily consisted of direct tactics—mainly the use of lobbyists, although organizations like the Washington State Medical Association and labor groups had also established political action committees (PACs) to raise funds for the election of their supporters or to defeat their opponents. At that time, the most powerful groups in Washington were natural resource interests (led by Weyerhaeuser), labor (blue and white collar), some agricultural interests, and business, including Boeing (Gissberg and Boswell 1996).

Washington's interest group system went through a major transformation after the 1960s in the wake of anti-Vietnam War protesters, the civil rights movement, and the rise of the environmental movement. The increased role of government through the mid-1960s Great Society programs produced changes. These developments inspired a range of new interests and stimulated others to become more politically active, including women, minority rights groups, environmentalists, advocates for various social causes such as pro-life and pro-choice groups, gay rights groups, and groups for the disabled. In addition groups representing public employees, universities, state agencies, and good government groups such as Common Cause became prominent. Many of these groups were single-issue groups, in contrast to the old, established interests that covered a range of issues.

Changes in Washington's economy also contributed to an increase in the number and types of groups represented in Olympia. Most notable was the establishment of Microsoft and the high-tech industry beginning in the late 1970s and Amazon in the 1990s, as well as the attraction of outside businesses such as WalMart, FedEx, and Verizon Wireless. Many of these became engaged in major lobbying activities (Johnson 2014). This expansion in group activity led to greater competition among groups and encouraged the use of a broader range of lobbying techniques defined below, especially the initiative and the formation of ad hoc coalitions (several groups coming together to promote an issue, but usually disbanding afterwards). It was a combination of the initiative process and a coalition that was behind the enactment of public disclosure laws. Before 1972, there had been minimal lobby regulation. Jolene Unsoeld, a political activist and politician, was a major force behind the enactment of comprehensive lobby regulation in Washington (Bone 1969; Cuillier, Dean, and Ross 2004). Initiative 276, passed by the voters in 1972, had been pushed by a broad coalition of good government groups named the Coalition for Open Government (Cuillier, Dean, and Ross 2004). From this initiative came the Public Disclosure Act of 1972 and the Public Disclosure Commission (PDC).

Subsequent new groups in Washington became active as political counter-weights to existing interests. These new groups range from environmentalists challenging developers, and groups opposing the use of fossil fuels, to those opposing the sale of genetically modified foods. These clashes of interests, combined with the increased number of interest groups, has led to constraints on those groups that for many years had free rein in their operations and influence.

Today, Washington's interest group system is one of the most diversified, developed, and professional of all 50 states. Due to its balanced economy, plus a degree of ethnic and demographic diversity, and a large, well-educated middle class, there are a wide range of interests operating in Olympia. In this regard, Washington is on a par with much larger states, like California and Florida, though on a smaller scale. Additionally, lobbying in Olympia by interests outside the state has a long history, and has increased considerably in the last 30 years. Out-of-state interests have included social issue groups, such as Mothers Against Drunk Driving; major economic interests, including the former energy giant, Enron, or outside beverage companies lobbying for favorable access to Washington markets; and ideological interest groups that push various causes such as restricting abortion rights or gay rights.

Developments in interest group activity since statehood have worked to enhance democracy in the Evergreen state. This has been particularly evidenced by a much wider range of interests represented and through public action, there is now a high degree of transparency and public accountability. But as we will see, both these developments only go so far in promoting democracy. And, while the number of groups in Olympia has grown, the groups and interests that are most influential have changed very little. Presence in Olympia and a high profile is one thing, actual influence is often quite another.

Interest Group Strategies and Tactics in Washington and Intergovernmental Lobbying

In Washington, as elsewhere in the country, for many years direct contact between the lobbyist and the policy maker was the only form of lobbying used by many organizations. But because of the increasing competition between groups, many organizations now undertake more complex lobbying campaigns, using a range of direct and indirect tactics including:

1. **Lobbying the legislature and executive branches of government**—direct contact by a lobbyist.
2. **Grassroots lobbying**—using group members to contact public officials.
3. **Lobbying through the courts**—cannot be lobbied directly, but many interest groups use the courts to obtain or oppose policy decisions that affect them.
4. **Affiliation with or support of a political party**—high profile interests, like labor, some businesses, many religious groups, and some minority groups, either affiliate with, or have strong leanings toward, one of the two major parties.
5. **Involvement in direct democracy campaigns**—use of the initiative, referendum, and recall.
6. **Financial contributions to help elect candidates**—One major source campaign of money is the political action committee (PAC).
7. **Non-financial contributions to help elect candidates**—including recruiting candidates, providing campaign workers, helping get out the vote, and providing political expertise from the group.
8. **Use of the media, public relations (PR), and advertising campaigns**—using print and broadcast media (including editorials and comments on stories), social media, and PR and advertising campaigns to get a message across to policy makers, and also to

create a perception that the public strongly supports or strongly opposes the policy concerned.

9. **Protests, boycotts, and demonstrations**—most often employed by outsider groups who do not have access to policy makers but want to attract their attention. Often they are tactics of last resort. Because of their often confrontational nature, they can backfire on a group but can also be successful at gaining the attention of the public and policy makers.

Direct contact by lobbyists with public officials is still the major tactic used by groups (Nownes, Thomas, and Hrebenar 2008) although the use of the initiative and judicial campaign activity are both noteworthy tactics in Washington.

When we think about interest groups, we often forget to include two related aspects of strategy and tactics. One is that many groups lobby at the three levels of government—state, federal, and local—so-called intergovernmental lobbying. For example, teachers, particularly the Washington Education Association, try to influence policy at all three levels, but they primarily lobby for funding at the state level. The second aspect is government agencies lobbying governments and their agencies. For example, state universities, which are highly reliant on state funding, press their claims in Olympia. The lobbying effort of state universities is considered in a case study below.

The Initiative

Use of the initiative has become an increasingly important tactic. It has been employed by the Washington Education Association (WEA) to reduce class sizes and protect teachers' pay; by those who want to restrict the rights of public employees to spend money on political activities; by those working to promote health care; and by both pro- and anti-tax interests. Tim Eyman is perhaps best known in the state for pushing many anti-tax initiatives in recent years (Herold and Gombosky 2004). Among his several successes was Initiative 1053, passed in 2010, requiring a two-thirds vote by the electorate to increase state taxes and fees, although it was later ruled to be unconstitutional.

The initiative process can be used to benefit citizens as a whole, as with Initiative 276 in 1972, which established public disclosure in the state. However, it has also become subject to very specific interests pushing narrow causes, such as Costco-funded initiatives to privatize liquor sales in Washington (see below). Plus, many businesses, including those from out of state, have used the initiative to promote their economic self-interest.

Judicial Selection and Retention

Who sits on the bench, particularly those on Washington's Supreme Court, can have a major impact on many interest groups as judges rule on the constitutionality of laws and executive actions. In Washington, judicial elections are nonpartisan. The intention was to insulate judges from political influence in order to protect their impartiality. However, state judicial elections have become increasingly politicized in recent years and have been the subject of targeted spending by interest groups.

A high profile judicial election in 2016 pitted incumbent Supreme Court Judge Charles Wiggins against challenger Dave Larson. Many in the business community, including Bill Gates, made major contributions to defeat Wiggins, in part, because he had been one of the majority votes declaring the state's charter school law unconstitutional. Despite this, and despite being outspent, Wiggins retained his seat on the bench (Miletich 2016).

Lobbyists

Olympia's lobbying community is not much different from those in other states. In 2015, a total of 958 lobbyists representing 1,437 employers registered with the PDC. While the number of lobbyists has increased only slightly since 2000, the number of those employing lobbyists has increased dramatically (Anderson 2011; PDC 2017), probably reflecting the increased need that many businesses and organizations see to deal with government.

The lobbying community in Washington State, as in all states, includes five types of lobbyists:

- **Contract lobbyists**—hired on contract for a fee specifically to lobby. They often represent more than one client. Many are former legislators, legislative aides, or have worked in the executive branch. These are required to register with the PDC.

- **In-house lobbyists**—employees of an association, organization, or business who, as all or part of their job, act as a lobbyist. These represent only one client—their employer. Most have to register with the PDC.
- **Legislative liaisons**—employees of state, local, and federal agencies who represent their agency to the legislative and executive branches of state government. They do not have to register.
- **Volunteer or cause lobbyists**—represent citizen and community organizations or informal groups. They rarely represent more than one interest and are usually unpaid. Most do not have to register.
- **Private individual lobbyists**—act on their own behalf and not designated by any organization as an official representative. Most do not register.

This means that the number of lobbyists registered with the PDC is far lower than those actually lobbying, and while they get the most publicity because of their often-high salaries, contract lobbyists constitute only about 20 percent of the lobbying community.

As a medium-sized state in population, Washington's lobbyists and contract lobbying firms tend to be generalists representing a range of interests and not specialized lobbyists, such as those found in large states like California and New York. In Washington, for example, a medium-sized firm could represent forestry, pulp and paper, telecommunications, banking, health care, mining, aviation, retail, water rights, the state lottery, land development, oil, taxes, alcohol, tobacco, and the environment. A single law and lobby firm in Seattle has close to 40 lobbying clients (PDC 2017).

In terms of how the composition and the operation of the lobbying community affects democracy in Washington, it is certainly biased in favor of those groups with resources, but the increasing range of active organizations means that a larger part of society is being represented. Additionally, the increased transparency of contract and in-house lobbyist actions means that they have much less leeway to undermine the public interest.

Money

A common belief is that lobbying is all about money; those who have a lot of it get what they want from government but those with little or none have minimal political influence. Although the reality is more complex, the most consistently successful groups are those with money, and lobbying expenditures in Washington have been rising as the competition between interest groups increases.

Figure 1: Washington State Lobby Spending for Selected Years, 2001-2015: Private, Public, and Total Outlays in $Millions

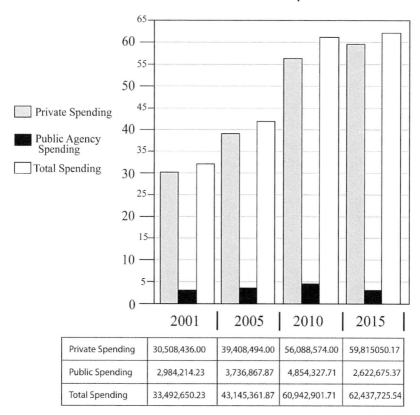

	2001	2005	2010	2015
Private Spending	30,508,436.00	39,408,494.00	56,088,574.00	59,815050.17
Public Spending	2,984,214.23	3,736,867.87	4,854,327.71	2,622,675.37
Total Spending	33,492,650.23	43,145,361.87	60,942,901.71	62,437,725.54

Source: Authors, from Washington Public Disclosure Commission data, www.pdc.wa.gov.

Figure 1 shows the trend in private, public, and total spending on lobbying between 2001 and 2015, showing a steady rise in spending. Much of the rise in spending is due to out-of-state interests. In 1980

Washington State expenditures were about $7 million (Peterson 1987, 125), but by 2006 when the money spent on lobbying across the 50 states passed the $1 billion mark for the first time (Laskow 2006), the total for that year in Washington State was $49 million.

Spending by Political Action Committees [PACs]

Political practitioners see PACs as important for access to decision-makers and a major factor in influence, hence the increasing use of PACs in recent years. By 1980 PACs were the main source of campaign funds in the state, and have been increasing in importance ever since (Peterson 1987). The total amount of money spent by PACs in Washington in the 2016 elections was almost $41 million, compared to just over $10 million in 2000 (PDC Committees).

One example of PAC spending in 2016 was Working Families, a PAC created by state Republicans to fund about $1,000,000 in negative TV ads targeting Democrats in two state senate races, with much of the money coming from out-of-state corporate interests. In both cases, the Democrats won. Another example was Citizens for Working Courts, created to fight Charles Wiggins' reelection to the State Supreme Court, which spent nearly $1 million and far outspent the pro-Wiggins supporters (Miletich 2016). These examples suggest that big money does not always sway an election.

It was noted earlier that Washington has been the target of spending by out-of-state money from certain interest group campaigns in recent years. As might be expected, issues that are largely of concern only in Washington, such as those regarding transportation (to reduce congestion), and health issues, attract less than 20 percent of out-of-state money.

In contrast, the 2010 Stop the Food and Beverage Tax Hikes initiative (I-1107) gathered more than $16 million in contributions, of which over 95 percent came from out of state (PDC 2014). Most contributions came from the American Beverage Association (ABA) based in Washington, DC. At that point, this was the most ever spent on an initiative by interest groups in Washington's history. It was surpassed in 2011 by Initiative 1183, which aimed to privatize sales of liquor in Washington, with almost $32 million spent by both sides on the ultimately successful campaign. Of the total expenditures, over $20 million was spent on the Yes campaign, mostly provided by Costco.[1]

Two years later Initiative 522, which would have required labeling of foods containing GMOs (genetically modified organisms), was defeated with more than $35 million spent against the initiative, including major contributions from out of state by food interests, particularly the Washington, DC-based Grocery Manufacturers Association (PDC Committees).

Regulation–the Public Disclosure Commission [PDC]

A major factor shaping the operating environment of interest groups in Washington State is the PDC. Among its regulatory responsibilities are the registration of interest groups and lobbyists and making this information available to the public. Although the PDC does not require those representing governments to register, it does require disclosure of the funds spent for such purposes, with the exception of local elected officials. The PDC makes the actions of groups and lobbyists transparent to the public and thus enables their actions to be monitored. This includes information about how much they spend on lobbying and whom they lobby.

Certainly, the media is also important in throwing light on the actions of interest groups' relations with public officials, but it is the PDC that provides reporters with much of the information they use in their stories. However, there is only so much influence the PDC can bring to bear on the operation of interest groups, and the agency is not immune from politics and political pressures. Nonetheless in several national surveys, the PDC was ranked as the most effective of such agencies across the 50 states by the Center for Public Integrity, a campaign and lobbying watchdog (CPI 2003; Anderson 2011).

Despite this recognition, continuing challenges in Washington include a lack of consensus and understanding on what regulation should and can achieve. Should it even-up the political playing field, prevent abuses by powerful interests, or inform public officials and the public of connections between those lobbying and those being lobbied? Whatever the perceived purposes, lobby laws cannot turn powerless groups into powerful forces, nor reduce the political clout of existing influential groups. However, with the right combination of laws and enforcement authority, the PDC can influence the actions of interest groups and their lobbyists by making nefarious and underhand activities by lobbyists less likely for fear of bad publicity or even prosecution.

The fact that the main driver for regulation is political scandal or public concern with the actions of public officials means that most lobby laws are enacted on an ad hoc basis and often within a highly charged political atmosphere. It also costs money to administer the laws, and such agencies are also often responsible for pressing campaign finance and conflict-of-interest laws, meaning that they are often not popular with politicians. Furthermore, it is not usually the public that makes use of the information made available, but rather the media and candidates running against incumbents. For these and other reasons, the PDC is often accused by politicians of being biased in its application of regulations (Brunner 2015). The agency has suffered budget cuts in the past five years and is rapidly becoming unable to fulfill its major role given increases in campaign and lobby spending and lack of funds to update its antiquated technology (Brunner 2016a).

Given these challenges, including the political fallout of regulation, discussions of lobby laws in Washington State revolve around the extensiveness of regulation and monitoring. Among public officials and those groups lobbying for regulation, there has been consensus on the role of regulation as partly restrictive but mainly as a monitoring device. Plus, more than most states, Washington has a systematic body of regulation that is well-enforced and, despite recent developments, generally less under attack to be changed.

Effects of Regulations on Interest Groups

Overall, within its constitutional and political limitations, increased regulation has had some impact in Washington State. As in all states, restraint in dealings with public officials, greater concern for their group's public image, and the increased professionalism of lobbyists appear to be the three major effects. Lobbyists, especially those representing powerful interests, are much less likely to use blatant strong-arm tactics. Lobbyists themselves are particularly concerned to change their image as wheeler-dealers and have an association called

The Third House, to promote professionalism. An increased level of professionalism and ethical standards among public officials since the 1960s has also made them less likely to deal with shady lobbyists and their organizations.

While there is no systematic research comparing the extent of corruption involving lobbyists across the states, research by the U.S. Justice Department and private organizations over the past 20 years or so indicate that the level of convictions of public officials ranks Washington as one of the cleaner states in the nation (Marsh 2008; CPI 2015; Mitchell 2015).

Additionally, judging by lobbying scandals that hit the media, and prosecutions by the PDC, the Evergreen State is very clean. Over the past 20 years or so, there have been relatively few lobbying scandals. One exception was the record-setting $18 million fine imposed in 2016 on the Grocery Manufacturers Association for illegal campaign contributions to defeat the 2013 GMO food-labeling initiative (Brunner 2016b). A less serious controversy surrounded State Senator Dino Rossi's 2008 bid for the governorship. The issue was the financial support extended to him by the Building Industry Association of Washington (BIAW). Following a complaint of state disclosure violations, the PDC cleared Rossi of any wrongdoing, but its report revealed how closely the BIAW skirted the law in promoting his candidacy (Brunner 2010). These cases notwithstanding, Washington is probably among the top ten of the cleanest lobbying states in the nation and on a par with states like Vermont, Maine, Nebraska, and Minnesota.

Two Case Studies

1. Carbon Tax Initiative

In many ways, Initiative 732 in the 2016 election highlights the complexity of the Washington State interest group system. To an outside observer, the passage of an environmental initiative that claimed to make progress towards climate change while also being revenue-neutral must have seemed an easy sell in a state like Washington.

The initiative proposed to raise a carbon emission tax on certain fossil fuels and fossil-fuel-generated electricity, while reducing sales tax slightly, increasing a low-income exemption, and also providing for a reduction in certain manufacturing taxes. However, the voters of

Washington delivered a resounding defeat to the bill, with almost 60 percent voting no (Kamb 2016). Why was this initiative so spectacularly unsuccessful?

First, this particular policy debate was complicated by the fact that rather than two opposing groups, there were three main competing factions. The Yes campaign was primarily concerned to bring an initiative to the voters that would have a good chance of passing. The initiative was one that garnered support from many scientists in the region, and also from numerous economists. However, the environment movement was deeply divided on this issue, and numerous environmental and general political interests refused to support the initiative, including the Sierra Club, the Washington State Democratic Party, labor unions, and the Washington Environmental Council. Their position was in part driven by suggestions that rather than being revenue neutral, it was likely that the 732 vision of carbon tax would be revenue negative, leaving what they said would be an $800 million hole over five years[2] in the state budget that would take away from other programs, and services. Additionally, there was a view amongst these groups that by striving to make the tax revenue neutral, it was failing to raise money to proactively address climate change through alternative energy investment.[3]

The third group in this equation was the No campaign, including industrial interests such as Kaiser Aluminum and Puget Sound Energy amongst others, while out-of-state opposition was represented by Koch Industries. With this array of forces divided, it is perhaps not surprising that the status quo was maintained due to a lack of unity in the environmental lobby.

2. Lobbying by higher education groups

There are many demands by state agencies on the state budget. For example, Washington's constitution places the education of children as the paramount duty of the state. With the state's Supreme Court finding the state out of compliance with this duty (see chapter 10), those pressures have only increased on other sectors looking for slices of the state budget. This includes state universities, and their faculty, students, and alumni who have lobbied in support of their interests, particularly regarding funding.

The aims of university students and those of faculty are not always complementary, with students looking for tuition cuts or freezes, and the institutions themselves looking for increases in funding either through more legislative support or through tuition increases. In recent years there has been mixed success for these two groups. Following cuts in legislative support, double digit tuition increases were instituted during the 2011–13 biennium at universities across the state. However, a rare tuition cut in 2015, funded by the legislature, was well-received especially by students, but also by administrators at the state's universities. It was one of only three states (the others being Maine and California) to institute a rollback of tuition.[4] While the tuition reduction was welcomed, legislative funding of Washington State's universities have not returned to pre-recession levels.

In a conversation with one of the authors, a Washington state legislator explained that the reason that universities have not received more support from the legislature is because those advocating on behalf of the universities have little leverage, and that those institutions don't bring anything to the negotiating table in terms of incentives, whereas tuition cuts are received well by all families of college-aged children. Both sets of interests organize in Olympia, but whereas the institutions' lobbying is usually carried out by small government relations teams, plus input from higher level administrators, the student associations comprise larger lobbying groups. Most student associations in the state participate in the Washington Student Association, conduct lobbying days in the capitol, and while legislators may not be as familiar with the individual student lobbyists as they are of university government relations members, their impact may be greater. Given that higher education is not emphasized in the way that K–12 education is in the state constitution, it is easier for the legislature to cut higher education support than many other budget items. Equally, tuition cuts are an easier way to garner support from a broader swathe of the population that does not see the immediate impact of overall cuts to a university budget that this may cause.

In many ways, these two case studies help to demonstrate the themes that we have discussed in this chapter. The tension between different higher education interests, and the compromise that was reached in 2015, shows the moderating influence that the interest group system can have in Washington, and how the system can work to represent large communities in the state. However, in sharp relief, the carbon tax initiative debate demonstrates the resilience of established interests in the state, especially in the absence of a united attempt to change policy. It takes significant momentum to change the status quo in politics, and with a divided set of interests, even a well-funded argument is unlikely to succeed. Money, while perhaps less of a factor here, is still an important feature in the initiative process as a whole. Outside money in the soda tax initiative made an enormous difference, as it did for the GMO food-labeling initiative. This latter initiative is also highly instructive in demonstrating the stability of Washington's institutional democracy. The Grocery Manufacturers Association's $18 million fine for deliberately hiding its donors also serves to validate the role of the PDC.

Conclusion: Democracy and Interest Groups

To what extent do interest groups promote or undermine democracy in the Evergreen State? In short, the answer is a mixed one, but veering toward the positive.

Today's state group system is a far cry from previous eras. The contemporary system is broadly representative of society, with far more constraints and counterbalancing forces on group and lobbyist activities, including increased competition among a much larger number of groups, increased professionalism of public officials, and greater media and public scrutiny of group activity. This combination of factors prevents any one group or a handful of groups from dominating politics and thus undermining democracy.

The developments have been largely the result of socioeconomic and political changes that have produced a more democratic Washington state in general. Of particular importance has been state policy on political ethics and conflict of interest, campaign finance laws, and the monitoring of lobbying activity through group and lobbyist registration. But there is only so much that public policy and even positive socioeconomic developments can do to deal with the elements of interest group activity that continue to work against the enhancement of democracy.

There are aspects of group and lobbying activity that are beyond the ability of public policy to address or which are a result of constitutional and legal provisions. No democracy guarantees equality of political resources and political acumen or political influence; and even if it did these would be impossible to enforce. In fact, by implication, pluralist democracy is founded on the fact that there will be an uneven distribution of political power or else there would be political deadlock. This gives some groups a major advantage over others.

At root, a successful lobbying operation involves utilizing a range of contacts in government and various political operatives, having adequate or preferably extensive resources, political know-how, and skills to exert influence and undermine the influence of opponents. The reality is that some groups and interests are more adept at acquiring and exercising these key aspects of political advocacy than others.

As a consequence, while some outsider groups and those with minimum resources will from time to time continue to score political victories, it will be those groups and interests with major financial and political resources that will exercise influence on a year-to-year basis. This means that, for some time to come, Washington's interest group system will continue to favor business (including many from out of state), the professions, some sectors of labor, and various government agencies.

Notes

1. Melissa Allison, "Costco's $22M for Liquor Initiative Sets Record," *Seattle Times*, October 20, 2011, www.seattletimes.com/seattle-news/costcos-22m-for-liquor-initiative-sets-record.
2. Jeff Johnson, "My Turn: I-732 Will Make Washington's Budget Deficit Worse," *Kitsap Sun*, October 11, 2016, archive.kitsapsun.com/opinion/MY-TURN--I-732-will-make-Washingtons-budget-deficit-worse-396666561.html.
3. "Why We Can't Support Carbon Washington's I-732," Fuse Washington, last modified November 1, 2016, fusewashington.org/why_we_cant_support_carbon_washingtons_i-732/.
4. "2016-17 Tuition and Fees at Public Four-Year Institutions by State and Five-Year Percentage Change in In-State Tuition and Fees," College Board, Annual Survey of Colleges, trends.collegeboard.org/college-pricing/figures-tables/2016-17-state-tuition-and-fees-public-four-year-institutions-state-and-five-year-percentage.

References

Anderson, Lori. 2011. Former Communications and Training Office, Washington State Public Disclosure Commission, personal interview, February 17, 2011, and subsequent phone contact and emails, April and May 2011.

Bone, Hugh A. 1969. "Washington State: Free Style Politics." In *Politics in the American West*, edited by Frank H. Jonas, 380–415. Salt Lake City: University of Utah Press.

Brunner, Jim. 2010. "PDC Clears Dino Rossi of Campaign Charges," *Seattle Times*, March 25, 2010.

_____. 2015. "State Public Disclosure Commission Director Resigns," *Seattle Times*, April 8, 2015.

_____. 2016a. "State GOP Says Campaign-Watchdog Agency Chief is Biased, Must Resign," *Seattle Times*. October 27, 2016.

_____. 2016b. "Food Lobby Fined $18 Million for Hiding Big Donors," *Seattle Times*, November 3, 2016.

Clark, Norman H. 1976. *Washington: A Bicentennial History*. New York: Norton.

CPI [Center for Public Integrity]. 2003. "Lobby Disclosure Rankings 2003." www.publicintegrity.org/2003/05/15/5908/hired-guns-initial-report.

_____. 2015. "State Integrity 2015," November 23, 2015. www.publicintegrity.org/2015/11/09/18693/only-three-states-score-higher-d-state-integrity-investigation-11-flunk.

Cuillier, David, David Dean, and Susan Dente Ross. 2004. "The History and Intent of Initiative 276." Pullman: AccessNorthwest, Edward R. Murrow School of Communication, Washington State University. www.courts.wa.gov/content/petitions/91442-7%20Petition%20for%20Review.pdf (45–50).

Gallup Poll. 2015. "Americans' Faith in Honesty, Ethics of Police Rebounds." December 21, 2015. www.gallup.com/poll/187874/americans-faith-honesty-ethics-police-rebounds.aspx?g_source=lobbyists&g_medium=search&g_campaign=tiles.

Gissberg, William A., and Sharon A. Boswell. 1996. *William A. Gissberg: An Oral*

History. Olympia: Washington State Oral History Project, Office of the Secretary of State.

Gray, Virginia, and David Lowery. 2001. "The Institutionalization of State Communities of Organized Interests," *Political Research Quarterly* 54 (2): (2001): 265–284, esp. Fig. 3.

Herold, Robert, and Jeff Gombosky. 2004. "Interest Group Politics in Washington State: Emergent Urbanization and the Continuing Struggle for the Public Domain." In *Washington State Government and Politics*, edited by Cornell W. Clayton, Lance T. LeLoup, and Nicholas P. Lovrich. Pullman: Washington State University Press, 45–71.

Johnson, Stephen F. 2014. Former executive director, Washington Public Utilities Districts Association, personal interview, November 5, 2014.

Kamb, Lewis, "Voters firmly Reject State 'Carbon Tax' on Fossil Fuels," *Seattle Times*, November 9, 2016.

Laskow, Sarah. December 20, 2006. "State Lobbying Becomes Billion Dollar Business," news release. Center for Public Integrity, Washington, DC. projects.publicintegrity.org/hiredguns/report.aspx?aid=835

Long, Carolyn N. 2004. "Direct Democracy in Washington." In *Washington State Government and Politics*, edited by Cornell W. Clayton, Lance T. LeLoup, and Nicholas P. Lovrich, 73–92. Pullman: Washington State University Press.

Marsh, Bill. 2008. "Illinois Is Trying. It Really Is. But the Most Corrupt State Is Actually…" *The New York Times*. December 13, 2008.

Miletich, Steve, "Wiggins Wins Despite Big Bid to Defeat Him," *Seattle Times*, November 9, 2016.

Mitchell, Anthea. 2015. *The Cheat Sheet*, "The Most Corrupt States in America." January 29, 2015. www.cheatsheet.com/politics/how-corrupt-is-your-state-what-can-america-learn-from-other-nations.html/?a=viewall.

Nownes, Anthony J., Clive S. Thomas, and Ronald J. Hrebenar. 2008. "Interest Groups in the States." Chapter 4 in *Politics in the American States: A Comparative Analysis*, 9th ed., edited by Virginia Gray and Russell L. Hanson. Washington, DC: Congressional Quarterly Press.

Nownes, Anthony J., and Patricia K. Freeman. 1998. "Interest Group Activity in the States." *The Journal of Politics* 60(1): 86–112.

PDC 2017. Registered Lobbyists, at web.pdc.wa.gov/MvcQuerySystem/Lobbying/Lobbyists?year=2017.

PDC 2014. Initiatives, at web.pdc.wa.gov/MvcViewReports/Committee/initiative_committees?year=2014&form=ALL.

PDC Committees, at web.pdc.wa.gov/MvcQuerySystem/Committee/continuing_committees.

Petersen, Anne. 2013. Journal clerk, Washington State House of Representatives, 1960–65, personal interview by Clive Thomas, November 11, 2013.

Peterson, Walfred H. 1987. "Washington: The Impact of Public Disclosure Laws." In *Interest Group Politics in the American West*, edited by Ronald J. Hrebenar and Clive S. Thomas. Salt Lake City: University of Utah Press, 123–31.

Thomas, Clive S., Ronald J. Hrebenar, and Anthony J. Nownes. 2008. "Interest Group Politics in the States: Four Decades of Developments—the 1960s to the Present." *Book of the States*, Vol. 40. Lexington, KY: The Council of State Governments, 322–31.

CHAPTER 5

Progressive Federalism: Washington State as a Protector of Civil Rights Progress?

María Chávez and Robin Dale Jacobson

Introduction[1]

Changing ethnic and racial demographics in Washington State, and across the nation, underscore some important political and cultural challenges and divisions in the United States. These were seen in the racially inflamed rhetoric employed throughout the 2016 presidential campaign and during President Donald Trump's first few months in office, and include his calls for constructing a border wall, ending sanctuary cities, ordering round-ups of undocumented persons, ending Deferred Action for Childhood Arrivals, and blocking the admission of refugees and visitors from a number of predominately Muslim countries. The Trump administration's actions toward minoritized groups throughout the United States led some to suggest that states with large minority populations and Democratic Party control may become more active in asserting state prerogatives and sovereignty to protect vulnerable minority groups from shifting federal policy.

During the first year of the Trump administration, Washington State appeared to exemplify this prospect. For example, in *State of Washington vs. Donald J. Trump* (2017),[2] Washington State, joined by Minnesota, challenged President Trump's Executive Order 13769 on immigration arguing that it was unlawful on both statutory and constitutional grounds. In support of Washington's lawsuit, *amicus* briefs were filed by 97 private corporations, Seattle University's School of Law, a large group of former state department and intelligence officials, and the state of Hawaii.

Calls for a strong state power that resists or pushes back against the federal government, however, have a long history in the United States of being associated with the oppression of racial, ethnic, and other minority groups rather than as protectors of civil rights. Indeed, the federal government's role in protecting civil rights during the twentieth century, and before that its role in ending slavery in the Civil War, were often criticized by proponents of states' rights as an over-reach of central authority and damaging to local-based democracy. Legal scholar Ilya Somin argues, however, that the sharp shift in federal policies under the Trump administration may occasion a *progressive* federalism, turning some states into protectors of diversity and the interests of minority groups against the federal government.[3] Heather Gerken, of Yale Law School, also suggests that "it is a mistake to equate federalism's past [of racial oppression] with its future. State and local governments have become sites of empowerment for racial minorities and dissenters" she contends.[4] How effective states will become in promoting a new progressive federalism remains to be seen, but Washington State's response to the Trump administration's early policy shifts makes clear that it may become a leader in the movement.

In this chapter, we examine the promises and challenges of Washington State's growing diversity at this time in the nation's history. We begin with a consideration of how states might become more vigorous champions of the rights of minority groups during a period when the federal government's role in the area recedes. We then turn to an examination of the growth among minority communities in Washington in recent decades and examine racial inequality across a range of indicators in the state—including in levels of poverty, unemployment, uninsured persons rates, educational attainment, and political representation. We also look at discrimination and hate crimes against minoritized communities. Finally, we conclude with a discussion of the challenges confronting Washington's immigrant and minoritized communities.

Part I: Prospects of a Progressive Federalism in Washington State

For more than a half century the federal government has been the major champion of the rights and interests of minorities living in the United States. From federal court decisions ending racial segregation and bans on interracial marriages, to sweeping federal civil rights statutes such as the 1964 Civil Rights Act, the 1965 Voting Rights Act, the Fair Housing Act, and the Americans With Disabilities Act, federal policies and programs have aimed at protecting minority groups and promoting equal opportunity. Often these federal advances came at the expense of state and local authority, and they were frequently challenged as violating the principles of federalism. More recently the federal government found itself partnering with states on policies aimed at reducing racial and ethnic inequality. While the outcomes of measures such as the Affordable Care Act (ACA) or No Child Left Behind are certainly debatable, written into the heart of those federal policies were attempts to increase access to health care and quality education for racial and ethnic minorities. However, in the wake of the 2016 presidential election the prospects for continued federal leadership on policies that target racial inequality and enhance civil rights seem less certain, and in some areas these federal programs may be retrenched and even reversed.

State legislatures, however, in recent decades have assumed a major role in enacting policies that protect and enhance the lives of minorities living within their states. During a period of federal retrenchment of civil rights, states may matter more than ever for understanding how racial and ethnic minorities fare in the United States, and prospects are ripe for a new form of *progressive federalism* to emerge. This may include refusing to partner with the federal government in some areas, creatively reinterpreting federal programs in others, filling in voids left by the federal government retrenchment, or mounting legal challenges against federal government actions.

Historically, state powers have played the dominant role in affecting the day-to-day lives of U.S. citizens. The Tenth Amendment reserved all police powers not explicitly granted to the federal government in the U.S. Constitution to the states, making their authority almost limitless and the purview of the federal government rather constrained. Through most of the nineteenth century, states controlled issues related to public welfare, economic regulation, and personal behavior (Moncrief and Squire 2017). While many scholars point to the Civil War as inverting the power relationship between the federal government and the states, historian Gary Gerstle (2010) argues it was only in the 1960s that such an inversion became a manifest reality. This inversion came in response to demands to address the systems of racial segregation and discrimination that were deeply entrenched in the South, lodging more control over the lives of citizens in the U.S. Congress than in their respective state legislatures.

The powerful central authority of the federal government is a relatively recent phenomenon in American politics, and while it was originally challenged by conservatives who opposed the liberal policies that it promoted in recent years, a progressive federalism has emerged, one in which those arguing for more robust state authority are developing expansive health care programs, such as Massachusetts before the Affordable Care Act, or promoting more progressive environmental protection measures such as those involving vehicle emissions in California. Examples such as these have led Gerstle to suggest that a federalism that "would stress the capacious power of government that resides in the states, would call on states to act in the public interest, and would seek to turn state governments into what the liberal jurist Louis Brandeis once celebrated as 'laboratories of democracy.'" Such a move would, she suggests, present the possibility of improving the lives of the most underprivileged people in those states and provide models for how to deal with problems across the nation.

The issue of immigration, however, demonstrates both the promise and the pitfalls of a strategy of relying on states as the principal champion of such rights. Starting in 2005 attention was given to the issue of immigration at the state level. State legislatures across the country considered a wide range of proposals about immigration enforcement and benefits and rights for immigrants. While some states denied access to state schools for undocumented immigrants, others secured in-state tuition for such immigrants. While some states provided state and local law enforcement officials with enhanced immigration authority or mandated reporting from state bureaucrats, others prohibited police and other state and local authorities from inquiring about immigration status. As the recent history of immigration law suggests, greater range of action at the state level could both restrict protections and equality of opportunity in some states and significantly enhance it in others.

Three distinctive aspects of Washington's political life, however, suggest that the Evergreen State could be one that advances civil rights and enhances the economic well-being of minoritized groups in major ways. These aspects are: (1) Washington is a solidly Democratic state in terms of statewide politics; (2) Washington provides a gateway to the Pacific Rim and is a vibrant player in the global market; and (3) Washington has a "moralistic" political culture that emphasizes the common good as the proper focus of government action. While Washington is fairly equally divided in partisanship, the state has voted for the Democratic presidential candidates in the last eight elections, it has had a long string of Democratic governors, and the Democratic Party has also controlled most statewide and many local elections in the influential Puget Sound region as well (see Chapters 2 and 3). Because the modern Democratic Party has generally taken a more progressive stance on civil rights, enhancing opportunities for minority groups and women, and on cultural diversity issues, including the view that government should play an active role promoting social and economic justice, it is likely that Washington will play a role in asserting federalism principles against any federal retrenchment of civil rights.

Additionally, the positioning of Washington as a global, high-tech leader on the Pacific Rim creates pressure from private and public officials who believe that in order to flourish the region needs to continue to attract creative and industrious people from around the world. This open-borders viewpoint is detailed in the state's lawsuit challenging President Trump's initial travel ban on immigrants. That lawsuit highlights the key role of immigrants in "high tech" industries, noting that Washington ranks ninth among the states in the number of high-skilled visas used in the country. The lawsuit mentions Amazon, Expedia, Starbucks, and Microsoft specifically in this regard. In addition to citing particular stories of individuals already employed suffering harm, the lawsuit also notes the harm done to the recruitment process. The following passage reflects these precise concerns:

> The market for highly skilled workers and leaders in the technology industry is extremely competitive. Changes in U.S. immigration policy that restrict the flow of people may inhibit these companies' ability to adequately staff their research and development efforts and recruit talent from overseas. If recruiting efforts are less successful, these companies' abilities to develop and deliver successful products and services may be adversely affected.[5]

Finally, as noted in the first chapter, the state's political culture can be defined as "the mix of shared attitudes, values, behaviors, and institutions that reflects a particular history and approach to politics." Lovrich, Pierce, and Elway apply Daniel Elazar's three types of political cultures in the United States—the individualistic, the moralistic, and the traditionalistic—to the Evergreen State, and show that the Moralistic/Individualistic label Elazar applies to the state based on its history of settlement works quite well down to the present (Elazar 1994b). They note the presence of "two Washingtons" with respect to geographic distribution of political culture orientations, one in the Puget Sound region, where moralistic culture reigns and the other in eastern Washington where a mix of individualistic and moralistic strains prevails. While the moralistic strain is heavily inclined toward a sense of the pursuit of the "common good" and dictates a dependence upon collaborative collective action to promote the general welfare, the individualistic is competitive and has a governmental *laissez faire* orientation. That established political culture might thus lead the state to actively protect and expand opportunities for minoritized communities within the state if their well-being is understood as a part of the common good.

The presence of the two Washingtons can be seen clearly in debates over how to address the large increase in diversity lying ahead. The overall result of the clash between a moralistic and an individualistic approach to this future in recent years has been one of a symbolic commitment to diversity accompanied by only limited movement towards substantive changes advancing social equity. A telling example is seen in the state's 1998 battle over affirmative action. Initiative 200 was placed on the ballot by citizen petition to prohibit state agencies from "granting preferential treatment based on race, sex, color, ethnicity, or national origin in the operation of public employment, public education or public contracting." This anti-affirmative action initiative was passed with large majorities in "the Other Washington" while losing in the Puget Sound area, indicating the potency of the individualistic strain of the political culture outside of that region.

The response to the passage of this measure is equally telling about the competing moralistic and individualistic goals in the Evergreen State. The Diversity Council was established in 2001 within the state Office of Financial Management (OFM), with human resource management leaders from all of the state's major agencies to help provide guidance on how state agencies and local governments could continue to make progress toward increasing diversity within the parameters of the new legal landscape prohibiting affirmative action. Microsoft, Boeing, Amazon, and other organizations joined the state's public universities to promote new diversity and inclusiveness initiatives of various kinds in an attempt to continue to foster an image of Washington being a progressive state open to all persons of good faith where the state government was acting as a progressive force for the advancement of the common good befitting its moralistic historical legacy.

But do racial and ethnic communities fit within Washington's moralistic political culture? Are their interests and voices adequately included within traditional notions of the common good? In the next section, we explore the changing demographics of Washington State, including political representation and policy options to protect and promote the well-being of minoritized groups.

Part II: Growing Diversity and Growing Inequality in Washington State

As with much of the rest of the nation, the 2010 census reveals that during the last decade Washington has experienced notable growth and profound shifts in its population. In 2000, it had a total population of 5,894,121; in 2014 its population rose to 7,061,410. Even more dramatic than this overall growth has been the growth in the diversity of the state's population. It is estimated that over 70 percent of all population growth in the state over the last decade was due to increases in its non-white population of racial and ethnic minorities. In 1970, communities of color were estimated to constitute only 6.5 percent of Washington's population and now they represent 31 percent. Latinos, the largest minoritized group in Washington State, comprised only 2.9 percent of the state population in the 1980s. As of 2015 they now comprise 12.5 percent of the state's population. In addition, "new Americans" comprise 13.2 percent of the population in the state, and 1 in 7 Washington residents are naturalized citizens.[6]

It is likely that this growth will continue well into the future. If current birth, death, and immigration rates are maintained, Hispanics/Latinos are estimated to comprise 14.5 percent of the population in

2020 and 17.8 percent in 2030. Asians were approximately 1.3 percent of the state population in 1970, and in 2010, 7.1 percent. If the Asian population continues to grow at the same rate, Asians are likely to comprise 8.7 percent of the population in 2020 and 9.7 percent in 2030. The non-Hispanic white population in the state has declined substantially since 1970, going from 95.6 percent in 1970 to 72.5 percent in 2010, and are likely to comprise 65.3 percent of the population in 2020 and 59.4 percent in 2030. The population of the state is becoming more ethnically and racially diverse, and less white, than ever before in its history since territorial days.

Figure 1. Population Growth in Washington, 1970–2030

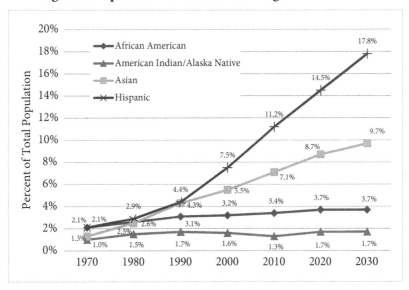

Source: Office of Financial Management, State of WA, and straight-line projections using 2010 Census data

While Washington becomes more diverse, inequality grows as a consequence of economic opportunities not being equally distributed. The median household income for whites in Washington in 2013 was $61,020, while the average income for Native Americans, African Americans, and Latinos was between $41,325 and $42,320, respectively, as the following charts reprinted from the Washington State Budget & Policy Center demonstrate:

Figure 2. Washington State Budget & Policy Center Figures on Economic Insecurity by Race[7]

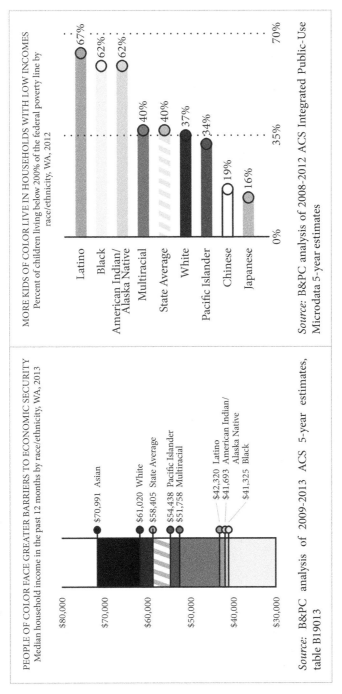

MORE KIDS OF COLOR LIVE IN HOUSEHOLDS WITH LOW INCOMES
Percent of children living below 200% of the federal poverty line by race/ethnicity, WA, 2012

- Latino — 67%
- Black — 62%
- American Indian/Alaska Native — 62%
- Multiracial — 40%
- State Average — 40%
- White — 37%
- Pacific Islander — 34%
- Chinese — 19%
- Japanese — 16%

Source: B&PC analysis of 2008-2012 ACS Integrated Public-Use Microdata 5-year estimates

PEOPLE OF COLOR FACE GREATER BARRIERS TO ECONOMIC SECURITY
Median household income in the past 12 months by race/ethnicity, WA, 2013

- $70,991 Asian
- $61,020 White
- $58,405 State Average
- $54,438 Pacific Islander
- $51,758 Multiracial
- $42,320 Latino
- $41,693 American Indian/Alaska Native
- $41,325 Black

Source: B&PC analysis of 2009-2013 ACS 5-year estimates, table B19013

Note about data: Disaggregated data is presented to provide a preliminary understanding of disparities by race and ethnicity. On its own, this data tells a limited story about the populations it represents. We encourage users of this data to engage with communities of color to develop a more accurate and meaningful understanding than the data allow.

Washingtonians of color make up a disproportionate share of those with low incomes or in poverty. In 2015, Washington ranked 17th in the nation with 12.2 percent of its residents living in poverty. A total of 11 percent of whites are in living in poverty in Washington, while 20.5 percent of Latinos, 23.1 percent of African Americans, and 24.4 percent of Native Americans make less than $24,250 for a family of four. Asian Americans have the lowest poverty rate at 10.5 percent. The racial disparity rises when considering children living with limited financial resources. Over two thirds (67 percent) of Latino children in Washington are growing up in low income households, while only 37 percent of white children grow up in such disadvantaged circumstances.

Statewide, both Hispanics and African Americans have unemployment rates that are noticeably higher than that of their white counterparts. It is estimated that 5.6 percent of whites across the state are unemployed, compared to 6.6 percent of Hispanics, 8.9 percent of African Americans, and 17 percent for American Indians/Alaska Natives.[8] Asian Americans have the lowest estimated unemployment rate of any racial/ethnic group, registering at 4.7 percent as of 2015.

Figure 3. Uninsured Rate by Race

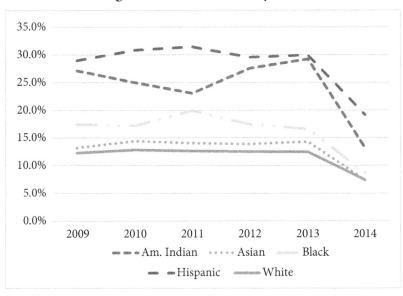

Source: Office of the Insurance Commissioner, Washington State, 2016.[9]

Unemployment and low incomes contribute to, and are compounded by, racially disparate access to important services such as health care and quality education. The percentage of Washington residents who do not have the benefit of health insurance is displayed in Figure 3.

Again, it is Washington's Latinos and American Indians who are among the groups with the most severe disparities relative to whites. While it is estimated that 8.2 percent of all residents in the state of Washington are currently uninsured, down from 13.9 percent before the ACA, close to 20 percent of Latinos are currently uninsured. In stark contrast, it is estimated that less than 10 percent of whites and African Americans in Washington do not have the benefit of health insurance coverage.

Similarly, an education gap exists, and this is both a cause and an effect of poverty in the state. However, while income does have a large impact on education, even controlling for poverty there is a strong and persistent racial education opportunity gap present in Washington.[10] Among students of similar income levels, whites and Asians score significantly higher on reading scores than African Americans, Latinos, and Native Americans alike.[11] This gap persists despite years of federal policy aimed at reducing that cross-group gap. These gaps are present in the important areas of math, reading, and other skills at all levels—including in kindergarten readiness. This continues through graduation and into higher education. Over 82 percent of whites in Washington graduate from high school in five years; around 70 percent of Hispanics and Blacks and less than 60 percent of Native Americans graduate in the same time frame.[12] Gene Balk of the *Seattle Times* reports that compared to the 200 largest school districts in the nation, Seattle ranks fifth in racial achievement gaps, with black students three and a half grades behind white students and Latino students two and a half grades behind white students.[13] Balk also notes that Seattle has among the most racially segregated schools in the nation, and has had for some time (see *Washington v. Seattle School Dist. No. 1* [1982]). The presence of such segregation in the public schools raises questions about how the interests of certain groups fit into the state's cultural commitment to "the common good."

In sum, measures of poverty and employment rates, the uninsured, and educational attainment all reveal that Latinos, Native Americans, and African Americans do considerably worse than whites in the State of Washington. Undoubtedly, similar patterns of systematic inequity in condition can be documented in virtually every state in the nation.

To further gauge the circumstances for minoritized communities in Washington State, we provide an overview of discrimination complaints and hate crimes documented in recent years. In 2015, hate crimes in Washington were slightly lower than the previous year, dropping to 282 incidents from 292 in 2014.[14] In these reported incidents, the majority of the bias motivations were related to race and ethnicity, with 158 offenses related to race or ethnicity. A distant second with a count of 55 was bias surrounding sexual orientation. Of crimes related to race and ethnicity, anti-African American bias was the most prevalent with 79 reported bias motivations against African Americans. Anti-Latino sentiment was reported in 13 incidents, and anti-Native American sentiment was reported in 20 incidents. Anti-Muslim bias motivations, recorded as religious hate crimes, were reported 20 times. Comparing Washington to the other 49 states, the state ranked 18th highest for the number of hate crimes per 100,000 residents in 2009. Similarly, Washington was 14th in number of discrimination complaints filed per 100,000 residents.[15]

Discrimination can also be institutionalized within state government. One site of state discrimination that has rightly received a lot of attention is found in the criminal justice system. As in the rest of the country, black and brown people have experienced higher rates of incarceration. In 1980, Washington had the highest discrepancies with the black population making up 9 percent of the prison population but only 3 percent of the general population. In 2005, Washington no longer has the most dramatic disparity in the nation, but still has significant racial disparities in incarceration rates. Blacks in Washington are incarcerated at 6.4 times the rate of whites. Latinos are incarcerated at 1.3 times the rate of non-Hispanic whites.[16] Discrimination in the workforce, in private settings, and through government bureaucracies are all real and present forces in Washington State contributing to the growing racial and ethnic inequality present in the state. While there is much work to be done furthering protections against discrimination, the state can also directly address the material well-being of racial and ethnic minorities (Moncrief and Squire 2017). In the next section we consider a number of ways the Evergreen State could intervene to alter the course of a growing racial gap in Washington State.

Part III: Challenges Confronting Washington's Immigrant and Ethnic and Racial Communities

Given the growing significance of immigrant and ethnic and racial communities in Washington State, the lack of economic, health care, and educational opportunities, and political empowerment and incorporation, underscore some important challenges confronting the state. To address these challenges would require Washington to direct additional public resources to these communities, as well as increase voter access and descriptive representation in the state's important political and social institutions.

Economic Protections and Opportunity

As documented above there are significant gaps between whites and non-whites in Washington on a range of economic indicators. The Washington Community Action Network (WCAN), in a report entitled *Facing Race* (WCAN 2014), suggests that to address these gaps the state needs to focus on benefits for low wage workers, specifically ensuring required sick leave and insurance for medical and family leave, and prevention of wage theft. Some cities within Washington State have provided models that might serve the state in this regard. For example, in 2016 Tacoma adopted an ordinance requiring employers to provide paid leave time for workers employed more than 80 hours in a year. Tacoma became the third city in Washington, joining 15 municipalities across the country and three states (Connecticut, Massachusetts, and California), that require paid sick leave for employees. Similarly, Seattle passed a historic secure-scheduling law protecting hourly workers at large employers in a variety of ways, most notably requiring two weeks advance notice of one's work schedule. Unpredictability in scheduling can have adverse impacts on family finances, health, and education. Having a predictable income and being aware of one's schedule is necessary for a person to arrange for childcare, transportation, and health care appointments, as well as to be able to engage in a modicum of financial planning. U.S. Department of Labor data indicate that the burden of unpredictability disproportionately falls on communities of color, immigrants, and women. A Seattle city council member has reported that half of African Americans and Latinos participating in a survey reported they received a week or less notice about their upcoming work schedules.[17] Such local measures could be considered at the state level to address racial economic inequality in the state.

Recognizing the close relationship existing between race and class, other policies that attempt to reduce overall economic inequality will also move Washington closer to racial economic equality. Washington State has the most regressive tax system in the country according to the nonpartisan Institute on Taxation and Economic Policy. In 2015, those making less than $21,000 a year paid 16.8 percent of their family income in taxes, while those making over $507,000 paid only 2.4 percent of their income in taxes.[18] Possible solutions include an income tax, a more progressive tax measure as used in most other states, closing of corporate loopholes, or a capital gains tax. None of these new tax measures have been popular in the state.

Health Care

People of color and immigrants experience greater health disparities and "greater barriers to care, lower quality of care, and a higher incidence of chronic disease than white people" (WCAN 2014). Under the Patient Protection and Affordable Care Act (ACA), enacted in 2010, Washington's Apple Health (Medicaid) program was expanded to cover more than half a million adults with incomes up to 138 percent of the federal poverty level.[19] A report by Washington State's Health Care Authority notes that because of the ACA, Apple Health now covers 25 percent of the residents of Washington State.[20] The Office of the Insurance Commissioner documented that Washington State's total uninsured population went from 13.9 percent to 8.2 percent after the ACA.[21] However, upwards of 160,000 people continue to fall through the cracks, and racial disparities persist as highlighted earlier. Racial disparities in health care may in fact worsen in light of the shifts in federal policy and the prospects of repeal of the ACA. Should that occur, Washington State would very likely lose the 90 percent federal dollars it receives for Medicaid expansion. The potential consequences of losing these federal funds would force the state to raise significant new revenues to continue coverage for these individuals or face the prospect of a large growth in the uninsured population in the state. With the pressures to fully fund K-12 education and comply with the state Supreme Court's 2012 *McCleary* decision,[22] this back-filling of federal funding is unlikely to happen. Thus, health disparities for the poor, communities of color, and immigrants are likely to continue, perhaps even worsen.

Education

Improving educational outcomes among minoritized communities is another challenge that faces the state. The benefits of improving educational outcomes, especially for minority communities in Washington, include increased social capital, reduced poverty rates, increased diversity in the professions and the opportunity for greater descriptive representation in government (Fraga 2010; Putnam 2015). The state's Educational Opportunity Gap Oversight and Accountability Committee[23] found that there are multiple overlapping reasons for low educational outcomes among minoritized communities. They provide eight recommendations for reducing racial gaps in education including disentangling punishment from loss of educational time, enhancing cultural competency within the system, increasing the number of educators of color, and improving English language instruction, to name a few. Their report concludes: "Closing the opportunity gap for our African American, Asian, Latino, Native American, and Pacific Islander students is a moral imperative and a civil rights obligation. The opportunity gap in Washington State is persistent, pervasive, and unacceptable." To address these disparities in education the committee made a series of recommendations for "mutually reinforcing and interdependent structural policy changes which if implemented entirely, will close the opportunity gap."[24] If adopted, the implications of these educational changes could be enormous for minoritized communities in Washington State, particularly if made in accordance with the requirements specified in the *McCleary* decision, which requires the state to equitably fund K–12 education.[25]

Political Influence and the Need for Further Political Incorporation

An important barrier to the adoption of policies such as those discussed above that would improve the economic and educational opportunities of minority groups in Washington is the lack of effective political participation and representation of these groups. Indeed, the dramatic population growth among the state's minority citizenry has not led to a concomitant growth in the level of political participation and political influence of ethnic and racial communities in the state's politics that would compel representatives to address the needs of these residents. Table 1 displays the rates of registration and voting in the 2008 presidential election as determined by responses to the Current Population Survey of the Census Bureau. Among citizens, significant disparities exist in the voter registration rates of African Americans, Latinos, and Asian Americans as compared to whites. The highest rates of voter registration among citizens who are 18 years of age or older are whites, at 73.3 percent. The registration rate for Asian adult citizens is 63.7 percent, for Latinos is 57.1 percent, and for African Americans is a surprisingly low 46.3 percent. It is interesting, however, that the disparities noted in voter registration reduce considerably when one compares rates of voter turnout among those who are registered. African Americans, for example, had the highest rates of voter participation in 2008 among registered voters. It is still the case that among the major impediments to the exercise of further electoral influence by ethnic and racial minority groups is the act of voter registration.

Table 1. Registration and Voting in Washington, 2008 (in thousands)

	Total Population	Total Citizen Population	% Registered Citizens
Total	4,912	4,600	71.7
White, non-Hispanic/Latino	3,801	3,729	73.3
Black	157	123	46.3
Asian	344	262	63.7
Hispanic/Latino (of any race)	404	280	57.1

	% Voted (Total 18+)	% Voted (Citizen 18+)	% Voted (Registered Citizens)
Total	62.6	66.8	93.1%
White, non-Hispanic/Latino	69.2	70.6	94.4%
Black	36.3	46.4	100.0%
Asian	38.5	50.5	79.0%
Hispanic/Latino (of any race)	36.6	52.7	92.5%

Source: U.S. Census Bureau, Current Population Survey, November 2008

It is also true that ethnic and racial minority groups in Washington are not well represented at any level of government. Currently, 91 percent of Washington legislators are white, while non-Hispanic whites compose only 77 percent of the population.[26] Latinos, while composing over 12 percent of the population, have the largest gap in representation, holding only 1 percent of the seats in the state's legislative chambers. At the local level, the prevalence of at-large voting systems in Washington allows for slim majorities to dominate representation and make it difficult for minorities to have a voice. It is the case that 99 percent of local elections in Washington are such at-large systems. In 2015 the Washington ACLU brought a federal lawsuit against Yakima contending that the at-large system resulted in violations of the Voting Rights Act by consistently denying Latino voters the ability to have an equal chance of electing a preferred candidate. The U.S. District court agreed and implemented a seven-district plan. This action led to calls for a state version of the federal Voting Rights Act that would allow for individuals to pursue changes to at-large and other local discriminatory election systems through state law rather than having to resort to the federal courts. This Washington Voting Rights Act has been debated during successive sessions, but has been stalled in the legislature. Such a law, if passed and signed into law by the governor, would not only enhance opportunities for more members of minority communities to be elected to office but might also promote confidence in the system and greater political participation more broadly by such groups. More racially inclusive leadership in local politics could also serve as fertile soil to grow a broader set of state politicians of color. Increasing political activity within minoritized communities would create pressure to enact policies that would promote progress toward economic, educational, and health equality and well-being for all Washingtonians (Lovrich and Newman 2004).

Conclusion: Moving Forward

We began our analysis with the important role state governments might play in protecting civil rights and advancing the economic well-being of racial and ethnic minorities in light of the possible retrenchment of policies at the national level. Given that Washington State is a strongly Democratic and liberal state overall with a moralistic political cultural heritage and is an important Pacific Rim trade player in the global marketplace, we argued that the state may be poised to become a leader in advancing a new progressive federalism.

After reviewing the pace and magnitude of growth in ethnic and racial communities and examining a number of dimensions of economic wellbeing and the patterns of incorporation, we conclude that there are still major challenges facing both immigrant and minoritized citizen communities in Washington. The rapid demographic changes taking place in the state raise very important issues of identity and commitment to equality. These are challenges that the state must confront in the coming years as Washington continues to attract settlement from migration and immigration alike. Despite becoming a much more ethnically and racially diverse state, and despite the fact that Washington is a strongly Democratic state with a persisting moralistic core in its political culture, when it comes to the equality and incorporation of communities of color it still has much more progress to make. Our analysis suggests that Washington is perhaps at a tipping point regarding its ultimate direction.

The state's role in challenging the Trump administration's immigration proposals and the fact that many cities and towns in Washington adopted sanctuary ordinances suggest that much of the state is on the path toward a progressive federalism. It remains to be seen, however, whether the state legislature, where political power is more closely divided and partisan control is currently split, will follow. Given other pressing budgetary issues, including *McCleary*, it is unlikely there is sufficient political pressure to pass new spending on programs aimed to reduce racial and ethnic inequalities in education, health care, and the workforce absent increased political participation and representation of the growing communities of color. At a minimum, targeted policies such as increasing funding for dual language programs or free naturalization and citizen education services could facilitate greater inclusion of the growing immigrant population. Additionally, passage of a Washington Voting Rights Act could promote greater representation of minority communities in political institutions across the state.

In our view, if Washington State does indeed make progress on inequalities in economic, social, and political incorporation it would reflect the deep-seated moralistic tradition in the state's politics dating from its territorial settlement and admission to statehood, making Washington State a clear protector of civil rights. Perhaps such actions would occasion another "turning point" in the Evergreen State's public life (Scott 2011). These actions would also provide protections for Washington's most vulnerable communities and enhance its attraction as a diverse and culturally vital place for all Washingtonians to live and work.

Notes

1. Parts of this chapter were published by Luis R. Fraga and Maria Chávez, "Changing Faces of Diversity in Washington State," in *Governing Washington: Politics and Government in the Evergreen State*, ed. Cornell W. Clayton and Nicholas P. Lovrich. Pullman: Washington State University Press, 2011, 87–108.
2. *State of Washington vs. Donald J. Trump, et al.* United States District Court Western Washington 2:17-cv-00141-JLR. www.uscourts.gov/cameras-courts/state-washington-vs-donald-j-trump-et-al.
3. Ilya Somin. 2016. "Trump, Federal Power, and the Left," *Washington Post*, December, 2016. www.washingtonpost.com/news/volokh-conspiracy/wp/2016/12/05/trump-federal-power-and-the-left-why-liberals-should-help-make-federalism-great-again/?utm_term=.1a3217a0031b.
4. Heather K. Gerken. 2012. "A New Progressive Federalism." *Democracy: A Journal of Ideas*, Spring 2012. hdemocracyjournal.org/magazine/24/a-new-progressive-federalism.
5. *State of Washington v. Donald Trump*, 3.
6. American Immigration Council. 2017. "Immigrants in Washington State." www.americanimmigrationcouncil.org/research/new-americans-washington.
7. Lori Pfingst, E. Hernandez, A. Nicholas, and K. Justice. 2015. "Economic Security" In *The Progress Index: Measuring Shared Prosperity in Washington State*. Washington State Budget & Policy Center, March 2015. budgetandpolicy.org/policy-areas/progress-index/PI%20Economic%20Security.pdf.
8. National Congress of American Indians. "Northwest Area Regional Profile: Idaho, Oregon, and Washington." www.ncai.org/policy-research-center/research-data/prc-publications/Northwest_Region.pdf.
9. Mike Kreidler. 2016. "The State of Washington's Uninsured 2014–2016: An Examination of the Health Insurance Market Before and After the Affordable Care Act." Office of the Insurance Commissioner, Washington State , February 3, 2016. www.insurance.wa.gov/sites/default/files/documents/2014-2015-state-of-uninsured.pdf.
10. Educational Opportunity Gap Oversight and Accountability Committee. 2016. "Closing Opportunity Gaps in Washington's Public Education System." www.k12.wa.us/Workgroups/EOGOAC/pubdocs/EOGOAC2016AnnualReport.pdf.
11. Educational Opportunity Gap Oversight and Accountability Committee, 2016.

12. Robin G. Munson, Deb Came, and Lisa Ireland. 2015. "Graduation and Dropout Statistics Annual Report." Olympia, WA: Office of the Superintendent of Public Instruction. www.k12.wa.us/legisgov/2015documents/GradandDropoutStats2015.pdf.

13. Gene Balk. 2016. "Seattle Schools Have Biggest White Black Achievement Gap in the State." *Seattle Times*, May 6, 2016. www.seattletimes.com/seattle-news/data/seattle-schools-have-biggest-white-black-achievement-gap-in-state.

14. Tonya Todd, Kellie Lapczynski, and Joan Smith. "2015 Crime in Washington Annual Report." Lacey, WA: Washington Association of Sheriffs and Police Chiefs, 70. http://www.waspc.org/assets/CJIS/crime%20in%20washington%202015.small.pdf.

15. The Daily Beast. 2011. "Ranking the Most and Least Tolerant States." January 16, 2011. www.thedailybeast.com/articles/2011/01/16/ranking-the-most-tolerant-and-least-tolerant-states.html.

16. Nationally, blacks are incarcerated at 5.6 times the rate of whites and Latinos at 1.6. "Preliminary Report on Race and Washington's Criminal Justice System." Task Force on Race and the Criminal Justice System, 2011, 9–10.

17. David Kroman. 2016. "Scheduling Law Could Set National Precedent to Combat Inequality." Crosscut, September 19, 2016. crosscut.com/2016/09/scheduling-law-could-set-national-precedent-combat-inequality.

18. Carl Davis et al. 2015. "Who Pays? A Distributional Analysis of the Tax Systems in All Fifty States," 5th ed. Washington, DC: Institute on Taxation and Economic Policy. itep.org/wp-content/uploads/whopaysreport.pdf.

19. Washington State Health Care Authority. "Eligibility Overview: Apple Health (Medicaid) Programs." Olympia, WA. April 2017. www.hca.wa.gov/about-hca/health-care-reform.

20. Washington State Health Care Authority. 2016. "Fact Sheet" (revised October 2016).

21. Kreidler, 2016.

22. Kim Justice, Michael Mitchell, Andy Nicholas, and Lori Pfingst. 2013. "A Paramount Duty: Funding Education for McCleary and Beyond." Washington State Budget & Policy Center. Policy Brief (February). budgetandpolicy.org/reports/a-parmount-duty-funding-education-for-mccleary-and-beyond.

23. The EOGOAC is comprised of members of the state legislature, representatives from the various minority commissions, a representative from the office of the education ombudsman, a representative from the office of the superintendent of public instruction, and a representative from the federally recognized Indian tribes.

24. Educational Opportunity Gap Oversight and Accountability Committee 2016, 7.

25. Justice et al. 2013

26. National Conference of State Legislatures. 2016. "Legislator's Race and Ethnicity 2015." www.ncsl.org/Portals/1/Documents/About_State_Legislatures/Raceethnicity_Rev2.pdf.

References

Bonilla-Silva, Eduardo. 2010. *Racism Without Racists: A Color-Blind Racism and Racial Inequality in Contemporary America*. New York: Rowman & Littlefield Publishers, Inc.

Chávez, Maria. 2011. *Everyday Injustice: Latino Professionals and Racism*. New York: Rowman & Littlefield Publishers, Inc.

Elazar, Daniel J. 1984. *American Federalism: A View from the States*. New York: Harper and Row.

Elazar, Daniel J. 1994. *The American Mosaic: The Impact of Space, Time, and Culture on American Politics*. Boulder, CO: Westview Press.

Erickson, Robert S., John P. McIver, and Gerald C. Wright. 1987. "State Political Culture and Public Opinion." *American Political Science Review* 81:797–813.

Feagin, Joe R. and José Cobas. 2014. *Latinos Facing Racism: Discrimination, Resistance, and Endurance*. Boulder, CO: Paradigm Publishers.

Fraga, Luis Ricardo, John A. García, Rodney Hero, Michael Jones-Correa, Valerie Martinez-Ebers, and Gary M. Segura. 2010. *Latino Lives in America: Making It Home*. Philadelphia, PA: Temple University Press.

Gerstle, Gary. 2010. "Federalism in America: Beyond the Tea Partiers." *Dissent* 57:4.

Hing, Bill Ong. 2004. *Defining America Through Immigration Policy*. Philadelphia: Temple University Press.

Jacobson, Robin Dale. 2015. "The Long American Tradition of Nativist Politics." *Religion and Politics*, December 15, 2015. religionandpolitics.org/2015/12/15/the-long-american-tradition-of-nativist-politics.

Kincaid, John. 1982. *Political Culture, Public Policy and the American States*. Philadelphia, PA: Institute for the Study of Human Issues.

López, Ian Haney. 2014. *Dog Whistle Politics: How Coded Racial Appeals Have Reinvented Racism & Wrecked the Middle Class*. New York: Oxford University Press.

Lovrich, Nicholas, and Meredith Newman. 2004. "Research Note. The Hearing of Local Government Interests in State Legislatures: The Effects of Prior Service in City or County Government." *State and Local Government Review*. 36:67–77.

Moncrief, Gary F., and Peverill Squire. 2017. *Why States Matter: An Introduction to State Politics*. Maryland: Rowman and Littlefield Publishing Group, Inc.

Nardulli, Peter F. 1990. "Political Subcultures in the American States." *American Politics Research*. 18:287–315.

Ngai, Mae M., and Jon Gjerde. 2011. *Major Problems in American Immigration History*, 2nd ed. Boston: Wadsworth/Cengage Learning.

Putnam, Robert D. 2015. *Our Kids: The American Dream in Crisis*. New York: Simon and Schuster.

Schmidt, Ronald, Sr. 2016. "The Quest for Racial Equality: A Public Policy Framework." *International Journal of Economic Development*. 10:1–31.

Scott, George W. (ed.). 2011. *Turning Points in Washington's Public Life*. Seattle: Civitas Press.

Scott, George W. 2012. *Governors of Washington*. Seattle: Civitas Press.

Smith, Rogers M. 1997. *Civic Ideals: Conflicting Visions of Citizenship in U.S. History.* New Haven, CT: Yale University Press.

Takaki, Ronald T. 1994. *A Different Mirror: The Making of Multicultural America.* Boston: Little, Brown and Company.

Verba, Sidney, Kay Lehman Schlozman, and Henry E. Brady. 1995. *Voice and Equality: Civic Voluntarism in American Politics.* Cambridge, MA: Harvard University Press.

WCAN. Washington Community Action Network. 2014. *Facing Race: Washington's Racial Equity Agenda.* washingtoncan.org/wordpress/wp-content/uploads/.../ FINAL-Facing-Race-report.pdf (January 18, 2017).

Welch, Susan, and John G. Peters. 1980. "State Political Culture and the Attitudes of State Senators Toward Social, Economic Welfare and Corruption Issues." *Publius* 10:59–67.

CHAPTER 6

The Washington Press and Politics: News Coverage in Changing Times

Sanne A. M. Rijkhoff and Jim Camden

Recent decades brought major and painful changes for the American news media transitioning from traditional media companies to digital-first. In the previous edition of this book, Searles and Jenkins (2011) noted that "market demands drive the American media system and Washington State is not immune to these pressures." In the current chapter, we show this trend has not stopped. While newspaper circulations are declining and some journals have completely disappeared, radio and television deal with budget cuts and layoffs and funding is lacking for nonprofit services.[1] In 2017 there were half as many journalists employed in the American news media as in 1990. Media outlets rely primarily on advertisements but companies shifted to online entertainment content. Overall, about 70 percent of the ad revenues go to just 10 companies, none of which produces news content (Shors and Blanks Hindman 2016).

Despite these changes, newspapers still give significant attention to government and public affairs. This is noteworthy because journalists are working with fewer resources to produce the same content. Although local television news still struggles to provide viewers with sufficient information on local and state politics, the addition of online content and widespread access to social media increasingly compensates for that gap (Gottfried and Shearer 2016).

In this chapter we provide a short historical overview of media and the most recent developments in Washington State. Then we focus on the relationship between reporters and politicians. Finally, we discuss what political news is covered in Washington State, particularly during elections.

Media Presence in Washington State

Newspapers

Looking back to the beginning of statehood in 1889, newspapers were the only commercial source of news. Any city of considerable size had at least two newspapers and many cities had three or four. Now, no city in the state has two competing daily newspapers.

This is true even in the largest city, where the *Seattle Times* is currently the only major daily newspaper in print since the *Seattle Post-Intelligencer* stopped printing and now delivers news solely online. At its founding in 1891, the *Seattle Times* was a four-page newspaper with a circulation of 3,500. Circulation as of 2017 was about 237,000. Currently the newspaper's parent company also owns two smaller papers in Washington, the *Yakima Herald-Republic* and *Walla Walla Union-Bulletin*. Starting in July 1995, the company also owned Issaquah Press Inc., with four more newspapers, but in February 2017 it closed this group and stopped those publications (McIntosh 2017). Although the *Seattle Times* is the largest print newspaper in Washington and places 26th in the United States (Mondo Times 2017a), its circulation, similar to other papers, is still declining. Although shortly after the 2016 elections its readership slightly increased, it is too soon to determine whether this is a temporary or a long-term growth. Circulation numbers of the five largest newspapers in Washington in 2011 and 2017 are shown in Table 1.

During the 2012 elections the *Seattle Times* itself became the subject of the news by making independent contributions of full-page ads supporting Republican gubernatorial candidate Rob McKenna and in favor of a state referendum on legalizing same-sex marriage. The $80,000 independent expenditure for McKenna was significant—only two contributions to his campaign were larger. This generated immediate criticism from journalists and political experts and more than 100 staffers signed a letter of protest about the independence and credibility of the paper (Brunner 2012a). Company officials responded that they published the ads to attract new revenue and to show "how effective advertising with *The Times* can be" (Brunner 2012b). Other news outlets also criticized the contributions and warned about potential boomerang effects if McKenna and the referendum lost the election

(Camden 2012, Gill 2012). As it turned out, it was a split decision: McKenna lost; same-sex marriage became law.

Washington's second largest newspaper, the *Tacoma News Tribune* can trace its roots back to 1883. The 1918 merger of three weekly newspapers—the *Tacoma Ledger*, *The News*, and the *Tacoma Tribune*—resulted in the *Tacoma News Tribune and Ledger*. It adopted the current name, *Tacoma News Tribune* in 1979 and was purchased by its current owner McClatchy Newspapers in 2008, a national chain which also owns the *Bellingham Herald*, the *Olympian* and the *Tri-City Herald* in Washington. In addition to print media, the paper's owners started two radio stations in 1948 and a television station in 1953, all now owned by other companies.

Table 1: Circulation of the five largest newspapers in Washington

	2011	2017
Seattle Times	251,697	236,929
Seattle Weekly (city guides)	109,000	109,000
Seattle Stranger (city guides)	90,309	74,074
Tacoma News Tribune	82,855	78,453
Spokane Spokesman-Review	74,386	69,161
Pacific Northwest Inlander (city guides)	n/a	49,768
Vancouver Columbian	n/a	48,078
Everett Daily Herald	n/a	46,481

Source: Searles and Jenkins, 2011, and www.mondotimes.com/newspapers/usa/ washington-newspaper-circulation.html.

The only daily newspaper remaining in Spokane is the *Spokesman-Review* which was established in 1894 with the merger of two competing newspapers, the *Spokane Falls Review* (1883–1894) and the *Spokesman* (1890–1893). It is owned by the Cowles Company, which owns newspapers in several states and also operates in forestry, a paper mill, broadcasting, real estate, and insurance. Until 1992, it also published the *Spokane Chronicle*, the city's afternoon daily, but declining circulation for afternoon papers prompted the company to shift its subscribers to the *Spokesman-Review* and close the *Chronicle*. The newspaper received national media attention in 2004 when it conducted a controversial online investigation of Spokane Mayor James E. West.

Allegations that he used city property to troll for young men on dating websites led to a recall campaign. Voters did recall West in 2004 but the FBI and local prosecutors declined to charge him.

In total as of 2017, Washington's 10 largest daily newspapers (the *Seattle Times, Tacoma News Tribune, The Spokesman-Review, Vancouver Columbian, Everett Daily Herald, Tri-City Herald, Kitsap Sun, Yakima Herald Republic, Snohomish Times,* and the *Olympian*) had a combined daily circulation of just over 615,000, with millions of online viewers per month (Mondo Times 2017b).[2]

Commercial Radio

Commercial radio broadcasting started in Washington in the 1920s with most stations providing music and entertainment rather than compete with newspapers to provide news. The 1930s and '40s are viewed as the golden age of radio with most families owning a radio and coming together to listen to it. The start of radio news broadcasts influenced the way the public experienced current affairs. For example, the radio was a key source of news during World War II, with correspondents like Edward R. Murrow reporting from the front.

Some stations that started in the 1920s still broadcast today, although their programs and focus changed over time. KOMO, a commercial station serving metropolitan Seattle, was founded in July 1926 with the call letters KGFA which became KOMO on December 31, 1926. In the 1940s and 1950s, KOMO broadcasted mainly entertainment such as game shows, music, and soap operas but also offered some news and talk radio. In 1995 KOMO transitioned to become an all-news radio station that follows a common format of broadcasting world and national news from an affiliated national network on a half-hour cycle with local updates in between for weather, traffic, sports, and other information. In addition, KOMO broadcasts two nationally syndicated news shows in the early mornings on weekdays and interviews and call-ins in the midday hours.

Public Radio

During that golden age of radio Washington news consumers did not have a major source of government news that today's consumers have—public radio. The current flagship station for public radio in Washington, Northwest Public Radio, is KWSU 1250, hosted by

Washington State University. Northwest Public Radio (NWPR) is an affiliate of National Public Radio (NPR), Public Radio International, and American Public Media. When NPR was established in 1970, KWSU became a member station. In 1982 KWSU started a network when the station from Richland signed on. Two years later, KWSU took over the station from the University of Idaho, which was facing budget cuts. Over the years, the network gathered more stations and as of 2014, NWPR had 152,050 weekly listeners, 2,760 local and regional news stories, and 297,681 unique visitors to nwpr.org (NWPR 2015). With 19 stations, it is the largest producer of public radio in Washington and had, of 2017, several credentialed radio reporters covering state government in Olympia including Austin Jenkins and Tom Banse.

The NPR member station in Seattle is KUOW, which started in 1952. The station changed its focus in 1992 to news radio. The station is now operated by KUOW Puget Sound Public Radio (PSPR) under an agreement with the University of Washington, KUOW's licensee and owner. Currently, they broadcast from Olympia to Bellingham and—in comparison with NWPR—KUOW reported in their 2015 annual report 311,800 listeners each week. In addition, their online presence continues to grow with 257,715 unique monthly visitors as of 2015, an increase of about 35 percent from 2014 (KUOW 2015).

A third major public radio station is KPLU, which started in 1966 and broadcasts from Seattle and Tacoma covering the entire Puget Sound area. In 2016, the station became KNKX, after ending its affiliation with Pacific Lutheran University and becoming a listener-owned station. The station is known for its jazz and blues programing and regional and national news coverage. KNKX plays a variety of NPR programs, including *All Things Considered*, *Car Talk*, and *Morning Edition*. For their audience online, they provide a regular station feed and Jazz24, a 24/7 free online jazz station.

Another community owned public radio station is KPBX, operated by Spokane Public Radio. This station is the only one that was never connected to a university. On January 20, 1980, the station made its debut as a true NPR member station. Currently it airs 24 hours a day with approximately 36 percent of the time dedicated to news; classical music receives 30 percent; a fifth of the time goes to folk and world music; and jazz and blues complete the schedule (Spokane Public Radio 2014).

Commercial Television

Television remains the main news source for older Washingtonians, although many, if not most, younger Washingtonians get their news online. Approximately half of all 18- to 49-year-olds often find their news online, while just 25 percent of 18- to 29-year-olds rely on TV as a regular news source (Mitchell, Gottfried, Barthel, and Shearer 2016).

Washington is divided into three television media markets and some regions, such as Vancouver, are covered by the Portland, Oregon, market. The largest media market is Seattle-Tacoma which covers over 1.8 million television households, 1.6 percent of the national total (Nielsen 2017). Washington has 17 local commercial television stations and 7 affiliates of Public Broadcasting Service. An overview of all media markets and their local stations is provided in Table 2.

Television coverage today is both better and worse than in "the good old days," whenever those were.[3] When TV still used film, reporters had to shoot, get back to the station, develop, and edit for the evening news. With digital equipment and satellite transmission, reporters can spend more time covering the Legislature, or be at a 4 p.m. gubernatorial press conference, go to the truck, edit the story, send it to the station, and do the live standup with the Capitol dome in the background.

There are also more TV newscasts in a standard weekday. At one time, evening newscasts consisted of 30 minutes around 5:00 p.m. and another 30 minutes at 11:00 p.m. Now local news at a national network's affiliated stations starts at 4:30 or 5:00 a.m. and goes on to 7:00 a.m. After that, the networks' shows take over, but local stations still have regular updates for news, traffic, and weather. Most stations start their local news again between 4:00 and 5:00 p.m. and some stations also have a half hour at noon. The evening broadcast now consists of at least an hour of local news wrapped around a half hour of national news provided by the network, plus a half hour broadcast at 10:00 or 11:00 p.m.

Several network affiliates like KING-TV in Seattle and KHQ-TV in Spokane also have a second digital channel where they have news for much of the day when their main stations have soap operas, talk shows, game shows, or prime time dramas from their network. Local news is made available to the public at a much faster pace and is offered throughout the entire day.

Despite this increase in news broadcasts, it is also fair to say that television news stories in general, including government news stories, have become shorter, more visual, and "punchier" to attract and keep viewers with short attention spans and remote controls. Most television stations use the same broadcast structure for local news: "mayhem at the top, teasable soft features at the end, and the rest of the day's news in the middle" (Rosenstiel et al. 2007). News on state and local public affairs competes with entertainment news, expanded weather and sports, traffic reports, and "news" taken from social media. Television coverage of state and local politics is minimal in quantity and lacks depth. As such, coverage of state politics has provocatively been nicknamed "Swiss cheese journalism." Doris Graber argued that "Swiss cheese has more substance than holes while the reverse is true for the press in their coverage of state government" (1993). Considering factors that go into television news selection (e.g. holding viewer interest), this neglect is not surprising.

Some of the most pressing issues facing state government are complicated. It is difficult to explain in two minutes competing sides of a legislative debate over changes to the school district property tax levy structure, even though this is key to solving the dilemma of adequate state support of public schools. State politics has many nuances and may be visually uninteresting for television. Politicians can influence the spin of the story as they provide the "facts" necessary for journalists (Renner and Lynch 2008, 142). Washington and other states, including Oregon, cannot escape this national trend (Rijkhoff 2018).

Public Television

This does not mean that there is no coverage of Washington state government on television at all. Washington also has TVW, a public affairs network some describe as a state version of C-Span (which broadcasts the U.S. Congress). During a legislative session, TVW shows floor debates from both chambers and some committee hearings live on a cable channel that most cable systems provide in their basic package to subscribers. On any given legislative day as many as 10 committee hearings can be taking place at the same time, or the House and Senate might both be debating issues simultaneously. Since TVW only has one cable channel it may flip back and forth between various debates

Table 2: Media Markets Covering Counties in Washington

Designated Market Area (DMA)	Counties (or county-equivalents) Covered	Television Homes (2015–2016)	Major Network Affiliates (ABC, CBS, Fox, NBC) (PBS excluded)
# 14 Seattle-Tacoma	Chelan, Clallam, Douglas, Grays Harbor, Island, Jefferson, King, Kitsap, Lewis, Mason, Pacific, Pierce, San Juan, Skagit, Snohomish, Thurston, Whatcom	1,808,530	KOMO-TV (ABC)[a] / KUNS-TV (Univision)[a] KCPQ (Fox)[b] / KZJO (MyNetworkTV)[b] KING-TV (NBC)[c] / KONG (Independent)[c] KIRO-TV (CBS)[j]
# 25 Portland, OR	Baker, Clackamas, Clark (WA), Clatsop, Columbia, Crook, Cowlitz (WA), Gilliam, Harney, Hood River, Jefferson, Klickitat (WA), Lincoln, Linn, Marion, Multnomah, Polk, Sherman, Skamania (WA), Tillamook, Union, Wasco, Washington, Wahkiakum (WA), Wheeler, Yamhill	1,143,670	KATU (ABC)[a] / KUNP (Univision)[a] KGW (NBC)[c] KPTV (Fox)[h] / KPDX (MyNetworkTV)[h] KOIN (CBS)[j]

Designated Market Area (DMA)	Counties (or county-equivalents) Covered	Television Homes (2015–2016)	Major Network Affiliates (ABC, CBS, Fox, NBC) (PBS excluded)
#73 Spokane	Adams, Asotin, Benewah (ID), Bonner (ID), Boundary (ID), Clearwater (ID), Columbia, Ferry, Garfield, Grant, Idaho (ID), Kootenai (ID), Latah (ID), Lewis (ID), Lincoln (MT), Lincoln, Nez Perce (ID), Okanogan, Pend Oreille, Shoshone (ID), Spokane, Stevens, Wallowa (OR), Whitman	422,550	KLEW-TV (CBS)[a] KREM (CBS)[c] / KSKN (CW)[c] KXLY-TV (ABC)[d] / KXMN-LD (MeTV)[d] KAYU-TV (Fox)[e] KHQ-TV (NBC)[f]
#122 Yakima-Pasco-Richland-Kennwick	Benton, Franklin, Kittitas, Morrow (OR), Umatilla (OR), Walla Walla, Yakima	230,950	KEPR-TV (CBS)[a] / KVVK-CA/KORX-CA (Univision)[a] / KIMA-TV (CBS)[a] / KUNW-CA (Univision)[a] KAPP (ABC)[d] / KVEW (ABC)[d] KCYU-LD (Fox)[e] / KFFX-TV (Fox)[e] KNDO (NBC)[f] / KNDU (NBC)[f]

*DMA numbers signify nationwide ranking of market by size.

Note: Letters in superscript indicate that television stations share the same owner company. a=Sinclair Broadcast Group; b=Tribune Broadcasting (sale to Sinclair Broadcast Group pending); c=Tegna Media Group; d=Morgan Murphy Media; e=Northwest Broadcasting; f = Cowles Company; h=Meredith Corporation; i=Cox Media Group, j=Nexstar Media Group.

Source: Nielsen Local Television Market Universe Estimates as of January 1, 2017 and used throughout the 2016-2017 television season.

and hearings. In addition, TVW streams as many as six committee hearings live online and all hearings held in the legislative office buildings are recorded and available in the TVW archives. During the 2016 elections, the channel provided the series *Your Voice, Your Vote* online, highlighting many local candidates and issues.

Digital/Online

The fastest changing component of the news industry is the online world. It is expected that by 2018 approximately 75 percent of younger news consumers will search online for information and news (Shors and Blanks Hindman 2016). Almost all traditional news outlets—newspapers, radio, and television—have some online presence. Many automatically transfer their stories to a website or have staff that repurposes it for the web. Some also "break" news on their website, something that would have been considered heresy just a generation ago in newsrooms. Nowadays a newspaper will routinely put breaking news online, with regular updates, and recast it for the next day's paper at the end of the news cycle, even if they have it exclusively before posting it. Online news also provides the possibility for hyperlocal news sites (i.e. attention to neighborhoods and streets): citizens can search for information about very specific regions and locations which can be updated every minute.

Most news websites are free, but some are not. Newspapers seem to vacillate on the issue of free versus paid access. The debate among newspaper executives continues over which is more important: more "eyeballs" on the website, which leads proponents to say the website should be free; or raising revenue to cover costs, which leads proponents to advocate for charging the public for access.

Despite large visitor numbers to online news sites of newspaper, radio, and television, their informational value is unknown because average visit to newspaper websites last only three minutes (Mackenzie 2016). Many digital visitors to these news websites are thus short-term visitors who are not loyal newspaper readers. In addition, even though revenue from newspapers' online sites reached 25 percent of newspaper advertising revenues by 2015, this had not made up for larger declines in print advertising. As a result, there were 40 percent fewer newsroom employees at U.S. newspapers in 2014 compared to 2004 (Barthel 2016).

Traditional news organizations are not the only ones in Washington offering state government coverage online. There are news websites like Crosscut, which is the most visible and largest, and PubliCola which aims to be a for-profit organization (Searles and Jenkins 2011). Slog is the website for the weekly newspaper *The Stranger*. In 2009 the *Post-Intelligencer* slashed its editorial staff of 165 to a total of 20 news and web producers when it became *Seattle PI*, the first major American newspaper to go online-only (Yardley and Pérez-Peña 2009). Some interest groups also support websites that aggregate news from other sources, offering their own slant on news as well as analysis or commentary. State government coverage on these online sources can resemble weekly magazines that mainly look for big feature stories or exposes. Finally, social media such as Facebook attracts more news consumers, including older ones, and they receive the majority of advertising revenue (Shors and Blanks Hindman 2016). None of these online outlets have a full-time reporter in the capital however.

Current State of Washington Media

Washingtonians currently have many more sources at their disposal than decades ago but this does not mean that they are better informed. In addition to gaps in the coverage of political news on television, news media also face budget cuts and layoffs; overall there are fewer full-time reporters covering state and local government. In January 2017, the *Seattle Times* announced it would lay off 23 people from its news operations (Seattle Times Staff 2017), a bit over 10 percent of newsroom staff, to deal with falling advertising revenue. Similarly, the *Seattle Globalist*, a nonprofit news website, lost its funding for 2017 from the University of Washington and could disappear within the year (Knauf 2016). In the same month KOMO TV disbanded its investigative team (Lerman 2017) and Northwest Cable News, which provided an "always-on CNN-like news outlet for the Pacific Northwest," fired about 20 employees and had its last broadcast day on January 6, 2017 (Day 2016). The major overhaul of the print news industry resulted in the departure of many experienced journalists from Olympia.[4] With so few positions remaining, the numbers of cuts are currently stable, with no signs of expansion.

The Relationship between Government and the Media

The relationship between government officials and the news media in Washington has always been adversarial, although the level of friction has varied over the years. Some unique examples from the last century show situations of a close cooperation as well as some high-profile conflicts. These two extremes are rare and nowadays the level of trust and comity differs between individual journalists and politicians, and changes on an almost daily basis.

In 1909, in the midst of the heated debates over Prohibition, newspaper reporter Joe Smith from the *Spokesman-Review* and a state representative, Republican James McArthur, came to blows on the floor of the House in Washington (Brazier 2000, 71). Accounts of the altercation vary over the exact cause and whether the reporter and legislator had two fist fights, or just one long one with a brief intermission. The House Journal[5] of the following day shows that while Smith offered a formal apology for his part, there is no corresponding apology on the record from McArthur, who only served a single term (Camden 2016). It is worth noting that despite this conflict between the media and the government, reporters still are granted access to the floors of both chambers, although it is limited and at the discretion of the Legislature. Although representatives and senators are expected to follow certain norms and protocols, ultimately they are answerable only to voters.

Governor Dixy Lee Ray and the press corps of the late 1970s provide another example of a hard-fought conflict. Democrat Ray, the state's first female governor, became a well-known scientist in the zoology department of the University of Washington in the early 1960s when she developed and hosted a television series *Animals of the Seashore* on KCTS-TV, the local PBS affiliate. Despite that early relationship with the media, as governor she was dismissive of the journalists who covered her. When a local television reporter Paul Boyd interviewed the governor, she was dressed in "a ratty Ban-lon sports shirt, sweat pants covered with dog hair, red socks, and tennis shoes" (Mungo 1977, 30). Her relationship with the press corps was so contentious that she told disfavored reporters she named pigs for them on her Fox Island farm, and gave the reporters sausage made from their namesakes after the porkers were slaughtered.

On the other hand, some might argue that reporters and elected officials have often worked too closely. A prominent example is the relationship between Republican Representative Al Canwell of Spokane and Ashley Holden, the *Spokesman-Review*'s political writer and legislative correspondent. In the late 1940s Washington had the Joint Legislative Committee on Un-American Activities, chaired by Canwell, which investigated communist influence in state agencies and academia. In his role as chairman, Canwell was aided and abetted in his pursuit of the Red Menace by his friend Holden. The two shared a longer history together as journalists before Canwell ran for office and it was in fact Holden who had encouraged Canwell to run in 1946 in the first place. Their relationship was a symbiotic one: Canwell leaked information from the committee and broke news on a cycle that benefited Holden's morning paper. The *Spokesman-Review* printed stories that gave Canwell the headlines for his crusade (Kienholz 2012).

The line between journalists and government officials also blurs as news media outlets shrink and government expands. In 2008 the Olympia capitol press corps experienced a mass exodus with many highly respected reporters leaving their jobs (Searles and Jenkins 2011). Many of the members of the capitol press corps found new positions and were working in state government ten years later. Most often, their positions put them in the world of journalism and communication from a different vantage. As example, David Postman, the former *Seattle Times* bureau chief, became Governor Jay Inslee's chief of staff after serving a stint as his director of communications. Ralph Thomas, another former *Times* reporter, was the spokesman for the state's budget office, and Adam Wilson went from the *Seattle Times* to the state auditor's office. The *Spokesman-Review*'s Olympia correspondent, Rich Roesler, was acting director of Results Washington, having spent time as that agency's communications director, and before that as spokesman for the Insurance Commissioner. Longtime Associated Press Bureau Chief David Ammons worked for two Washington Secretaries of State, and in 2017 was appointed to the state Public Disclosure Commission after retiring from the state. Chris Mulick of the *Tacoma News Tribune* became a spokesman and lobbyist for Washington State University. Karina Shagren, an experienced television journalist for KXLY in Spokane, was a spokeswoman for Governor Chris Gregoire, and later for the state Emergency Services Department.

Leaving journalism for government work is not a new phenomenon. For decades Washington reporters who covered the election campaigns for governor or for Congress were recruited to run the press office when the candidate became the office holder. Spokane reporter Bill First covered the 1964 campaign of a young attorney against an 11-term veteran Republican congressman. When the young attorney won, First became his press secretary, a post he held for more than 20 years as his boss, Tom Foley, was on his way to become the Speaker of the House. Even when First retired from the daily job of press secretary, he served as a consultant on Foley's biennial re-election campaigns and on other political issues in Spokane.

Some reporters also decided to run for office. The previously mentioned Al Canwell started as a general assignment reporter of the *International News Service* and returned to Spokane in 1938 where he became a photojournalist in addition to his written journalism before running for office. Seattle television newsman Rod Chandler won a seat in the state House in 1975, and moved on to the U.S. House of Representatives in 1983. Al Swift, who won an Emmy as a broadcast journalist, later represented Bellingham in the U.S House between 1979 and 1995. Jack Geraghty went from newspaper reporter in Spokane to county commissioner, to public affairs consultant, to Spokane mayor. Finally, Joe Smith, the reporter who slugged the legislator on the floor of the state House of Representatives in 1909, became one of the most celebrated journalists of his day. He co-founded Seattle's Municipal League, worked for mayors and governors, and even ran for office several times. He never won, but in each case he put up a good fight.

Coverage of Politics in Washington State

Candidates have multiple ways of campaigning during elections: through paid media such as advertising, through free media obtained by news coverage (Iyengar 2011), and by artful use of social media. Local and state elections receive less attention from the media than national and presidential elections. Although presidential candidates receive significant attention and take full advantage of that free exposure, that situation does not really exist for candidates for state and local offices. There can, however, be extensive coverage of a few competitive state and local races, although typically local newspapers—with limited readership—provide more in depth information on those races than local television can. Although the focus on local television news is often on campaign "horse race" and strategy, Fowler (2013) shows that in the last weeks before an election, coverage of some local races is substantial. However, most political news covered by the TV stations listed in Table 2 involves the major races in the main city of that particular media market, with the vast majority of local and state legislative races being largely ignored.

Whether television stations mainly cover the issues at stake or the game of the elections depends largely on the competitiveness of the races in their area, the competitive pressures of the size of the market and the commitment of the station to politics. Local television news attracts the largest audiences among media outlets, but its audience often pays little attention to politics (Fowler 2013, 56). Since the advertising revenue that funds television is directly linked to viewership, a lack of interest from low-information viewers weakens incentives TV stations have for airing news of state and local politics. Nonetheless, any information helps these low information citizens to become familiar with the candidates, especially for the down-ballot races.

Although advertising costs are decreasing, candidates remain strategic in where they spend their money. The gubernatorial races and ballot initiatives are the campaigns that typically rely on significant television advertising in Washington. They are also usually among the most covered by free media, so they benefit from both. Candidates for the state legislature traditionally place significant importance on direct contact with the voters but even in these races, campaign ads are becoming increasingly central (Renner and Lynch 2008). Competitive legislative races, which are rare, find hundreds of thousands of dollars spent on direct mail, TV ads, and paid voter contacts.

Local news broadcasts attract large audiences and candidates often select local television for their advertisements. However, buying television ads on broadcast stations for local and legislative races comes with disadvantages. Television broadcasts are divided by media markets, but a candidate's district may bear little relationship to the market, or is spread over multiple markets. As a result, candidates may exclude vital supporters and waste money on non-eligible voters.

Some newspapers publish endorsements of candidates and ballot measures in addition to reporting on elections. These recommendations are not news but are expressed as editorial opinions from the papers' editorial teams that provide voters with cues as to the candidates' qualifications and political acceptability. These newspaper endorsements matter in local elections (Lieske 1989, 167), especially for first-time candidates because they provide name recognition. A 2003 study revealed that the majority of people who at least occasionally read a newspaper also actually read an endorsement for a gubernatorial or congressional candidate. During the 2002 election season this was 66.6 percent, and of these people, a significant portion (about 12 percent) said that their voting decision was affected by the endorsement article (Meltzer 2007).

Nowadays the impact of endorsements on citizens' voting behavior is less clear. Given that most newspaper readers are older, better educated, and more politically aware, the endorsements seem to reach the people who least need newspaper endorsements. Despite this, these readers often take them most seriously, regarding them as a useful evaluation by a trusted source (Meltzer 2007). Editorial boards often view endorsements as a public service and most feel that it is their civic and journalistic duty to guide the public because they believe that they are better informed than the general public. In addition, it is a tradition that most editorial boards prefer to continue (Meltzer 2007).

All major newspapers in Washington published endorsements in 2016. The *Seattle Times* editorial board interviewed more than 180 candidates running in Washington for the state and local races in 2016. On November 4, 2016, the *Times* published an updated list with their endorsed candidates. The most impactful endorsements are arguably those for the ballot measures as these often involve complex decisions. Now, high profile ballot measures frequently have their own media campaigns, including many television advertisements, which are another source of information for voters. Accordingly, as shown in Table 3, voters do not blindly follow the endorsements from newspapers' editorial boards. The 2016 election outcomes of Initiative 1501 on protecting seniors from identity theft and Initiative 732 on carbon tax were not in line with any of the newspapers' recommendations.

Table 3: Washington State Ballot Measures and Newspaper Endorsements during the 2016 Elections

	Vote	Seattle Times	Tacoma News Tribune	Spokesman Review	Vancouver Columbian	Everett Daily Herald
1433: Minimum wage	Yes	Yes	No	No	No	No
1464: Campaign finance	No	No	No	No	No	No
1491: Extreme-risk protection orders for removing guns	Yes	Yes	Yes	Yes	Yes	No
1501: Identity theft and open-records measure	Yes	No	No	No	No	--
732: Carbon Emission Tax	Yes	No	No	No	No	No
735: Citizens United	No	No	Yes	No	Yes	No

Note: Italicized endorsements indicate correspondence with the election outcome.

Sources:

www.seattletimes.com/opinion/the-seattle-times-endorsements-for-the-nov-8-general-election

www.thenewstribune.com/opinion/article109461157.html

www.spokesman.com/sections/opinion-2016-endorsements

www.columbian.com/news/2016/nov/08/in-our-view-our-voting-guidance

www.heraldnet.com/opinion/the-herald-endorses-the-editorial-boards-recommendations-for-the-nov-8-general-election

Conclusion

In recent decades, news media in Washington followed the national trends: the circulation of print media decreased; options for television viewers increased while at the same time their coverage of (state) politics declined; and remaining reporters shifted to online content such as blogs in answer to the direct demand of the readers for news. This shift to digital news reporting will likely expand in the future but we are confident that the decline of print media will come to a halt as we expect there will always be readers who prefer print over other media.

The results and aftermath of the 2016 elections may, however, spark more political interest in both news media and its audience. While accusations of political bias against the national news media are not new, the recent claims of the deliberate reporting of "fake news" are. Under those circumstances, the relationship between the press and government is shaky at best and the importance for quality reporting on public affairs is only increasing.

In fact, newspaper circulation is currently increasing in Washington, not declining.[6] This is true for the *Seattle Times* and the *Spokesman-Review* and likely for other Washington newspapers as well. Nationally the *New York Times* and *Washington Post* show an increase in circulation as well. It is too early to tell whether this is a temporary anomaly or the start of a long-term trend.

Notes

1. When writing this chapter, circulation numbers of newspapers in Washington were actually increasing again. This may have been influenced by the 2016 election campaigns and results, the focus on fake news, and the demand for quality information.
2. For more information about older newspapers in Washington, please view the Washington Digital Newspapers program, which has the largest collection of Washington state and territorial newspapers (www.sos.wa.gov/library/newspapers/newspapers.aspx). Since 2009 the Washington State Library has digitized over 30 distinct newspaper titles.
3. While people often refer to these "good old days," they rarely specify what era they are referring to.
4. See Searles and Jenkins 2011 for a thorough overview of the exodus of experienced reporters in Washington.
5. In order to keep an official record, the House Journal captures the proceedings of all House meetings.
6. While it is too early to show up in the numbers of the Audit Bureau of Circulation, it is worthy of mention in light of discussions about the media during and after the 2016 presidential elections.

References

Barthel, Michael. 2016. "Newspapers: Fact Sheet." State of the News Media 2016, Pew Research Center, June 2016. www.journalism.org/2016/06/15/newspapers-fact-sheet.

Brazier, Don. 2000. "History of the Washington Legislature, 1854–1963." Olympia: Washington State Senate. leg.wa.gov/LIC/Documents/Historical/HistoryoftheLeg.pdf.

Brunner, Jim. 2012a. "Seattle Times Co. Launches Ad Campaigns for McKenna and Gay Marriage, Draws Criticism." *Seattle Times*, October 17, 2012. blogs.seattletimes.com/politicsnorthwest/2012/10/17/seattle-times-co-sponsors-full-page-newspaper-ad-for-rob-mckenna.

_____. 2012b. "Seattle Times News Staffers Protest Company's Political-Ad Campaign." *Seattle* Times, October 18, 2012. blogs.seattletimes.com/politicsnorthwest/2012/10/18/seattle-times-news-staffers-protest-companys-political-ad-campaign.

Camden, Jim. 2012. "Sunday Spin: Times Wades into McKenna, Ref. 74 Campaigns." *Spokesman-Review*, October 21, 2012. www.spokesman.com/blogs/spincontrol/2012/oct/21/sunday-spin-times-wades-mckenna-ref-74-campaigns.

_____. 2016. "Spin Control Files: Legislator, Reporter Engaged in Fist Fight on House Floor in 1909." *Spokesman Review*, January 4, 2016. www.spokesman.com/stories/2016/jan/04/spin-control-files-legislator-reporter-engaged-in-.

Day, Matt. 2016. "Northwest Cable News Pulling the Plug Next Year. *Seattle Times*, October 28, 2016. www.seattletimes.com/business/northwest-cable-news-pulling-the-plug-next-year.

Fowler, Erika F. 2013. "Making the News: Is Local Television News Coverage Really that Bad?" In *New Directions in Media and Politics*, edited by Travis N. Ridout, 45–60. New York: Routledge, 47.

Gill, Kathy. 2012. "Seattle Times Ad Buy Leads To Newsroom, Reader Protests," *Seattle Times*, October 22, 2012. blogs.seattletimes.com/uwelectioneye/2012/10/22/seattle-times-ad-buy-leads-to-newsroom-reader-protests.

Gottfried, Jeffrey, and Elisa Shearer. 2016. "News Use Across Social Media Platforms 2016." Pew Research Center (May 26). www.journalism.org/2016/05/26/news-use-across-social-media-platforms-2016.

Graber, Doris A. 1993. "Swiss Cheese Journalism." *State Government News* 36:19–21.

Iyengar, Shanto. 2011. *Media and Politics: A Citizen's Guide*. New York: W.W. Norton & Company, Inc.

Kienholz, Mary, L. 2012. *The Canwell Files: Murder, Arson and Intrigue in the Evergreen State*. Bloomington, IN: iUniverse.

Knauf, Ana Sofia. 2016. "UW Budget Cuts Throw Local News Nonprofit into an 'Existential Crisis.'" *The Stranger*, December 8, 2016. www.thestranger.com/slog/2016/12/08/24734716/uw-budget-cuts-throw-local-news-nonprofit-into-an-existential-crisis.

KUOW. 2015. "The Story of Us." KUOW Annual Report 2015. www2.kuow.org/reports/AnnualReport_2015.pdf.

Lerman, Rachel. 2017. "KOMO Cuts Positions in Newsroom." *Seattle Times*, January 7, 2017. www.seattletimes.com/business/technology/komo-cuts-positions-in-newsroom.

Lieske, Joel. 1989. "The Political Dynamics of Urban Voting Behavior." *American Journal of Political Science* 33:150–74.

Mackenzie, William. 2016. "The Long, Slow, Agonizing Death of the Oregonian." *Thinking Oregon,* January 7, 2016. thinkingoregon.org/2016/01/07/the-long-slow-agonizing-death-of-the-oregonian.

McIntosh, Andrew. 2017. "Seattle Times Co. Plans Closure of Issaquah Press Group Community Newspapers." *Puget Sound Business Journal*, January 19, 2017. www.bizjournals.com/seattle/news/2017/01/19/seattle-times-plans-closure-of-issaquah-press.html.

Meltzer, Kimberly. 2007. "Newspaper Editorial Boards and the Practice of Endorsing Candidates for Political Office in the United States." *Journalism* 81:83–103. DOI: 10.1177/1464884907072422.

Mitchell, Amy, Jeffrey Gottfried, Michael Barthel, and Elisa Shearer. 2016. "The Modern News Consumer: News Attitudes and Practices in the Digital Era." Pew Research Center, July 7, 2016. www.journalism.org/2016/07/07/the-modern-news-consumer.

Mondo Times. 2017a. "Highest Circulation Newspapers in the United States." www.mondotimes.com/newspapers/usa/usatop100.html.

————. 2017b. "Highest Circulation Washington Newspapers." www.mondotimes.com/newspapers/usa/washington-newspaper-circulation.html.

Mungo, Raymond. 1977. "Dixy Lee Ray: How Madame Nuke took over Washington." *Mother Jones Magazine*, May 1977:29–31, 39–40.

Nielsen. 2017. "Local Television Market Universe Estimates." Estimates as of January 1, 2017 and used throughout the 2016–2017 television season. Estimates are effective September 24, 2016. www.thevab.com/wp-content/uploads/2016/09/2016-2017-nielsen-local-dma-ranks.pdf.

NWPR. 2015. "Annual Report 2014." mediad.publicbroadcasting.net/p/nwpr/files/201503/nwpr_2014_annual_report_mur_web.pdf.

Renner, Tari and Patrick G. Lynch. 2008. "A Little Knowledge is a Dangerous Thing: What We Know about the Role of the Media in State Politics." In *Media Power Media Politics*, edited by Mark J. Rozell and Jeremy D, Mayer, 137–157. Lanham, MA: Rowman & Littlefield Publishers, Inc., 2008, 142.

Rijkhoff, Sanne A.M. 2018. "Media in Oregon: Doing a Lot More with a Lot Less." In *Oregon State and Local Politics: Continuity and Change*, edited by Richard Clucas, Mark Henkels, Priscilla Southwell, and Ed Weber. Corvallis, OR: Oregon State University Press.

Rosenstiel, Tom, Marion R. Just, Todd L. Belt, Atiba Pertilla, Walter C. Dean, and Dante Chinni, editors. 2007. *We Interrupt This Newscast: How to Improve Local News and Win Ratings Too*. New York: Cambridge University Press, 33.

Searles, Kathleen, and Austin Jenkins. 2011. "Media and Politics in Washington in the Post-Post-Intelligencer Age." In *Governing Washington: Politics and Government in the Evergreen State*, edited by Cornell W. Clayton and Nicholas P. Lovrich, 109–124. Pullman WA: Washington State University Press.

Seattle Times Staff. 2017. "*Seattle Times* to Cut Newsroom Jobs," *Seattle Times*, January 7, 2017. www.seattletimes.com/business/seattle-times-to-cut-newsroom-jobs.

Shors, Ben, and Douglas Blanks Hindman. 2016. "Future of Journalism." 2016. Edward R. Murrow College of Communication, Washington State University (June). communication.wsu.edu/news-events/future-of-journalism.html.

Spokane Public Radio. 2014. "SPR Believes in Variety." spokanepublicradio.org/spr-believes-variety

Yardley, William, and Richard Pérez-Peña. 2009. "Seattle Paper Shifts Entirely to the Web," *New York Times*, March 16, 2009. www.nytimes.com/2009/03/17/business/media/17paper.

Government Institutions

CHAPTER 7

Washington's Constitution: The Politics of State Constitutional Interpretation

Cornell W. Clayton and Gerry Alexander

Introduction

The United States is a system of dual constitutionalism. State constitutions pre-existed the federal document and in many ways are more important in determining how governments function. Despite their history and importance, most Americans know little about their state charters. Constitutional commentaries focus almost exclusively on the federal document, and polls indicate a majority of Americans do not even realize their states have constitutions.

State constitutions do not simply mirror their federal counterpart, however, but rather differ in important ways. They have their own histories, structures, and concerns, and they restrict power differently. The unfamiliarity Americans have with them undoubtedly is the result of the nationalization of politics during the twentieth century, a period that also saw the U.S. Supreme Court expand federal constitutional law into many areas formerly left to state and local control. But a revival of federalism in recent decades has brought with it a revitalization of the role of state constitutions and courts. Under this "new judicial federalism" state courts have discovered new rights and liberties under their own constitutions, often providing greater protections than those afforded under federal law (Tarr 1997). For example, decisions by high courts in Massachusetts, California, Iowa, and elsewhere extended the right of same-sex couples to marry under state constitutional protections well before the U.S. Supreme Court did so under the federal constitution in *Obergerfell v. Hodges* in 2015, and those state court decisions served as catalysts for the latter.[1]

The "rediscovery" of state constitutional rights, however, has not been without critics (Gardner 1992; Kahn 1996). An early leader in this movement, the Washington Supreme Court's development of an independent constitutional jurisprudence is also controversial (Clayton 2002; Spitzer 1998; Utter 1992). Understanding these debates tells us much about politics in Washington State as well as about the promise and problems of a system of dual constitutionalism in the twenty-first century.

Washington's Constitutional History and the Concerns of its Framers

Efforts to create a state in the territory that eventually became Washington began immediately following the Civil War. Measures calling for a constitutional convention appeared on territorial ballots as early as 1869, and one finally passed in 1876. The first convention was held in Walla Walla in June 1878. After 40 days, the delegates produced a draft constitutional document, but the statehood effort stalled in a closely divided Congress that was unwilling to admit new states into the Union. Democrats who were in control of the House of Representatives refused to admit new states that were perceived to be Republican-leaning (including Washington), while Republicans controlled the Senate and refused to acquiesce to states that might elect Democrats to their chamber. The impasse broke in 1888, when Republicans gained control of both houses of Congress, and on February 22, 1889, Congress passed statehood-enabling legislation for Washington and several other western states.

A second constitutional convention convened in Olympia on July 4, 1889. The 75 delegates to this convention were selected by a special election; two-thirds were Republican and one-third Democrat. The constitution they drafted was approved by a wide margin of voters, 40,152 to 11,879, during a special election in October 1889. A month later, on November 11, 1889, President Benjamin Harrison proclaimed Washington the 42nd state of the union (Beckett 1968).

Although a transcriber took detailed notes during the convention, these notes were lost. Contemporaneous news accounts, however, shed light on the attitudes of those in Olympia; they echoed those expressed in other state conventions during the same period.[2] Indeed, late nineteenth-century state constitution-makers operated self-consciously in a context of constitutional pluralism and liberal borrowing. The delegates in Olympia were familiar with the federal constitution and borrowed many of its features, such as a separation of powers into three branches, a bicameral legislature, and language for many rights provisions, such as the due process protections found in article I, § 3 of the state constitution, declaring "No person shall be deprived of life, liberty, or property, without due process of law."

The delegates also borrowed systematically from other state constitutions. In fact, prior to the convention, former territorial judge W. Lair Hill drafted a complete model constitution which he distributed to delegates that drew heavily on California's constitution from 1879, and provided the wording for as many as 45 provisions in Washington's constitution (Utter and Spitzer 2002). Oregon's constitution supplied wording for another 23 provisions, Wisconsin's for 27, and Indiana's for at least 7 more (Clayton 2002). Indeed, few of the provisions in Washington's constitution can claim originality.

The structural features of Washington's constitution were also borrowed. A bicameral legislature that included a House of Representatives, consisting of between 63 and 99 members, each serving two-year terms (art. I, § 2); and a Senate, one-third to one-half this size, each serving four-year terms with half its seats elected every two years (art. I, § 6). Regular legislative sessions would be biennial and limited to 60 days (art. I, § 12).

The constitution disperses the executive authority among the office of governor, elected to a four-year term (art. III, § 2), and seven other independently elected officers, including the lieutenant governor, secretary of state, treasurer, auditor, attorney general, superintendent of public instruction, and the commissioner of public lands (art. III, § 1). There was a lively debate over the veto power, but in the end the governor was granted the power to veto any bill or single item of any bill, with a two-thirds vote of both legislative chambers required to override (art. II, § 12).

The court system drew heavily on the California model. It consisted of a supreme court with five members (later expanded to nine) and lower superior courts (art. IV). Supreme Court justices are elected to six-year terms, and superior court judges to four-year terms (art. IV, § 3, 5). Again, none of these structural features are original to Washington.

The social and political attitudes of late nineteenth-century America were also apparent during the convention (Spitzer 2008). Women's suffrage and the prohibition of alcohol were contentious issues nationally at that time, and they were the subjects of heated debates in Olympia. Articles dealing with these issues were narrowly defeated by voters, but other social and political attitudes of the period found their way into the constitution.

America was going through wrenching social and economic change in the late nineteenth century, moving from an agrarian economy and localized politics to industrial capitalism and political nationalization. The period was marked by concentration of wealth, rising corporate power, and a good deal of corruption in government. In response, populist and progressive third parties sprang up throughout the United States. Chapters of the Grange, the People's Party, the Union Labor Party, the Farmers Alliance, and the Knights of Labor were all established in territorial Washington and their ideas animated many of the debates during the second constitutional convention (Schwantes 1982).

The delegates in Olympia thus had very different concerns than did the framers of the federal constitution a century earlier (Spitzer 2008). While the federalists were strongly influenced by the ideas of civic republicanism and a fear of populist majorities, delegates in Olympia were advocates of popular sovereignty and direct forms of democracy. Liberty, they believed, could best be secured through open, democratic government that was powerful enough to regulate corporations and private economic power (Dolliver 1992; Snure 1992).

Similar to other state constitutions during this era, Washington's thus sought to balance economic development with protections against concentrations of private power and wealth (Bakken 1987; Tarr and Williams 1998). Understanding this historical milieu helps explain many of the prominent, but otherwise disparate, provisions of Washington's constitution.

Individual Rights

Unlike the federal constitution where a bill of rights was an afterthought, protecting individual liberties was the first concern of those in Olympia. Article I is a broad declaration of rights containing 35 separate sections. The rights guaranteed range from traditional legislative prohibitions on bills of attainder and *ex post facto* laws (§ 23), to specific proclamations of liberties, such as a right to assemble (§ 4), a right to speak freely (§ 5), a right to religious freedom (§ 11), rights to trial by jury and due process (§ 3, 21, 22, 26), a right to bear arms (§ 24), and a right to privacy (§ 7). Also, unlike the federal bill of rights which is formulated as restrictions on Congress's power (e.g. "Congress shall make no law…"), the rights in Washington's constitution are often phrased as positive affirmations of liberties (e.g., "Every person may freely speak…") and therefore can be interpreted as protections against both the government and private power.

Democracy

In contrast to the republican institutions in the federal constitution (e.g. the Electoral College, the election of senators by state legislatures, the appointment of judges, etc.), Washington's constitution provides for direct democratic control of all three branches of the government. This includes direct election of both houses of the legislature (art. II, § 4, 6), popular election of judges (art. IV, § 3, 5), and separate election of all major offices in the executive branch (art. III, § 1). Direct democratic control was enhanced further by passage of the Seventh and Eighth Amendments, in 1912, which allow citizens to directly legislate through the initiative and referendum process (art. II, § 1) and made statewide elected officials subject to popular recall (art. I, § 23).

The Legislature and Special Interests

The delegates in Olympia specifically sought to prevent the legislature from becoming a tool of corporate interests. It is prohibited from lending public money or credit to private companies (art. XII, § 9; art. VIII, § 5), contracting convict labor (art. II, § 29), and passing "private or special legislation" involving taxes, highways, mortgages, corporate privileges, deeds and wills, interest rates, fines and penalties, or civil and criminal actions (art. II, § 28).

The constitution also imposed structural restrictions on the legislative process to guard against corruption; requiring open meetings (art. II, § 2), forbidding bribery or unwarranted influence of public officials (art. II, § 30 and 39), and prohibiting legislative "log-rolling" by preventing bills from embracing more than one subject (art. II, § 19).

Restricting Corporate Power

An entire article is dedicated to restricting private corporations. Article XII bars the formation of monopolies and trusts (§ 22), prohibits discrimination in the rates companies may charge (§ 15), prohibits railroads from consolidating lines (§ 16), requires stockholders to assume liability for corporate debts (§ 4, 11), and forbids the use of eminent domain powers on behalf of private interests (art. I, § 16).

A unique provision in Washington's constitution also prohibits private companies from "organizing, maintaining or employing an armed body of men" (art. I, § 24). This restriction sought to prevent the reoccurrence of an event in 1888, when mining companies in Cle Elum and Roslyn employed armed strikebreakers to resolve a labor dispute (Dolliver 1992).

Structural Differences between the State and the Federal Constitution

In addition to reflecting its distinct history and the political attitudes of the period, Washington's constitution, like all state constitutions, differs from the federal document in structural respects as well. These differences are crucial to understanding constitutional politics at the state level and the interpretation of state constitutions.

Restricting or Empowering Government?

It is well-known that the federal constitution created a government of limited or "enumerated powers," so that when Congress regulates it must be pursuant to an explicit grant of authority under the document. The opposite is true of state governments, which are assumed to possess plenary legislative authority ("police powers") unless those powers are explicitly restricted or limited (Grad 1968).

Delegates in Olympia understood this structural difference, which is why the restrictions they placed on state government are more detailed and specific than those found in the federal document (Utter 1985). Constitutional challenges to state laws turn on whether the Legislature is specifically prohibited from doing something, not explicitly authorized, and the burden falls on those challenging the government action to find the restriction on the state's power (Grad 1968). This difference is articulated in *State v. Gunwall* (1986), where Justice Andersen explained:

> [T]he United States Constitution is a grant of limited power authorizing the federal government to exercise only those constitutionally enumerated powers expressly delegated to it by the states, whereas our state constitution imposes limitations on the otherwise plenary power of the state to do anything not expressly forbidden by the state constitution or federal law (815).

This difference also affects how judges interpret grants of power. Under the federal document government power is often interpreted expansively, but under state constitutions they are more often interpreted narrowly (an authorization to pursue one course of action by negative implication is often interpreted as precluding others). It also affects interpretation of individual rights. The absence of a federal plenary legislative power acts as an implicit protection of individual liberty by denying government power to make laws. At the state level, however, protection must be found in the express affirmations of liberties (Tarr 1998; Utter 1985).

Positive Rights

In contrast to the federal constitution which mostly frames rights as *negations* or *restrictions* on government authority, state constitutions often contain "positive rights" or provisions that *require government action*. Indeed, of the 35 sections in Washington's Declaration of Rights only three are expressed as restrictions on government (art. I, § 8, 12, 23), the others are phrased as affirmations of rights requiring government enforcement. For example, article II, § 35 provides that the "Legislature shall pass necessary laws for the protection of persons working in mines, factories and other employments dangerous to life or deleterious to health."

Several provisions in the state constitution also confer an entitlement to public resources. Article XIII, § 1, for example, provides that educational, reformatory, and penal institutions, as well as state mental hospitals, "shall be fostered and supported by the state," while article IX, § 1 declares it "the *paramount duty* of the state to make ample provision for the education of all children residing within its borders."

These *positive rights* raise special problems for courts in their relationships with the other branches. Decisions about taxing and spending are usually thought to be legislative function under the purview of the legislature. Sensitive to this, judges in Washington traditionally were reluctant to enforce the positive rights provisions in the constitution (Talmadge 1999). Yet, such concerns may not be warranted if judges can point to clear textual commands in the constitution that require government to provide certain resources and when judges in Washington are elected and can be voted out of office if citizens believe they are abusing their authority (Clayton 2002).

Length and Fluidity

As with most state constitutions, Washington's document is longer and more detailed than its federal counterpart. It contains 32 separate articles and features 108 amendments, compared to the 7 articles and 27 amendments in the federal document. The state constitution runs to nearly 40,000 words, compared to 6,000 in the federal constitution. The provisions of the state document range from clear and specific commands (e.g., article III specifies the governor's salary), to open-ended clauses that require pure political judgment to interpret (e.g., article I's statement that a "frequent recurrence to fundamental principles is essential to the security of individual rights and the perpetuity of free government").

Even more vexing is the state constitution's fluidity. The more than 108 amendments to the constitution vary in detail and subject matter. The area eliciting the most change are provisions involving government expenditure and finance, where there have been more than 25 separate amendments. Other areas provoking frequent amendment include courts and judges (11), local governments (9), compensation of public officials (5), and voter qualifications (5). More than 80 of the constitution's 247 original sections—nearly one-third of the entire document—have been altered by amendment, and a quarter of these amendments have been themselves subsequently amended or repealed.[3]

While historians point to the overhaul or reconstruction of the federal constitution during periods such as the Civil War or the New Deal, when multiple amendments or landmark judicial decisions fundamentally changed its architecture (Ackerman 1991), no such periods of reform or reconstruction have brought coherence to the development of Washington's constitution. In fact, several reform efforts to do so failed. In 1918, the Legislature actually recommended a third constitutional convention to update the document, but that proposal was rejected in a referendum vote. In the 1930s a Constitutional Revision Commission appointed by the governor recommended nine sweeping reforms to the document (including a controversial move to a unicameral legislature), but none of these were adopted by the Legislature. In 1965, a second Constitutional Advisory Council proposed a series of reforms, but these too failed to elicit action by the Legislature. Governor Daniel Evans, a strong advocate of constitutional reform, created three separate constitutional revision committees between 1967 and 1975, all of which recommended changes, but none were adopted (Beckett and Peterson 1985).

The 108 amendments to Washington's constitution are thus separate, unrelated alterations. Some parts of the document have remained unchanged since 1889, while others have been altered on a regular basis. Some sections embody a coherent constitutional perspective, while others reflect a hodge-podge of inconsistent views and values accreted over time. Judges who interpret the constitution thus often confront the task of *constructing* rather than *discovering* coherence. Moreover, to the extent the individual provisions do not embody a coherent set of values, interpreters cannot look to the whole to illuminate the meaning of parts. State judges are thus often forced to adopt a "clause-bound" interpretive methodology in which each provision is interpreted in isolation rather than relying on a uniform or integrative approach.

An Independent State Constitutional Rights Jurisprudence

The promise and pitfalls of state constitutional interpretation are illustrated by efforts to develop an independent constitutional rights jurisprudence in Washington. In a 1977 speech, former justice William Brennan urged state judges to look beyond the federal constitution to the individual rights guaranteed in their own state charters. He especially urged them not to interpret state constitutional rights provisions in lock-step fashion with how federal courts interpret analogous federal provisions (Brennan 1977). That call was echoed three years later by the U.S. Supreme Court in *Pruneyard v. Robins* (1980), where it said each state has a "sovereign right to adopt in its own Constitution individual liberties more expansive than those conferred by the Federal Constitution." This invitation began a renaissance in state constitutional development as one state high court after another began plumbing the language and history of their constitutions to develop new rights (Tarr 1997; Williams 1996).

Washington's high court was an early leader in this movement (Utter 1984). As early as 1981 it had begun interpreting the state constitution to confer greater rights on Washington's citizens. In *Alderwood v. Washington Environmental Council* (1981), the court held that the free speech clause of Washington's constitution required owners of a private shopping center to accommodate the free expression rights of political activists. The First Amendment of the federal constitution only protects against government suppression of speech, but, writing for the court, Justice Utter said the federal bill of rights only "establishes the minimum degree of protection" of free speech rights and state courts "are obliged to [independently] determine the scope of protections in state constitutions."

Washington's high court began asserting the primacy of state constitutional rights over federal ones in other areas as well. In *State v. Coe* (1984), it bypassed the federal First Amendment to instead apply the state's free speech provisions barring a trial judge's gag order in a highly publicized murder trial. The court said "by turning first to our own constitution we can develop a body of independent jurisprudence" and that moreover it would be "improper and premature" to apply the federal constitution if the case could be resolved under state constitutional law alone.

From the outset, however, this new judicial federalism carried substantial political undercurrents. Advocates hailed it as a boon to expanding individual rights, but critics saw it as unprincipled, result-oriented, constitution shopping. Justice Brennan's call was especially viewed by political conservatives as part of a liberal agenda to use state constitutions to counter the retrenchment of individual rights by an increasingly more conservative federal judiciary.

The effort by Washington's high court to develop an independent rights jurisprudence was not exempt from these debates (Spitzer 1998). In *State v. Ringer* (1983), Justice Dimmick chided her colleagues for their "sudden leap to the sanctuary of our own state constitution" in a search and seizure case. Adopting different interpretations of analogous state and federal provisions, she said, only "confound(s) the constabulary and, by picking and choosing between state and federal constitutions, change(s) the rules after the game has been played in good faith."

Critics of the court's new rights jurisprudence introduced measures in the legislature to curb its power (Talmadge 1999). Although these efforts failed, a more serious challenge came in the mid-1980s when four new justices were elected to the court (Spitzer 2006). These new justices were critics of the new jurisprudence and led a retreat from some of the court's earlier decisions.[4] In one highly publicized case, *Southcenter Joint Venture v. National Democratic Policy Committee* (1989), for example, the court reversed its *Alderwood* decision applying the state's free speech protections against private property owners. Appealing to the "general principles of constitutionalism," the court's new majority held that the state constitution's free speech protections only applied to "state action" after all.

To convince critics that its jurisprudence was principled, the court developed a set of criteria to guide its decisions. In *State vs. Gunwall* (1986) the court articulated "six neutral and nonexclusive criteria" for when to invoke an independent interpretation of the state's constitutional protections: (1) the text of the state provision; (2) differences in the text of the parallel federal provision; (3) differences in the history of the two constitutions; (4) differences in preexisting state law; (5) differences in the structure between the two constitutions; and (6) differences that emerge from matters of particular state interest or local concern.

Although these criteria were intended to assuage its critics, a debate broke out immediately on the court about their application. Justices Utter and Madsen in particular argued that the *Gunwall* criteria were merely interpretive tools that should be used by judges to advance an independent state jurisprudence. On the other side, Justices Durham and Guy argued that the criteria were procedural hurdles that litigants must pass before courts could move beyond the federal constitution to consider independent state grounds (Spitzer 2006).

Initially, those who saw the criteria as hurdles prevailed. In *State v. Wethered* (1988), for example, the court refused to even consider a state constitutional claim raised by a criminal defendant because the attorney failed to brief all six of the criteria, indicating that all had to be briefed in each case. A study of decisions between 1986 and 1997 found that of the 109 cases where the high court cited *Gunwall,* it refused to interpret the state constitution 65 percent of the time, and, when it did, it reached a different result from a federal analysis only eight times (Spitzer 1998).

The debate over the use of criteria came to a head in *State v. Gocken* (1995), a case involving double jeopardy. Writing for the court, Justice Guy decided the case on federal constitutional grounds, but conducted a perfunctory examination of the *Gunwall* criteria to conclude no basis existed for broader protection under the state's double jeopardy clause. In dissent, Justice Madsen criticized the majority for using "*Gunwall* as a talisman" preventing independent analysis of the state's document. The state's constitution should come first, she argued. The court should not leave the constitutional rights of Washington's citizens "lost somewhere in the ever-shifting shadow of the federal courts which are no less political and perhaps more so than our own state courts."

Justice Madsen's dissent would eventually become the accepted view on the court. All five of the justices in the *Gocken* majority left the court by 2003, and new justices since that time have mostly adopted the state primacy view. In *State v. Jackson* (2003), the court held that once a state provision had been interpreted to confer greater rights than its federal counterpart, a *Gunwall* analysis was no longer necessary in subsequent cases under that provision. In *Woodinville v. Northshore United Church of Christ* (2009), the court went further, chastising a lower court for using the criteria to prevent an interpretation of Washington's religious freedom provisions. Requiring a complete *Gunwall* analysis in every case, it said in uncharacteristically colorful language, would turn "briefing into an antiquated writ system where parties may lose their constitutional rights by failing to incant correctly."

Indeed, in contrast to the first decade under *Gunwall,* a study of the court's decisions citing it between 1997 and 2010 found that in 101 cases the court interpreted the state constitution 60 percent of the time, and in those cases held that the state provision provided greater protection 40 percent of the time (Clayton and McMillan 2011).

The Court and Constitutional Politics

If Washington's Supreme Court is no longer self-conscious in developing an independent rights jurisprudence, its constitutional decisions are not without controversy. Two areas of state constitutional development especially have brought the court into protracted conflict with the other branches and with organized political groups—public school funding, and ballot initiatives seeking to limit state taxes.

Public Schools

The high court was originally drawn into the school funding controversy in *Seattle School District v. State* (1978), when parents and educational groups sued the state for not adequately supporting public education. Agreeing with the plaintiffs, the court held that the state had failed to meet its "paramount duty" under art. IX, § 1, "to make ample provision for the education of all children."

Rejecting the state's argument that the issue was "political not judicial," the court went on to say that the judiciary must provide a remedy as part of its "duty to interpret, construe, and give meaning to words, sections and articles of the constitution." Although it required the legislature to meet its obligation by 1981, it did not retain jurisdiction in the case and refused to define what constituted adequate support for a "basic education." Deferring to the "traditional roles" of each branch, the court instead expressed "trust" in the legislature to make "good faith efforts" to provide a "basic program of education" for all of Washington's children.

The legislature addressed the issue by passing the Basic Education Act in 1978, which was later comprehensively amended in 2009. Under the statutes the legislature explicitly defined a "basic education," imposed new requirements on school districts, and listed programs that the state would support with funding. These new standards, slated to go into effect in 2011, however ran up against a deep economic recession that kept the legislature from funding the law. Without the funding, the state was again challenged for breaching its "paramount duty," now under standards that it had set itself. In *McCleary v. State* (2012), the court unanimously held that the state failed to comply with its constitutional duty, and, in contrast to 1978, it retained jurisdiction in the case and ordered the state to comply with its ruling by 2018 and provide the court periodic progress reports until that time.

After several unsatisfactory progress reports by the legislature, the court in 2014 held the state in contempt for failing to implement program of basic education, but delayed imposing a penalty to give the legislature time to address the matter in the next legislative session. A divided legislature, however, could not come to an agreement on a detailed plan to meet the state's funding obligations, so in 2015 the court imposed a remedial penalty against the state of $100,000 a day "until it adopts a concrete plan for complying" with its constitutional duty.

The court's action was not well received by legislators, many of whom saw it as an affront to their prerogatives. Indeed, even as they struggled to find a partisan compromise to fund education and comply with *McCleary*, legislators sought to retaliate against the court with a series of measures aimed at reducing the court's size, cutting its budget, or stripping its authority. Although these measures did not pass, the legislature signaled its displeasure in 2016 when it refused to invite the Chief Justice to present the traditional State of the Judiciary message to a joint session.

As of this writing in 2017, the legislature is in special session still trying to address *McCleary*. How any resolution it reaches will fare against future court challenges is uncertain. It can, however, be said that in the area of school funding at least, the court has eschewed its reluctance to actively enforce the positive rights provisions in the constitution.

Taxes and Ballot Initiatives

A series of decisions regarding the constitutionality of ballot initiatives limiting taxes has also thrust the court's role into sharp political relief. A populist era reform, ballot initiatives were intended to allow citizens to bypass corrupt elected officials and enact direct legislation. In recent years, however, initiatives have increasingly become tools used by special interests to enact policies that lack legislative support. Tim Eyman, a conservative political activist, is a major sponsor of initiatives aimed at restricting taxes in Washington. Since 2000, Eyman's group has sponsored more than 20 ballot initiatives, half of which were passed by popular votes; and eight were subsequently invalidated in whole or part by the state's high court as violating the constitution.

Eyman's first tax initiative, passed in 1999, cut the state motor vehicle excise tax (the yearly car tabs) and required voter approval for all future tax increases. I-695 was challenged in *Amalgamated Transit Union v. State* (2000), and struck down as violating the constitution's single subject rule and the requirement that the subject of an act appear in the measure's title. The court said that the title of I-695 failed to advise the public that it also applied to fees and other government charges not "traditionally considered to be taxes." After the decision the Legislature and the governor abolished the unpopular car-tab tax, but took no action to limit other tax increases.

Eyman returned the following year with I-722 (the "Son of I-695"), which capped property tax increases at 2 percent and retroactively repealed tax increases adopted during the previous year. It passed with 56 percent of the vote, but it was struck down again by the court for violating the single subject rule. Writing for the majority, Justice Johnson said "we cannot know if either subject of I-722 would have garnered popular support standing alone, so we must declare the entire initiative void."

Eyman responded in 2010 by gaining the passage of I-1053, which required a two-thirds vote by both legislative chambers for any tax increase. In *League of Education Voters v. State* (2013), the court found that the supermajority requirement violated art. II, § 22 of the state constitution, which provides "no bill shall become law unless a majority of each chamber votes in favor of it." Writing for the court, Chief Justice Madsen said the initiative was essentially a backdoor effort to amend the constitution. In a dissent, however, Justice Johnson criticized the majority for getting involved in the "political arena in unwise and unprecedented fashion, misreading the constitution and overriding case law and the clear wishes of the electorate."

Undeterred, Eyman sponsored I-1366 in 2015, which passed with just over 51 percent of the vote. In an effort to circumvent the court, it forced a reduction in the state's sales tax from 6.5 percent to 5.5 percent (causing a loss of about $1 billion in revenue) unless the legislature referred a constitutional amendment to the ballot requiring a two-thirds vote in the legislature or voter approval for future tax increases. In *League of Education Voters v. State* (2015), the court struck down this initiative too. Writing for the court, Chief Justice Madsen said "the 'do this or else' structure of the initiative" effectively violated the single subject rule. It also violated art. XXIII, which does not permit constitutional amendment through ballot initiatives. By "pair(ing) one drastic or undesirable measure with an ultimatum that it go into effect unless a specific constitutional amendment is proposed to the people," I-1366 "amounted to a small percentage of voters effectuating a constitutional amendment by two majority votes" Madsen said. Concurring, Justice

Gonzalez called the initiative an attempt to turn the constitutional amendment process "on its head," emphasizing that ballot initiatives "are not the proper vehicle to amend the constitution."

Other Constitutional Developments

Other recent constitutional decisions have had important political ramifications as well. In *Gerberdine v. Munro* (1998), for example, the court threw out a ballot initiative that imposed term limits on elected officials. I-573 prevented a candidate's name from appearing on the ballot after specified periods in office. The court struck the law down as a backdoor constitutional amendment violating art. XXIII. Justice Talmadge said the law "improperly attempts to add qualifications to constitutional offices by statute. A statute, whether adopted by the Legislature or the people, may not add qualifications for state constitutional officers where the Constitution sets those qualifications."

More recently the court incurred the wrath of charter school supporters, including some of the state's wealthiest business leaders. Charter schools receive public funding, but operate independently of the public school system and are exempt from many state laws and administrative regulations governing public schools. Supporters see charter schools as an important part of school reform as they provide parents "more options" for schooling. Opponents oppose them as an effort to privatize public education.

In Washington, charter schools were authorized by a ballot initiative that narrowly passed in 2012. The initiative, I-1240, designated charter schools part of the state's system of "common schools," thus authorizing them to receive public funding. In *League of Women Voters v. State* (2015), however, the court struck down that provision as violating art. IX, § 2 of the constitution, which requires a "general and uniform system of public schools." The court reasoned that charter schools are not "public schools" because they are not governed by elected boards and not accountable to voters.

The court's decision broke with high courts in some other states, which had upheld charter schools, and came just weeks after nine charter schools were authorized to operate and had enrolled students. One state representative called it "a slap in the face to the people we're supposed to be serving" (Pettigrew 2015). The legislature acted swiftly to address the problem in 2016, authorizing charter schools to receive funding from state lottery proceeds rather than the general fund. However that fix in the law was also immediately challenged, and, in the meantime, the court's decision helped fuel a well-financed campaign to defeat three sitting justices up for reelection in 2016. According to public disclosure reports, wealthy business leaders such as Microsoft's Bill Gates and Paul Allen poured more than $1.7 million into independent PACs which worked to defeat the justices. Although all three justices won reelection, the campaigns were some of the most expensive in the history of the state (Miletich 2016; see also chapter 10 in this volume).

Conclusion

Constitutional scholar Edward Corwin once observed that "one of the greatest lures to the westward movement of population was the possibility which federalism held out to the advancing settlers of establishing their own undictated political institutions" (1950, 22).

Washington's constitution has a distinct history, and its structure and purposes differ in important respects from the federal constitution. The promise of dual constitutionalism is that states can learn from each other and from the federal experience. Justice Utter recognized that promise when he wrote in his *Southcenter* opinion: "Federalism allows the states to operate as laboratories for more workable solutions to legal and constitutional problems. As part of our obligation to interpret our State's constitution, we have the opportunity to develop a jurisprudence more appropriate to our own constitutional language" (1303).

Washington's effort to develop an independent constitutional rights jurisprudence, however, also illustrates the problems attendant with dual constitutionalism. Political commitments to federalism are often politically strategic. Conservatives, for example, might favor federalism when it comes to abortion rights, but want strong national control when it comes to the war on drugs. Liberals hold the opposite views about the role of the federal government in these disputes. It is not surprising that strategic commitments to constitutional principles might also apply at the state level, leading partisans to favor judicial enforcement of state constitutional provisions when it advances their policy agenda, and to oppose it when it does not.

Interest in state constitutions and the role of state judiciaries in interpreting them is nevertheless here to stay. As with other constitutional developments, it is linked to broader developments that have forced Americans to rethink the locus and forms of governmental power. As in the past, this challenge will require new generations of Washington citizens to define for themselves and give voice to their political goals and aspirations. That voice, as in the past, will continue to be reflected in the state's constitution and debates over its meaning.

Notes

1. See *Goodridge v. Dept. of Public Health* (2003); *In re Marriage Cases* (2008); *Kerrigan v. Commissioner of Public Health* (2008); *Varnum v. Brien* (2009).
2. The best general discussions of the convention and prevailing attitudes of the day are found in two unpublished sources Fitts (1951) and Airey (1945). See also Dolliver (1992). For an account of the convention's day-to-day actions see Rosenow (1962).
3. An up-to-date listing of amendments to Washington's constitution can be found at https://lib.law.washington.edu/content/guides/waconstAmend.
4. For example, *State v. Stroud* (1986); *State v. Kennedy* (1986); and *Southcenter Joint Venture v. National Democratic Policy Committee* (1989).

References

Ackerman, Bruce. 1991. *We The People. Vol. 1: Foundations*. Cambridge, MA: Harvard University Press.

Airey, Wilfred J. 1945. *A History of the Constitution and Government of Washington Territory*. Thesis (Ph.D.). Seattle: University of Washington.

Bakken, Gordon Morris. 1987. *Rocky Mountain Constitution Making: 1850–1912*. New York: Greenwood Press.

Beckett, Paul Louis. 1968. *From Wilderness to Enabling Act: The Evolution of a State of Washington*. Pullman: Washington State University Press.

Beckett, Paul L., and Walfred H. Peterson. 1985. "The Constitutional Framework." In *Political Life in Washington: Governing the Evergreen State*, edited by Thor Swanson et al., 19–34. Pullman: Washington State University Press.

Brennan, William J. 1977. "State Constitutions and the Protection of Individual Rights." *Harvard Law Review* 90(3): 489–504.

Clayton, Cornell W. 2002. "Toward a Theory of the Washington Constitution." *Gonzaga Law Review* 37(1): 41–88.

Clayton, Cornell W., and Lucas McMillan. 2011. "The Politics of State Constitutional Interpretation." In *Governing Washington: Politics and Government in the Evergreen State*, edited by Cornell W. Clayton and Nicholas P. Lovrich. Pullman, Washington: Washington State University Press.

Corwin, Edward S. 1950. "The Passing of Dual Federalism." *Virginia Law Review* 36(1): 1–24.

Dolliver, James M. 1992. "The Mind of the Founders: An Assessment of the Washington Constitution of 1889." In *Washington Comes of Age: The State in the National Experience*, edited by David Stratton, 135–51. Pullman: Washington State University Press.

Fitts, James Leonard. 1951. "The Washington Constitutional Convention of 1889." Master's Thesis, University of Washington.

Gardner, James A. 1992. "The Failed Discourse of State Constitutionalism." *Michigan Law Review* 90(4): 761–837.

Grad, Frank P. 1968. "The State Constitution: Its Function and Form for Our Time." *Virginia Law Review* 54(5): 928–73.

Kahn, Paul. 1996. "State Constitutionalism and the Problems of Fairness." *Valparaiso University Law Review* 30 (2): 459–75.

Miletich, Steve. 2016. "Supreme Court: Zempel, other challengers face uphill run." *Seattle Times*, September 24, 2016. www.yakimaherald.com/news/elections/supreme-court/article_c621b144-82c6-11e6-aa22-87e507c7f1ff.html.

Pettigrew, Eric. 2015. "Charter ruling hurts poorer students." *The Olympian*, September 17, 2015. www.theolympian.com/opinion/opn-columns-blogs/article35481888.html.

Rosenow, Beverly. 1962. *Journal of the Washington State Constitutional Convention, 1889*. Seattle: Book Pub. Co.

Schwantes, Carlos A. 1982. "Protest in a Promised Land: Unemployment, Disinheritance, and the Origin of Labor Militancy in the Pacific Northwest, 1885–1886." *Western Historical Quarterly* 13(4): 373–90.

Snure, Brian. 1992. "Comment: A Frequent Recurrence to Fundamental Principles: Individual Rights, Free Government and the Washington State Constitution." *Washington Law Review* 67(3): 669–90.

Spitzer, Hugh D. 1998. "Which Constitution? Eleven Years of Gunwall in Washington State." *Seattle University Law Review* 21(4): 1187–1215.

_____. 2006. "New Life for the 'Criteria Tests' in State Constitutional Jurisprudence: 'Gunwall is Dead—Long Live Gunwall!'" *Rutgers Law Journal* 37(4): 1169–1202.

_____. 2008. "Washington: The Past and Present Populist State," in *The Constitutionalism of American States*. George E. Connor and Christopher W. Hammons, eds. 771–84.

Talmadge, Philip A. 1999. "Understanding the Limits of Power: Judicial Restraint in General Jurisdiction Court Systems." *Seattle University Law Review* 22(3): 695–739.

Tarr, G. Alan. 1997. "The New Judicial Federalism in Perspective." *Notre Dame Law Review* 72(4): 1097–1118.

_____. 1998. *Understanding State Constitutions*. Princeton, NJ: Princeton University Press.

Tarr, G. Alan, and Robert F. Williams. 1998. "Forward: Western State Constitutions in the American Constitutional Tradition." *New Mexico Law Review* 28 (1): 191–97.

Utter, Robert F. 1984. "Freedom and Diversity in a Federal System: Perspectives on State Constitutions and the Washington Declaration of Rights." *University of Puget Sound Law Review* 7(3): 491–525.

_____. 1985. "Swimming in the Jaws of the Crocodile: State Court Comment on Federal Constitutional Issues When Disposing of Cases on State Constitutional Grounds." *Texas Law Review* 63 (5): 1025.

_____. 1992. "The Practice of Principled Decision-Making in State Constitutionalism: Washington's Experience." *Temple Law Review* 65 (1): 169.

Utter, Robert F., and Hugh D. Spitzer. 2002. *The Washington State Constitution: A Reference Guide*. Westport, CT: Greenwood Press.

Williams, Robert F. 1996. "Looking Back at the New Judicial Federalism's First Generation." *Valparaiso Law Review* 30 (2): xiii.

Cases Cited

Alderwood Associates v. Washington Environmental Council, 635 P.2d 108 (1981).

Amalgamated Transit Union Local 587 v. State, Not Reported in P.3d (2000).

City of Woodinville v. Northshore United Church of Christ, 166 Wn.2d 633 (2009).

Goodridge v. Department of Public Health, 798 N.E.2d 941 (Mass. 2003).

In re Marriage Cases, 183 P.3d 384 (Ca. 2008).

Kerrigan v. Commissioner of Public Health, 957 A.2d 407 (Conn. 2008).

League of Education Voters v. State of Washington, 176 Wn.2d 808 (2013).

League of Education Voters v. State of Washington, 355 P.3d 1131 (Wash. 2015).

McCleary v. State of Washington, 269 P.3d 227 (Wash. 2012).

Obergerfell v. Hodges, 135 S. Ct. 2584 (2015).

Pruneyard Shopping Center v. Robins, 447 U.S. 74 (1980).

Seattle School Dist. No. 1 v. State, 90 P.2d 71 (1978).

Southcenter Joint Venture v. National Democratic Policy Committee, 780 P.2d 1282 (Wash. 1989).

State v. Coe, 679 P.2d 353 (Wash. 1984).

State v. Gocken, 896 P.2d 1269 (Wash. 1995).

State v. Gunwall, 720 P.2d 808, 815 (Wash. 1986).

State v. Jackson, 150 Wn.2d 251 (2003).

State v. Kennedy, 726 P.2d 445 (Wash. 1986).

State v. Ringer, 674 P2d 1240 (Wash. 1983).

State v. Stroud, 720 P.2d 436 (Wash. 1986).

State v. Wethered, 755 P.2d 797 (Wash. 1988).

Varnum v. Brien, 763 N.W.2d 862 (Iowa 2009).

CHAPTER 8

Governing the Evergreen State: The State Legislature

Hans Zeiger and Sara Singleton

The legislature consists of 147 citizens—98 in the House of Representatives and 49 in the Senate—who represent their fellow Washingtonians in crafting the state's public policies and budgets. Following redistricting in 2011 on the heels of the 2010 Census, each legislative district has 137,236 constituents (Ballotpedia 2017). The "redistricting wars" were often brutal affairs that occupied much legislative business until the entire process was placed under a bipartisan, fairly independent commission process in 1982 (McCurdy 2011). As is the case in many states, there is considerable variation in the political culture and partisanship of the state's 49 legislative districts, ranging from blue-collar Democrat-leaning districts on the coast, to progressive Democrat-dominant districts in Seattle, Tacoma, Everett, and Olympia, to conservative Republican districts spread across most of eastern Washington. The urban districts in the Puget Sound region tend to favor Democrats, the rural districts in "the other Washington" tend to favor Republicans, and the suburban districts are often the swing districts. Democrats have had a majority in most legislative sessions over the past twenty years, but in recent sessions the legislature has been nearly evenly split along party lines. The House is currently controlled by the Democrats, with a Democratic-Republican vote split of 50–48, and the Senate has a one-seat Democratic majority. From the 2012 election until 2017, the Senate was controlled by the Majority Coalition, which in its latest form was made up of 24 Republicans and one Democrat who caucuses with the Republicans in the chamber.

Legislators come to serve from a wide variety of backgrounds and perspectives. In recent years, the legislature has included the usual collection of lawyers from both the prosecutorial and defense bars, but also many public school teachers, nurses, fire fighters, law enforcement officers, small business owners, former Microsoft employees, technology entrepreneurs, a Boeing test pilot, farmers, foresters, labor union leaders, military veterans, public health administrators, and retirees. Some legislators begin their journey in public service as planning commissioners, fire commissioners, city council members, school board members, or county commissioners. Others make the legislature their first public office. Almost all were deeply involved in their respective communities before seeking a legislative seat. Most have college degrees, and a few have PhDs, but there is no legal prerequisite for legislative service beyond being at least 18 years old, a U.S. citizen, and a registered voter in their legislative district (Washington State Constitution, Article II, Section 7).

As with state legislatures across the country, Washington's legislators generally do not reflect the composition of the state in terms of *descriptive representation*—that is, the extent to which legislators possess the same gender, ethnic, racial, or age characteristics as the state's population as a whole. Nonetheless, with respect to gender, historically, Washington has been something of a pacesetter. In 1854, the Territorial Assembly first proposed that women be given the vote. The measure lost by a single vote, but in 1883 a similar measure passed, making Washington the first state to grant suffrage to both Caucasian and African American women. That victory for gender equity was short-lived, however, because the statute granting that voting right was subsequently overturned by the Washington Supreme Court (Scott 2011; Ballotpedia 2017). Today, one-third of the state legislative seats are occupied by women, a considerably larger percentage than the national average of 25 percent (Kurtz 2015). In terms of race and ethnicity, the state's population has a higher than average percentage of Caucasians, and the gap between actual representation and descriptive representation is even larger. For example, nationally, Hispanics make up about 17 percent of the population and 5 percent of state legislators. In Washington, the equivalent figures are 12.2 percent and 1 percent (Kurtz 2015).

The Campaign

Candidates run for legislative office either of their own volition, as a result of recruitment by others, or some combination of the two. Some candidates position themselves for legislative service over many years, while others seem to fall into the role through a succession of community activities or by learning to navigate the legislative process from the outside. Current legislators, local and state party officials, and interest groups take part in the candidate recruitment process, suggesting connections, facilitating introductions, and passing along their suggestions about effective practices for campaigning. Both liberals and conservatives have state-level programs to identify, train, and provide mentorship to prospective candidates. Two of the most important of these are the Institute for a Democratic Future for liberals and the Jennifer Dunn Leadership Institute for conservatives. Legislative leaders seeking to keep or gain a majority make it their business to find candidates who "fit" their district. For example, it helps if a legislative candidate in the 28th District, a swing district which covers Joint Base Lewis-McChord (JBLM) and surrounding areas, has a very strong connection to the military. Candidate recruiters try to discern issues in a prospective candidate's background that could cause potential problems in the heat of the initial campaign to win the seat, and party recruiters seek candidates they believe can hold their seats and contribute meaningfully to the legislative process over time once their name recognition is established in their districts.

Candidates for legislative offices spend the better part of a year, sometimes more, raising funds and contacting voters. A candidate may spend much of their campaign going door-to-door to talk with voters. It may take a failed election or two before a candidate succeeds in winning a legislative seat. It may cost several hundred thousand dollars to reach voters in a hotly-contested race. In 2014, the total average contributions of Washington state senate campaigns was $191,419, and for house members, $71,175 (Ballotpedia 2017). The highest cost legislative race in state history was a special State Senate election in 2017 between Democrat Manka Dhingra and Republican Jinyoung Englund in the 45th District, which includes Kirkland, Woodinville, Duvall, and Sammamish. Republican Andy Hill was first elected to the Senate seat in 2010, but when he passed away from cancer in 2016, Republican Dino Rossi was appointed to fill the vacancy. If Dhingra won, she would not only flip the seat from Republican to Democrat, but she would give Democrats a majority in the Senate. The money spent by the rival campaigns and independent expenditures by interest groups amounted to more than $8.5 million (Public Disclosure Commission 2017). Dhingra won the election.

The Job of a Legislator

The legislative session begins on the second Wednesday of January. In even-numbered years, the session runs for 60 days; in odd-numbered years, the session runs for 105 days. If there are significant unresolved issues, a special session may be called, either by the governor,or by a two-thirds vote in either chamber. A special session lasts for 30 days, but the governor or the legislature may call yet another session. Special sessions have become more common in recent years. In the seven years from 2003 to 2009, the legislature convened for regular or special sessions 11 times. In the following seven years from 2010 to 2016, the legislature convened for regular or special session 20 times (Washington State Legislature 2016).

Occasionally, special sessions are called for economic development reasons, such as in October 1995, when the legislature came together and authorized funding for construction of a new baseball stadium for the Seattle Mariners baseball franchise (*Seattle Times* 2005). And again in November 2013, Governor Jay Inslee called the legislature into special session to pass a package of tax and regulatory incentives for the aerospace industry, designed largely to secure construction of the Boeing 777X in Washington State; two negotiated incentive bills passed with strong support on the third day of the special session (Garber 2013). Most special sessions, however, have to do with passage of the state budget. The legislature faced difficult budget choices and took its time resolving them during and following the most recent recession. With the Senate controlled by Republicans and the House by Democrats since 2013, partisan divides have made it more difficult to reach agreement, and budget talks and negotiations have often stretched into the summer. In 2013, lawmakers deliberated until June 29. In 2015, the third special session did not adjourn until July 10, setting a new record of 176 days that the legislature had been in session (Washington State Legislature 2016).

What is the actual job of a legislator once elected to office? Practically, a legislator must develop a variety of skills and capabilities related to the establishment of a reputation among his or her fellow legislators. Not counting the civic leadership roles that legislators may have in their home districts, there are a variety of roles that a legislator plays within the legislative process in Olympia. First, at the most basic level, legislators are *voters*—they cast policy and budget votes on behalf of their constituents for or against bills in committee and on the floor, and they develop criteria for how they will decide on the multitude of issues that come before them. Second, they are *proponents*, proposing bills, amendments, and resolutions, sometimes trying to solve some big problem, sometimes trying to fix a small error in the law, sometimes carrying the water for a constituent or an interest group. Third, they are *communicators*—floor orators, op-ed writers, and sources of sound bites in press releases or the evening news, delivering the message of their party or a favored cause to the various audiences who will pay attention. They communicate with fellow legislators, the governor, agency executives, constituents, or the citizenry of Washington State. Fourth, legislators may be *chairs or moderators*, holding formal power in a committee or caucus, or informally convening stakeholders to build consensus on an issue. Fifth, they are *negotiators*, working amid often-competing interests, parties, and personalities to find a way forward on a bill or a budget. Sixth, they are *parliamentarians*, working within the established parliamentary rules of the House or Senate to conduct the business of the people of the State of Washington. Finally, they are *strategists*—they are charting their own course in a complex process, figuring out how to make the best of time, knowledge, reputation, coalitions, and the various other resources available to legislators to change state policy, advance their own political career, cultivate a movement, serve their constituents, or do all of the above at the same time.

The Cycle of Lawmaking

"Writing a bill, even a good bill, doesn't guarantee it will get anywhere," wrote Mary Ellen McCaffree, a prominent legislator who served in the 1960s. She wrote a highly detailed account of her service in the House, tracing the written and unwritten rules, personalities, relationships, and conflicts that characterized the legislative process as she had experienced it. She perceptively observed: "It is the next steps—the education and negotiating, the convincing and the compromise, the persistence and rewriting yet again—that transform a good idea from possibility into law" (McCaffree 2011, 181).

The cycle of legislative work begins long before session convenes in January of each year. Members, lobbyists, and legislative staff are researching and discussing ideas and refining language for upcoming bills throughout the year. Membership associations and other interest groups vet proposals through their boards of directors and compile legislative agendas for the upcoming session months in advance of its commencement. Legislative committee chairs convene interim work sessions to study an emergent issue and to hear updates from agency directors. Lobbyists visit legislators in their home districts to secure commitments for or against a forthcoming bill. Legislators encounter one another on panels at association conferences, at fundraising breakfasts, or at political party meetings and talk about ways they might work together as session nears. Even during the session, legislative policy conversations are not confined to caucus, committee, and the floor. These conversations often happen informally, at off-campus receptions, in the stairwell or the hallway, or increasingly in recent decades over email.

What McCaffree noted about the 1960s concerning informal communication still obtains. She opined in this regard: "The banter outside organized session work is a valuable part of the legislative process, and though this type of wheeling and dealing carries with it a certain stigma, I believe it should be accepted for what it is—a chance for human legislators to express their very human ideas" (McCaffree 2011, 360). Most legislators have found that receptions and other social activities with an abundance of seemingly idle chatter were in fact highly conducive to frank talk among colleagues. "Legislators are loathe to talk frankly with a lot of other people around," she wrote. "They have constituent interests to protect, partisan allegiances to honor. And in the House, where we serve single two-year terms, there's always another election to win. To have a real conversation, therefore—true back and forth, real argument—it's often best to track down someone socially, and chat within the buzz of a lively room" (McCaffree 2011, 360). So it was in McCaffree's time, and so it is today.

Social life in Olympia is critical to the story of the legislature. As

Gordon Newell opined, "From its opening in 1920, the Hotel Olympian was, for four decades, the second capitol of the state of Washington. More laws were passed or rejected and more political careers decided there than in either the old sandstone statehouse across the street or the splendid new Legislative building on the hill. The Olympian was *the* hotel and all the important legislators and lobbyists made it their headquarters" (1975, 333). Later, when the Tyee Motel in Tumwater opened in the late 1950s, it became the "new social center" of legislative life, wrote Northwest historian Daniel Jack Chasan (2011, 138).

There is probably no present-day social equivalent to the Hotel Olympian or the Tyee Motel, but the relational element of policymaking is no less important today. "Ultimately, the Legislature is about people and the relationships they form," wrote Allen Hayward. "More legislation passes or fails because of those personal relationships than the brilliant arguments drafted for or against a measure's passage" (2014, 65–66).

Legislative Staff

When it comes time to formally propose a bill, legislators work with legislative policy staff to craft ideas, refine legal language, and draft amendments. The nonpartisan policy staff of the House is called the *Office of Program Research*, and in the upper chamber the *Senate Committee Services* staff fulfills this role. Both caucuses have their own partisan policy staff personnel who can discuss political considerations and offer informed opinions. Caucuses also employ communications staff, and each legislator has an individual legislative assistant who handles scheduling, correspondence, constituent casework, and other tasks relating to community relations. The House is administered by the *Chief Clerk*, who is elected by the members, and works closely with the Speaker to manage the affairs of the body. The Senate is administered by the *Secretary of the Senate*. Senate offices differ from House offices in that they have legislative assistants as well as session aides and interns assigned to each office.

The modern staff structure of the Washington legislature took shape in 1973 during the Speakership of Leonard Sawyer and the Senate leadership of August Mardesich. This was also the Watergate era, a time when many Americans looked on executive power with suspicion and when "legislatures all over the country became more assertive," according to Chasan. "Washington's legislature became as assertive as any. It not only had the desire but it finally had the tools to compete on even terms with the executive branch" (Chasan 2011, 153).

Structuring the Work: Leadership and Committees

The House and the Senate function somewhat differently with respect to their leadership. The House elects its leader and presiding officer, the Speaker, first through a majority caucus vote, and then by a vote of the whole body. The Speaker is the leader of the majority party, the presiding Officer of the House, and the chair of the Rules Committee. As one commentator put it, "It's a little like having the coach of the home basketball team also be the referee of the game" (Seeberger 1997, 127). The Senate's presiding officer, in contrast, is the President, who is the *Lieutenant Governor* chosen by statewide election. Accordingly, the President of the Senate is not necessarily from the party that holds the majority in the Senate. While the President presides over the sessions of the Senate, she or he only votes if there is a tie. The *President Pro Tempore* shares in the duties of presiding over the Senate. He or she is chosen by an election within the majority party, and then is confirmed by a floor vote of the entire body at the beginning of the session following an election (Washington State Legislature 2015).

A number of other leadership positions are also chosen at the start of the session by the majority and minority caucuses in each chamber. These leadership slots in both parties include the majority and minority caucus chairs, majority and minority whips, assistant whips, and various deputy leaders and assistant leaders as each party decides on how to apportion its ranks to accomplish their goals for the session in question.

Much of the actual work of legislating is done within committees, which cover the wide variety of substantive policy areas that affect the state. Committees consider bills and hold public hearings in which stakeholders and members of the public are allowed to testify for, against, or "other" regarding a particular bill. Ultimately, the members of the committee vote on whether or not to recommend passage of a bill. Committees also hold work sessions during which state agencies or other parties may be invited to present background information or status reports of previously identified issues. Newly-elected members are anxious to serve on committees that are relevant to their constituents since the committee structure allows those members whose districts are most affected by decisions made in particular areas the greatest opportunity to influence those decisions. The committee system is generally successful in encouraging a certain degree of specialization and expertise formation, promoting better-informed policymaking overall. The Senate maintains 15 standing committees, and the House maintains 20. In addition, there are a number of joint committees or taskforces that are created in one session to delve into a problem, compile information, and then present a report to the relevant standing committees in a subsequent session. For example, joint committees or taskforces that were created in the 2016 session included the Education Funding Task Force, the Children's Mental Health Work Group, the Task Force on the Use of Body Worn Cameras, and the Joint Legislative Task Force on the Use of Deadly Force in Community Policing (Washington State Legislature 2017).

The Journey of a Bill

Once the prime sponsor of a bill has gathered signatures from legislative co-sponsors and filed the bill in the bill introduction box known as the "hopper," he or she asks the chair of the relevant policy or fiscal committee to schedule a hearing. A bill will typically begin its journey in a policy committee. If a bill has a "fiscal note" (price tag) as determined by the relevant state agencies impacted under the proposal, it will continue on for a second hearing in a fiscal committee.

Committee chairs in both chambers generally hold broad authority over the policy or fiscal matters within their purview. As chair of the House Revenue and Taxation Committee in the late 1960s, McCaffree was "no pawn of an executive dictate," she later wrote. "I've been given the issues to address, but it is up to me to examine them, to hear the sides, to propose a route to completion, and then to guide the compromise that will eventually lead to new law" (McCaffree 2011, 395). While a chair can establish an agenda and pass bills they favor through their committee, those bills may encounter difficulties later in the process. The power of a committee chair may be exercised in killing a bill by denying it a hearing or a vote, even if the bill came over from the other chamber with unanimous support, and even if there is strong support for that bill among other legislators on the committee.

In describing the prerogatives of the committee chair, McCaffree noted: "Serving as chairman of a major committee requires a distinctive combination of leadership skills—in-depth knowledge of a particular subject, the ability to referee negotiations and compromise, and to keep the process moving forward to accomplish legislative goals" (2011, 235). She added that the chair is "also the committee's conduit to the media, to lobbyists, to fellow legislators, to our leadership in the House and Senate, to the Governor and his aides, and to the people of the state—our public" (2011, 244).

Once a bill has come through the committee process, it moves into the Rules Committee. If a bill is not voted out of the Rules Committee by an established cutoff deadline, no action can be taken unless it is ruled by House or Senate leadership as "necessary to implement the budget" or "necessary to the pass the budget," or unless it is held over from an odd-year session to an even-year session. In the House, the Rules Committee is chaired by the Speaker of the House, and the Speaker, who also governs the floor calendar, has ultimate say in whether any bill comes to the floor for a vote.

The office of Speaker of the House has become increasingly important in the direction of Washington State government. In the first decades after Washington became a state, it was common for a speaker to serve just one term before letting someone else have a turn (Newell 1975, 412). Most of the speakers' portraits hanging in the House Rules Room of the State Capitol pre-date World War II. John L. O'Brien's speakership set a new record of eight years, from 1955 to 1963 (Chasan 2011, 130; Sharp and Sharp 1997). Today, the current Speaker Frank Chopp holds the record as the longest-serving Speaker of the House, having served as co-speaker from 1999 until 2002 and as speaker from 2003 to the present.

The Washington Legislature is governed according to a parliamentary book known as *Reed's Rules*. The Rules promote unity and fidelity to the institution of the legislature. Rule 49 says, "The duties of each member are based upon the considerations which arise from his being a component part of the assembly, which desires to act together and which, in order to act together, must come to some agreement" (Reed 2016). According to Allen Hayward, a former speaker's attorney and counsel to the House Republicans, these formal rules result in at least three informal rules that legislators should know:

- It is the right of the majority to decide what bills will pass.
- It is the right of the minority to decide how long that will take.
- It is the duty of leadership to avoid irreconcilable conflict between the two (Hayward 2014, 37).

Various motivations exist for individual legislators to support or not to support a particular bill. A legislator might be said to "answer" to three different authorities in this regard. First, there is the matter of a legislator's conscience, or sense of moral obligation, as they consider a policy proposal. Second, a legislator answers to their constituents, the people of their district who called upon the individual to represent them. Third, a legislator answers to their caucus, the party organization to which they belong and are held accountable, both by their colleagues and by their partisan political supporters.

There are pronounced patterns present in the public aspects of the legislative process as witnessed from the gallery. Gordon Newell offered a comedic description of the cycle of public consideration of bills in his 1975 book *Rogues, Buffoons and Statesmen.* "From territorial days to the present, the legislative time table has changed little if at all," wrote Newell. "Following pious promises of a businesslike, no-nonsense session, legislators become political tortoises, pursuing a leisurely and rambling course. Then in the final days, with the adjournment deadline staring them inexorably in the face, they metamorphize into hares, leaping wildly toward *sine die*, passing bills in a dazed state and with few having the vaguest idea what they are voting upon" (Newell 1975, 403). While somewhat overstated, this depiction of what citizens experience in the operation of their state legislature remains largely accurate.

In addition to devising legislative solutions to state issues, the legislature plays a key role in drafting and passing the state's budget. The budget cycle begins in September when state agencies submit their budget requests. In December, the governor submits a proposed budget. The two chambers then release their own budgets and negotiations commence. Once a deal is struck, there is an urgency to pass the budget and get it to the Governor's desk. The more time passes, the more likely it is that interest groups will rally their members against some part of the deal and that leadership will lose votes in their caucuses. According to Hayward, "the rule of politics is: When you have the votes, vote. A budget is like a fish; if you let it sit in the sunshine it rapidly begins to stink" (2014, 87).

Constituent and Interest Group Communication

In the past, telegrams and letters, then phone calls, were conventional ways for citizens to voice their positions on legislation (see for instance the Western Union telegrams that came in following Governor Evans's environment appeals—McCaffree 2011, 415). Today, emails are a significant means of citizen communication with legislators. Legislators are increasingly active on social media as well.

The ability of citizens to watch the legislative process unfold was transformed by the creation of TVW in the mid-1990s. "TVW is a good idea simply because in this day and age, given the relatively limited expense required, people just have a right to watch their government in action (or inaction)," wrote Denny Heck, who co-founded the network (Heck 2014, 140–41). Heck was elected to serve in the U.S. House of Representatives in 2012 and continues to represent the 10th district in Washington, DC.

Lobbyists have always played a major role in the legislative process in Olympia. Lobbyists may work to bring representatives of industry or association members to the capitol to spend time with their legislators. They may serve as liaisons between the board of an association, union, or business coalition and members of the legislature, as well as maintain contact with other lobbyists with whom they may be working to advance legislation of shared interest. They may speak on behalf of a client in a committee hearing in support or opposition to a bill, or sometimes to express concerns; lobbyists will often suggest amendments and alternatives if they don't like the way a bill is presented in a hearing. Interest group lobbyists may even choose to work behind the scenes, speaking with majority leadership or committee chairs to kill or slow down the progress of a bill. Lobbyist Jim Metcalf and State Senator Ken Jacobsen quipped in Rule 51 of their maxims of the legislative process, "If your bill is in trouble for no discernible reason, big timber is against it. If your bill dies for no discernible reason, Boeing is against it" (Hayward 2014, 290).

Direct Democracy

The legislative function of state government is not limited to the House and the Senate. It also includes the initiative, referendum, and recall, legislative powers granted to the people under Article II of the State Constitution. There are most assuredly tensions between representative democracy and direct democracy that play out frequently in Washington. Sometimes the voters reject actions by the legislature, and other times the legislature suspends or even repeals actions by the voters. In the wake of the recession and declining state revenues in 2010, the legislature approved taxes on bottled water, candy, and gum. Subsequently, citizens filed Initiative 1107 to repeal these taxes, and voters passed the initiative. In 2014, voters passed Initiative 1351 to reduce class sizes in schools, but with the added costs of the measure, the legislature voted in 2015 to put the initiative on hold (Dake and Associated Press 2015).

A two-thirds vote of the legislature is required to suspend or amend an initiative of the people within two years after its passage; after two years, an initiative can be changed (and very often is modified or nullified) with a simple majority vote (Washington State Constitution, Article II, Section 41). An interesting historical account of such modifications and nullifications can be found in Daniel Jack Chasan's account of the state's experience with "ultimate democracy" (2011, 191–218). A good account of the way in which the initiative process has become an increasingly important part of public finance and state budget processes is presented by Jenny Holland and Steve Lundin (2011; 246–48).

The Continuity of the Legislature

There will always be a need for a state legislature—and states legislatures will display the same public drama of noble intentions at the outset of each session, followed by what will appear to be aimless wandering through the landscape of public policy for a good portion of the session, and then ultimately pass a good number of bills in what seems like a mad flurry of last-minute action. It is likewise the case that even if the legislature of one biennium takes bold actions to solve a pressing problem of governance, the next legislature may (and often does) find flaws in those actions and propose new solutions of their own. Budget writers come and go, each with different priorities for the spending of public dollars. An issue may not get much legislative attention for years on end, then a major public crisis, a budget emergency, or an event in the news may spur the legislature to take the issue up again and take decisive action.

The legislative issues of one generation often reappear in the next. Former State Representative Denny Heck, now a member of the U.S. Congress, wrote about the Basic Education Act of 1977 as a response to a ruling by Thurston County Judge Robert Doran that the state was not adequately funding its schools in accordance with the constitutional directive to support public education [understood as public schools, grades K-12]. The Basic Education Act "was good legislation," he wrote, "and it was durable, but not permanently so. Eventually, the state would fall behind again in its obligation and find itself back in court. Legislatively, nothing lasts forever. Nothing" (Heck 2014, 51). Indeed, the State Supreme Court ruled in *McCleary v. State of Washington* decades later in 2012 that the legislature had once more failed to properly fund basic education. The court called on the legislature to "demonstrate steady progress" toward full funding of a school funding model that had been adopted by the legislature in 2009, setting a deadline of 2018 for compliance with the state constitution's mandate of "ample provision" for the education of Washington children. The legislature devoted significant additional money to K–12 education in the 2013, 2015, and 2017 budgets, reformed the state's property tax to increase state funding to schools, and restricted the use of local property tax levies to spending outside of teacher salaries and other "basic education" purposes. As of this writing, the legislature has yet to respond to a State Supreme Court mandate to expedite $1 billion in education spending to meet the 2018 deadline.

Conclusion

Every January, Washington's 147 legislators come to Olympia on behalf of their fellow citizens to make their mark on the state. Some legislators keep this up for a few years, others for a few decades. In the course of their public service, these legislators interact with thousands of their constituents, along with legislative staff, lobbyists, state employees, civic leaders, and legislative colleagues. They gather input, discuss problems, and learn about ways to improve our representative democracy. This ongoing series of interactions makes up the legislative process.

The capacity of the legislature to work effectively for the citizens of Washington will be tested in its response to *McCleary*, just as it is tested in any year for its work on policies and budgets. In times of deep political polarization in Washington, DC, will legislators in Olympia practice civility and strive for collaboration with each other? In times when great educational, environmental, fiscal, or economic challenges face the state, will legislators find ways to set aside their party allegiances and personal ideologies and embrace some sense of common good? These are among the questions that face the electorate from time to time. After all, it is the voters who have the final say in the performance of their legislators—they have input in who will represent them in the House every two years and who will represent them in the Senate every four years.

References

Ballotpedia. 2017. "Washington State Legislature," ballotpedia.org.

Benjamin, Francis, and Nicholas Lovrich. 2011. "The State Legislature." In *Governing Washington: Politics and Government in the Evergreen State*, edited by Cornell W. Clayton and Nicholas P. Lovrich. Pullman: Washington State University Press, 207–231.

Chasan, Daniel Jack. 1990. *Speaker of the House: The Political Career and Times of John L. O'Brien*. Seattle: University of Washington Press.

———. 2011. "Ultimate Democracy: Initiatives and Referendums." In *Turning Points in Washington's Public Life*, edited by George W. Scott. Seattle: Civitas Press, 191–218.

Dake, Lauren, and The Associated Press. 2015. "Washington Senate Approves Class-size Deal," *Columbian*, July 10, 2015. www.columbian.com/news/2015/jul/09/washington-senate-oks-class-size-deal.

Donovan, Todd. 2004. "The Legislature." In *Washington State Government and Politics*, edited by Cornell W. Clayton, Lance T. LeLoup, Nicholas P. Lovrich, 165–87. Pullman: Washington State University Press.

Garber, Andrew. 2013. "Legislature approves tax breaks to secure Boeing 777X," *Seattle Times*, November 9, 2013. www.seattletimes.com/seattle-news/legislature-approves-tax-breaks-to-secure-boeing-777x.

Hayward, Allen. 2014. *My Ride: The People, Procedures, and Politics of Lawmaking at Our State Capitol*. Centralia, WA: Gorham Printing.

Heck, Denny. 2014. *Lucky Bounce*. Centralia, WA: Gorham Printing.

Holland, Jenny, and Steve Lundin. 2011. "Public Finance and Budgeting in Washington State." In *Governing Washington: Politics and Government in the Evergreen State*, edited by Cornell W. Clayton and Nicholas P. Lovrich. Pullman: Washington State University Press, 233–58.

Kurtz, Karl. 2015. "Who We Elect: The Demographics of State Legislatures." *State Legislatures Magazine*. www.ncsl.org/research/about-state-legislatures/who-we-elect.aspx.

McCaffree, Mary Ellen. 2011. *The Politics of the Possible: The Decade Our American Democracy Worked*. Bainbridge Island, WA: Island Penworks.

McCurdy, Howard E. 2011. "Redistricting Wars." In *Turning Points in Washington's Public Life*, edited by George W. Scott, 219–46. Seattle: Civitas Press.

Newell, Gordon. 1975. *Rogues, Buffoons and Statesmen: The Inside Story of Washington's Capital City and the Hilarious History of 120 Years of State Politics*. Seattle: Superior Publishing.

Public Disclosure Commission of Washington State. 2017. Legislative Candidates. www.pdc.wa.gov/browse/more-ways-to-follow-the-money/candidates/legislative?category=Candidates

Reed, Thomas Brackett. "Reed's Parliamentary Rules." Washington State Legislature. leg.wa.gov/LawsAndAgencyRules/ReedsRules/Pages/default.aspx. [Original source: *A Manual for General Parliamentary Law with Suggestions for Special Rules*, Thomas Brackett Reed, Speaker of the U.S. House of Representatives 1889–1891 and 1895–1899.]

Scott, George W. 2011. "The Rise of Women in Washington's Politics." In *Turning Points in Washington's Public Life*, edited by George W. Scott, 157–90. Seattle: Civitas Press.

Seattle Times. 2005. "About Safeco Field." old.seattletimes.com/sports/mariners/safecofield/history.html.

Seeberger, Edward D. 1997. *Sine Die: A Guide to the Washington State Legislative Process*. Seattle: University of Washington Press.

Sharp, Nancy Weatherby, and James. R. Sharp, editors. 1997. *American Legislative Leaders in the West, 1911–1994*. Westport, CT: Greenwood Press.

Washington State Constitution. http://leg.wa.gov/lawsandagencyrules/documents/12-2010-wastateconstitution.pdf.

Washington State Legislature. 2015. "Permanent Rules of the Senate." leg.wa.gov/Senate/Administration/Pages/senate_rules.aspx.

Washington State Legislature. 2016. "Session Dates of the Washington State Legislature."

Washington State Legislature. 2017. "Legislative Committees." leg.wa.gov/legislature/Pages/CommitteeListing.aspx.

CHAPTER 9

The Governor and Other Statewide Executives

Carolyn N. Long and David Ammons

Introduction

Governmental power in Washington State is divided among three co-equal, powerful branches, the Executive, Legislative, and Judicial. Power is further divided among nine separately elected statewide officials, including: the Governor, Lieutenant Governor, the Secretary of State, Attorney General, State Treasurer, Auditor, Commissioner of Public Lands, Superintendent of Public Instruction, and the State Insurance Commissioner. Each of these officers has jurisdiction over important sectors, such as education, elections, and enforcement of our laws. Yet despite that dispersal of power established by the founders and the unusually large number of independently elected officials, the governor is invariably seen as the central player, with broad portfolio, powers, and visibility.

Washington, like Oregon, is characterized electorally by an urban-rural divide, with self-identified Democrats dominating the Seattle area and its suburbs, and Republicans dominating counties east of the Cascades. However, party identification has declined at a faster pace than other states in the last twenty years, and the growing number of independents has led to some volatile statewide races, particularly for governor.

The Chief Executive

Like the Schoolhouse Rock description of the president wearing five "presidential hats" to describe that office's myriad duties, Washington's governor serves a broad array of roles and functions. Describing some of these roles provides a useful look at the powers and challenges of being governor of a growing and complex state.

Political and Party Leader

In a state with a history of close gubernatorial elections and a closely divided legislature, a governor's role as both head of state and leader of their party is both significant and circumscribed. As a single individual, the governor has great access to public and media attention—Teddy Roosevelt's "bully pulpit"—and the ability to set an agenda for Olympia.

As titular head of his or her political party, the governor must be able to maintain partisan support while also reaching across the aisle to pursue a policy agenda, including the state's budget. Given the increasingly polarized political climate in Olympia and beyond, and the large number of unaffiliated voters, this often requires deft political footwork. As a political leader, the governor may also embrace the regional or national stage. For instance, Governor Jay Inslee garnered national attention in 2017 when he and Attorney General Bob Ferguson successfully launched a court challenge to the Trump administration's travel ban from seven mostly Muslim countries. Similarly, Inslee grabbed the national spotlight in 2016 when he banned state-funded travel to North Carolina and Mississippi to illustrate his administration's objection to these states' allowing businesses to refuse service, on religious grounds, to LGBTQ individuals. Washington was also one of the first states to tackle the issue of gay rights and marriage equality, both in the Legislature and by referenda.

The governor's role as party leader, however, can be difficult in independent-minded Washington. Voters do not indicate a party preference when they register, making it hard to assess the strength of party loyalty. One glimpse is when public opinion surveys ask voters how they describe their party preference. Although the numbers fluctuate considerably, in recent years between 37 and 42 percent identify as Independents (Elway 2012). While these voters likely lean in the direction of one political party, the high percentage who identify as independents indicates that party identification is not as strong as in other states. Some argue that the state's unusual top-two primary, where the top two vote getters advance to the general election without respect to party label, also weakens party identification, possibly further undermining the governor's power to lead their party.

The governor must also navigate the state's stark rural-urban divide. As described in Chapter 1 of this volume, Washington politics is often described in terms of a west-east divide or the "Cascade Curtain." The urbanized, populous western part of the state, particularly Seattle and King County, trend Democratic, and the more rural eastern part typically votes Republican. Washington is heavily "blue" in metropolitan areas and red in much of the rest of the state, meaning the governor and other statewide Democrats often win by carrying just a handful of populous counties. The divide also affects the policy issues of interest to voters, including initiatives and issues they want Olympia to consider. So the combination of the declining strength of partisan identification, amplified by the geographic divide, can make it especially difficult for governors to act as a cohesive party leader.

Governors do play a ceremonial role as titular head of the party during party conventions and at other times. And, because the state Legislature is organized as party caucuses, there is also plenty of opportunity for a governor to reach out and rally partisans to pursue their policy agenda. Their success, however, may be limited and will often depend on circumstances beyond their immediate control.

Legislator-in-Chief

Governors cannot, of course, achieve policy success on their own. While they may command the bully pulpit and enjoy media attention, their ability to capitalize on statewide support depends heavily on a good working relationship with all four legislative caucuses—House and Senate, Democrat and Republican. This is no easy task in an era of partisan polarization.

Polarization at the national level is higher than any other time since the late 19th century, and it has reached Olympia as well, making it difficult to develop bipartisan consensus in addressing policy needs. Indeed, Washington has been rated as having one of the nation's most polarized legislatures (McCarty et al. 2015). Despite the many political tools at their command, governors can find it hard to push through a policy agenda if the Legislature is divided or controlled by the other party, and historically Washington has often had divided government, with at least one chamber controlled by the opposition party.

Because of the polarized state legislature, and an electorate characterized best by an urban-rural divide, the governor plays a key role in setting the policy agenda and proposing solutions. The public views the governor as the chief legislator, and they expect the chief executive to campaign and deliver on a set of policies once in office.

Putting signature issues aside, the governor has the prime task of making sure the government has adequate financial resources. The governor introduces a biennial budget, including all state expenditures and any requested revenue increases. This has historically been a difficult endeavor in the Evergreen State for a number of reasons, including the fact that the state has no income tax, which means its revenue streams are less diversified than in many other states and is less stable during economic downturns (see Chapter 11).

The largest budget-related debate in recent years has been over the adequacy and equity of state funding for education, highlighted by efforts to satisfy the state Supreme Court's decision *McCleary, et al. v. State of Washington*. In 2012 the court held that the state was in violation of the State Constitution by not adequately financing public K–12 education. In 2014, the court held the Legislature in contempt for not coming up with a comprehensive way to meet its constitutional obligations and imposed a $100,000 daily fine for lack of progress. In 2016, an election year, the governor and Legislature were still unable to come up with a plan to satisfy *McCleary*, but the matter was finally resolved in the summer of 2017 when lawmakers approved a bipartisan funding plan with a price tag in the billions. The package was sent to the state Supreme Court for review.

While governors campaign on major policy issues, their success in implementing them largely depend on the political climate and the resources available. Governor Inslee, for instance, campaigned on addressing climate change, but most of his proposals were blocked by a divided Legislature. He enjoyed greater success with transportation funding, brokering a $16 billion bipartisan package in 2016. The latter was due to strong support for investment in transportation infrastructure, including from major employers Amazon, Microsoft, and Boeing, to help address traffic congestion in the Seattle metro area.

Administrator and Chief Executive

Washington governors oversee a large administrative state with thousands of employees working in dozens of agencies. They work in social services, health care, law enforcement, environmental protection, transportation, parks, prisons, and much more. As chief executive, the governor is tasked with implementing state laws and making sure employees do their job effectively.

One of the governor's most important duties is to appoint the heads of state agencies and commissions. In general, governors seek individuals who are competent but who also share their political and policy perspectives to fill such positions. This is because they will be acting in the governor's name and must be trusted to act on the governor's priorities. Many of these posts must face Senate confirmation. The governor also plays a crucial role in appointing judges when a vacancy arises midway through a judge's term. Although any judge appointed by the governor must subsequently seek election, running as an incumbent provides a distinct advantage and usually leads to their retention (see Chapter 10).

The governor also has a key role in intergovernmental relations among federal, state, local, and tribal governments. Ideally, they will work collaboratively, but on occasion the governor may strike out on his own, using executive orders or other action. Compared to other states, however, the executive order powers of Washington's governor are rather limited. They cannot, for example, reorganize the executive branch, create administrative agencies, or respond substantively to federal programs (Council of State Governments 2014).

Washington's governors have varied greatly in their use of executive orders. Some have resorted to their use when unable to achieve goals legislatively, or to highlight issues in hopes of prompting lawmakers into action. Frustrated by a lack of legislative action, Governor Inslee issued 21 executive orders during his first term, more than either of his two predecessors during their two full terms in office (Gregoire 16 and Locke 13). Some of Inslee's orders were significant. When he was unable to get a "cap and trade" bill passed, for example, he issued an executive order to reduce the state's carbon emissions among the heaviest polluters (O'Sullivan 2016b). He also signed an executive order to strengthen background checks on gun buyers, which initiated a statewide plan to reduce suicides by gun violence, and he used an executive order to impose a moratorium on use of the death penalty while he is in office.

Executive orders may also be a way that the governor expresses unhappiness with the federal government. In the ongoing tension between Washington State, and the Trump administration over immigration, Inslee in 2017 restricted state officials from using state resources to assist the federal government in its enforcement of federal immigration laws.

Ceremonial Leader/Head of State

Because of their visibility, governors are often seen as Washington's head of state. The governor represents the state during important ceremonies such as dedicating buildings or ribbon cutting ceremonies, and represents state interests to other state's leaders, federal officials, and to international trading partners.

Washington is one of the most trade-dependent states in the nation, so modern governors have prioritized trade and investment relations with other countries. One of Governor Inslee's first actions after taking office in 2013 was to lead a 100-person trade delegation to China, the state's top trading partner. He also led trade missions to Japan and Korea. In 2015, he combined trade and his favorite issue, climate change, when he and business leaders hosted China's President, Xi Jinping (Lee 2016).

Governors also must respond to crises or natural disasters that effect the state, including wildfires, landslides, and severe storms. During such events, governors not only must coordinate the state and federal resource response, but engage with media to inform the public and reassure people affected by the disaster.

Gubernatorial History

There have been 22 governors in Washington's history; 11 Republicans and 11 Democrats, one of whom, John Rogers, the third governor, was previously a member of the People's Party. Arthur B. Langlie (R) served non-consecutive terms of office (1941–1945 and 1949–1957), and he and Dan Evans (R) (1965–1977) are the only governors to serve three terms. The seat has been in Democratic hands since 1984, when Republican John Spellman, the 18th governor, lost to Booth Gardner (D).

Most governors have been white men, but in 1977 Dixy Lee Ray became Washington's first female governor, and only the second woman governor in the nation elected in her own right, rather than succeeding her husband. A former zoology professor at the University of Washington, Ray had never run for elective office and had little experience in state politics, although she had served as the first chair of the U.S. Atomic Energy Commission (1973–1975) and for a six-month stint as Assistant Secretary of State for Oceans and International Environmental and Scientific Affairs during the Nixon administration. An "outsider" candidate, Ray defeated Republican King County Executive John Spellman in a close election, but served only one term in office. Considered a brash but honest leader, she had an acrimonious relationship with the press, legislators, and lobbyists, and in 1980 lost her Democratic primary to Jim McDermott, who later lost in the general election to Spellman.

Christine Gregoire became the state's second female governor when she was elected in 2004. She went on to serve two terms before stepping down in 2013. In 1996, the state elected Gary Locke (1997–2005), the nation's first Chinese-American governor. Born to first-generation immigrants, Locke previously worked as a deputy prosecutor in King County before being elected to the state House of Representatives, and later, chief executive of King County. A popular governor, Locke initially won election against Republican Ellen Craswell in 1996, and easily won reelection in 2000 against Republican radio talk-show host John Carlson. Locke was later appointed by President Obama to serve as U.S. Secretary of Commerce in 2008, and then as U.S. Ambassador to China from 2011 through 2014.

Washington's former governors come from a variety of different professional backgrounds. With the exception of Ray, most have had broad governmental service, often in the legislature or county government. Two recent governors, Mike Lowry and Jay Inslee, both served in Congress. Many—such as governors Spellman, Locke, Gregoire, and Inslee—have also had law degrees and come from the state's legal community.

Close Elections

Modern gubernatorial races are typically competitive and sometimes extraordinarily close. Although in recent years the state usually votes Democratic for president, the governor's race does not always follow that pattern and very close races have become increasingly expensive. The 2004 gubernatorial race between Christine Gregoire (D) and Dino

Rossi (R) was the closest in U.S. history, and the most expensive in state history at the time, with each candidate spending over $6 million in the campaign.

On election night the contest ended in a virtual dead heat; Gregoire led by about 7,000 votes out of 2.8 million cast, a considerably smaller margin than most predicted. By the initial certification of the vote on November 17, however, Rossi had pulled ahead of Gregoire by 261 votes, triggering a mandatory machine recount that narrowed his lead to 42 votes. Rossi was declared the winner by the Secretary of State Sam Reed, but Democrats requested a hand recount, which flipped the vote again to Gregoire by a mere 10 votes. During the manual recount, King County election officials also discovered 732 ballots mistakenly rejected. Litigation ensued, and after the state Supreme Court allowed the newly discovered ballots to be counted, Gregoire's lead expanded to 129 votes. Reed certified her victory and Gregoire took the oath of office in January 2005.

The Republicans filed an unprecedented election challenge that took months to resolve. Chelan County Superior Court Judge John Bridges eventually held in favor of Gregoire, determining that she won by 133 votes. Rossi did not appeal.

Rossi ran against Gregoire for a second time in 2008. The race was even more expensive than in 2004, as the two candidates spent a combined $25.3 million. Gregoire won more easily with 53 percent of the vote.

When Gregoire announced she would not stand for re-election in 2012, Jay Inslee, a veteran Democratic congressman, ran against Rob McKenna, a two-term Republican attorney general. Inslee garnered 47 percent of the vote in the primary with McKenna receiving 43 percent. Both advanced to the general election, where Inslee narrowly won, 51.5 percent to 48.5. Together the two candidates and outside groups spent over $40 million, making it the most expensive in Washington State history and, at the time, one of the most expensive races in the country.

When Inslee ran for reelection in 2016, he faced Republican Bill Bryant, a former Seattle Port Commissioner (2008–2015) and founder of a trading company. During the campaign, which largely became a referendum on Inslee's first term, Inslee touted the state's rebounding economy and his transportation package. Bryant charged the governor had done a poor job managing state government, especially the state's department of transportation, prison agencies, and psychiatric facility, all of which had been subjects of scandal, and that he had failed to adequately address the school funding crisis under the *McCleary* decision. A clear underdog in the race, however, Bryant only raised $3.9 million, compared to the $10 million raised by Inslee. Inslee easily won a second term, 54 percent to Bryant's 46 percent.

Beyond the Governor's Mansion

Governors sometimes extend their work to the national stage. During the first month of the Trump presidency, for instance, Inslee, as noted above, grabbed national attention for taking on the president's executive order banning travel from seven majority-Muslim countries and a ban on Syrian refugees. And, in his leadership role with the National Governor's Association, Inslee held a platform to articulate opposition to the new president on a range of issues from health care to immigration policy, to the environment.

The higher visibility brought him the attention of major political donors and national media, with some suggesting he might be a serious contender for the Democratic presidential nomination in 2020 (Chuang 2017).

There are other opportunities for former governors. As mentioned above, Gary Locke served as Barack Obama's Secretary of Commerce (2009–2011) and then Ambassador to China (2011–2014). Booth Gardner served as trade representative in Geneva, and Christine Gregoire was often mentioned to be on the short list for cabinet positions in the Obama administration. Other governors found themselves moving to Congress or other plum positions in the public and private sector after holding office. Daniel J. Evans became president of The Evergreen State College and served in the U.S. Senate (1983–1989) and was considered for the Republican vice presidential nomination in 1968 and again in 1976.

Other Statewide Elected Officials

There are eight other executive officials elected by statewide ballot in Washington. Each has authority to run important sectors of state government. Their offices range in size from 65 staffers at the state treasurer's office to more than 1,100 lawyers and support staff in 27 legal divisions that work in the office of the attorney general. The Washington state constitution defines the duties of these offices broadly and most of their responsibilities are established in more detail under statutes, which means that their responsibilities have also evolved over time.

Since statehood, many elected to these positions have enjoyed long tenures in office, but 2016 was an unusual election year because five of the eight positions were "open" seats with no incumbent running, and therefore more competitive than past election cycles.

Lieutenant Governor

The office of the lieutenant governor is different from what might be seen as a vice president of the state. Candidates do not run on the same ticket with the governor but are elected independently. That raises the potential of a partisan split between the offices, such as when Democrat John Cherberg served as the lieutenant governor under Republican Dan Evans, or when Republican Joel Pritchard served under Democratic governors Booth Gardner and Mike Lowry. As with all statewide offices, lieutenant governors are directly elected every four years during presidential elections, and there are no term limits.

If the governor is unable to serve, or leaves office by resignation or death, the lieutenant governor is first in the line of succession. As acting governor, the lieutenant governor's role is thought to be circumscribed by political tradition to using the authority lightly. As one profile of the office described, "the lieutenant governor typically would not make or propose policy changes or new initiatives while serving as acting governor, but does hold that authority" (Washington State Office of the Lieutenant Governor 2017). Perhaps the only exception to this norm would be if the state was experiencing a "state of emergency" or crisis when a central executive authority was needed.

The lieutenant governor's main responsibilities are legislative. Article III, section 16 of the state constitution makes it the presiding officer over the state Senate, and permits "other duties as may be prescribed by law." The lieutenant governor is often the most visible player in the Senate when it is in session, guiding debate and serving as chair of the powerful Senate Rules Committee (Washington State Office of the Lieutenant Governor 2017). The lieutenant governor also serves as chair of the Legislative Committee on Economic Development & International Relations, and is a member of the State Finance Committee.

Despite its visibility, the office is not traditionally used as a stepping-stone to higher office. Since statehood, there have been fifteen lieutenant governors; three of these, Henry McBride (R) (1901), Marion E. Hay (R) (1909), and Louis F. Hart (R) (1913–1919), ascended to the office of governor upon the death of the sitting governor, but only one of these, Louis Hart, subsequently ran for re-election and was elected in his own right. Instead, many past lieutenant governors have enjoyed a long tenure in office, including John Cherberg (D) who served for eight consecutive terms, the longest of any lieutenant governor of any state (Washington State Office of the Lieutenant Governor 2017).

Brad Owen (D) (1997–2016) also was one of the state's longer-serving lieutenant governors. When he served in the Washington House (1976–1983) and Senate (1984–1996), Owen took a leading role in the field of public health and safety, and played a strong role in promoting Washington trade. When Owen retired from office in 2016, 11 candidates competed in the primary. Cyrus Habib, a Democratic state senator and former law professor, and Marty McClendon, a Republican Gig Harbor pastor and talk show host with no previous government experience, advanced to the general election. Habib won with 54 percent. His victory was yet another example of the state leading the way electing diverse candidates to office. Habib, a cancer survivor who is legally blind, is the first and only Iranian-American elected to statewide office in the United States (Washington State Office of the Lieutenant Governor 2017).

Secretary of State

The Secretary of State, third in line of succession to the governor, is also elected by partisan ballot to a four-year term. Article III, section 17 of the state constitution states that the secretary "shall keep a record of the official acts of the Legislature, and the executive department of the state, and shall, when required, lay the same, and all matters relative thereto, before either branch of the legislature, and shall perform such other duties as shall be assigned him by law."

Other duties of the office are prescribed by statute, and most of these focus on running and ensuring the integrity of state and local elections, including those involving initiatives and referenda. Indeed, as the use of these forms of "direct democracy" by citizens and interest groups has grown in recent years, so too has the secretary's responsibilities, which include signature verification and certification of ballot measures. The secretary also ensures that voters are provided access to election materials, including print and online voters' pamphlets. Other duties include registering corporations, partnerships, and trademarks as well as individuals and organizations involved in charitable solicitation. The secretary also oversees the State Archives and the State Library.

Close elections, such as those in 2000 and 2004, and concerns about potential electoral fraud and cybercrime have focused greater public scrutiny of the office and its role. The state's 14th Secretary of State, Sam Reed, attracted national attention during the contested 2004 gubernatorial race. He later led a number of voting innovations aimed at encouraging greater political participation, including vote-by-mail and online voter registration, and gained national prominence, serving as president of the National Association of Secretaries of State.

Reed was succeeded in office by Kim Wyman (R), only the second woman to serve in the office. The first, Belle Reeves (D), a veteran legislator, was appointed as secretary in 1938 and was then subsequently elected to two terms. Wyman, one of only a few statewide elected Republicans in recent years, won a close contest against Democrat Kathleen Drew in 2012, and was reelected in 2016 against Democrat Tina Podlodowski. Like Reed, Wyman views the office's role in nonpartisan terms and has focused on civic engagement, ensuring access to voter information, modernizing the election process, and expanding voter registration.

Attorney General

The office of attorney general is more visible than other constitutional officers because their work is frequently in the public eye. There have been 17 attorneys general, all men with the exception of Christine Gregoire, the 15th attorney general, who served from 1993 to 2004. Five former attorney generals have run unsuccessfully for governor, but only Gregoire made the leap.

The attorney general is elected to a four-year term. Article 11 Section 21 of the state Constitution says the attorney general "shall be the legal adviser of the state's officers, and shall perform such other duties as may be prescribed by law." Those duties mostly include representing the state departments and agencies in court. The attorney general oversees many deputy attorneys general and may initiate prosecutions, or instigate civil or criminal proceedings. The office is also assisted by a Solicitor General's office, which is appointed by the attorney general to assist with appellate litigation.

Past attorneys general have distinguished themselves thorough their initiation of high-profile cases. For instance, in 1999, Gregoire led the successful lawsuit against the tobacco industry. She argued that because the state finances health care, bearing the cost of treating diseases caused by tobacco, that the tobacco industry should be held liable. The $206 billion settlement was largest civil settlement in history.

Rob McKenna (R), who succeeded Gregoire, argued cases before the United States Supreme Court multiple times. He was one of 26 state attorneys general who challenged the Affordable Care Act, which was largely upheld by the Supreme Court (*National Federation of Independent Businesses v. Sebelius* 2012). He was more successful defending public records disclosure of voters who sign ballot initiative petitions and the state's top-two primary system (*Doe v. Reed* 2010; *Washington State Grange v. Washington State Republican Party et al.* 2007).

Bob Ferguson, the state's 18th attorney general elected in 2012, has been involved in several high profile issues which have put the state at odds with the federal government. For example, in 2012 Washington voters passed ballot Initiative 502 which made the state one of the first to decriminalize possession of small amounts of marijuana. It became a legal issue because the law conflicts with the federal Controlled Substance Act, which lists marijuana as a Schedule I drug and criminalizes its possession and use. After passage of the initiative, then-Governor Gregoire and Ferguson met with members of the Obama administration to discuss implementation of the law. The Justice Department announced that it would not challenge legalized recreational marijuana, but might step in if states failed to adequately regulate use of the substance (Office of Public Affairs 2013).

In another high-profile case, Ferguson argued that a florist's refusal to provide flowers for a same-sex wedding violated the state's anti-discrimination and consumer protection laws that make discrimination on the basis of sexual orientation illegal. The florist argued that servicing their wedding would violate her Christian beliefs and that her floral arrangements were a form of expression protected by the First Amendment. The Washington State Supreme Court unanimously ruled against her (Thompson 2017).

Ferguson also made headlines when he became the first attorney general to file a lawsuit challenging President Donald Trump's executive order to temporarily ban entry into the United States by individuals from seven majority-Muslim nations, and indefinitely block entry for Syrian refugees.

Treasurer

Article III, section 19 of the constitution provides little guidance to the duties of the state treasurer, stating that the officeholder "shall perform such duties as shall be prescribed by law." These laws direct the treasurer to oversee the state's financial accounts, which held more than $408 billion in 2015, make short term investments with cash on hand, manage the state's debt, and provide guidance on the management of the state's investments and debt as a member of the State Investment Board, the Economic and Revenue Forecast Council, and the Economic Development Finance Authority (Washington State Office of the Treasurer 2017). The office also regularly updates the governor and Legislature about the state's financial status.

Although elected by partisan ballot to a four-year term, the position is not one that is usually tied to partisan politics. The current treasurer, Duane Davidson (R) was elected in 2016 with 58 percent of the vote against a fellow Republican Michael Waite. It was the first time in which the top-two primary had produced a statewide contest with two candidates from the same party. Davidson succeeded Jim McIntire (D), who retired after two terms.

Davidson, the rare Republican from eastern Washington elected to a statewide office, joined Kim Wyman, the Secretary of State, as two of only three Republicans to hold statewide office on the West Coast.[1] Davidson's successful bid was attributed to his success as auditor and treasurer in Benton County, his three terms of service as president of the Washington State Association of County Treasurers, and the endorsement of 35 of 38 fellow county treasurers.

Davidson is unlikely to make waves in office, stating once that "I think the state treasurer's office should be boring. You should stick to the numbers" (Culverwell 2016). This is in comparison to his predecessor, McIntire, who called for a state income tax to diversify the state's tax system and provide funding so the state could comply with the *McCleary* decision.

Auditor

The state auditor's role is also not well defined under the constitution. Section 20 of article III says he or she "shall be auditor of public accounts, and shall have such powers and perform such duties in connection there with as may be prescribed by law."

The auditor oversees financial audits of over 2,400 local and state government units, including schools and colleges, to ensure they comply with local, state, and federal laws and regulations (Office of the Washington State Auditor 2017). The office holds government officials accountable for public resources and is empowered to initiate investigations of potential fraud. The auditor regularly issues reports and is authorized to conduct performance audits. The auditor also sets standards for accounting and budgeting and provides training and technical assistance (Office of the Washington State Auditor 2017). Given the breadth of these responsibilities, it is a fairly large office, with about 350 employees located across the state.

The auditor's office rarely receives much attention, and many incumbents have enjoyed lengthy tenures, including Brian Sonntag, the state's ninth auditor who served five terms between 1992 and 2011. The only auditor to receive a great deal of press attention did so because he was indicted and tried for federal crimes. Democrat Troy Kelley, who succeeded Sonntag in 2012, was indicted by the Department of Justice in 2015. He was charged on 15 counts alleging that he stole over $3 million from clients of his private real-estate conveyance business which he owned prior to being elected to office (Carter 2016). After the indictments, Kelley took a seven-month leave of absence, but refused to resign from office, despite calls from the Governor and other elected official from both parties. On April 26, 2016, a federal jury deadlocked on 14 of the felony charges and acquitted him on one charge, for making false statements about his income to an IRS officer. The day after the verdict he returned to his office and was again in the spotlight when he fired three senior staff (O'Sullivan 2016a). Federal prosecutors announced that they would retry the case in 2017. He did not seek re-election.

In 2016 Pat McCarthy (D) was elected to a four-year term. McCarthy was previously Pierce County Auditor, overseeing elections and licensing, and Pierce County executive from 2009 to 2017. She was second in the primary against state Sen. Mark Miloscia (R), but went on to defeat him in the general election with 52 percent of the vote.

Commissioner of Public Lands

The state commissioner of public lands is elected in presidential election years and serves a four-year term. The office has evolved through statute, with guidance from article III, section 23 of the state constitution. The commissioner heads the state's Department of Natural Resources and carries out the policies set by the Legislature and the state Board of Natural Resources, which the commissioner chairs.

The commissioner is steward of about three million acres of forests, parks, and properties, including agricultural and grazing lands. Of the total, about two million acres of state-owned forests are held in trust for K–12 schools and other state institutions, and produces revenue for school and university construction. The commissioner also is responsible for 2.6 million acres of aquatic lands under Puget Sound, the coast, lakes, and rivers. Conservation of native plant habitats and wildlife and the preservation of the near-shore ecosystem are primary goals.

The commissioner oversees fire prevention and protection of these public lands as well as private and tribal lands in the state, a duty that has become increasingly important as the frequency of large wild-fires has had a serious impact on the state's budget in recent years (see Chapter 11). Washington has large fishing, timber and agriculture industries, and the commissioner has a good deal of policy influence of these industries that is shared with the board. The current commissioner is Hilary Franz (D), who was elected in 2016.

Superintendent of Public Instruction

The superintendent of public instruction is the only nonpartisan state-wide elective office. Article III, section 22 of the state constitution notes that superintendents "shall have supervision over all matters pertaining to public schools and shall perform such specific duties as may be prescribed by law." The superintendent (SPI) has oversight of the state's K-12 basic education and implementing educational reform, working with the state's 295 school districts within the funding and policy decisions of the Legislature. The superintendent also serves as a liaison between the schools and the governor and Legislature, and maintains records, including the state's common school code, teacher's certificates, student assessment, and the School Report Card on student and staff performance. Over a million students are taught by almost 54,000 teachers in over 2,300 public schools in the state.

Because financial management of schools rests with locally elected school boards, the Superintendent does not have a direct role in funding public schools, but does supervise school district budgeting, accounting and reporting to ensure responsible fiscal management (Office of Superintendent of Public Instruction 2017).

Randy Dorn served for two terms as superintendent from 2008 to 2016. His final years in office were frustrating as the governor and state legislature struggled to come up with a plan to fully fund K–12 education in response to the *McCleary* decision. He chose not to seek re-election, saying a "new face" might be a good idea. Chris Reykdal, a former teacher, school board member, and Democratic state representative, was elected to the office in 2016 (Ballotpedia 2016).

Insurance Commissioner

The Office of Insurance Commissioner was created by statute, rather than by the Constitution. The state's first Legislature made the function part of the Secretary of State's office, but it became a separate statewide office in 1907.

The commissioner regulates the insurance industry and protects consumers by ensuring that companies follow state insurance rules and regulations. The office also licenses insurance providers in the state, and can revoke licenses or issue fines against industry violators (Office of the Insurance Commissioner 2017).

In addition to a staff of 242, about 400 volunteers work as statewide health insurance benefits advisors (SHIBA) to provide free help with Medicare and health care choices.

Mike Kreidler is the state's eighth insurance commissioner. He served 20 years in the state Legislature, and eight years as member of Congress, before being elected commissioner in 2000. He was re-elected to a fifth term in 2016.

Conclusion

Despite Washington's reputation as one of the nation's most consistently "blue" states, a historical look at modern gubernatorial and other

statewide election contests reveals an occasional surprise. Close gubernatorial races and the recent selection of two of only three Republicans
to hold statewide office on the West Coast illustrates Washingtonians'
independence when casting their ballot. Citizens have also broken new
ground by electing diverse candidates to state executive positions, and
those elected often find themselves on the national stage through their
policy positions or legal challenges. On the other hand, Washington also
resembles other states because its politics can be described most easily by the urban-rural divide and an increasingly polarized Legislature,
which makes governing, and the work of the Governor, more difficult.

Note

1. The third is Oregon's secretary of state, Dennis Richardson, who in 2016 became
   the first Republican in 14 years to win a statewide Oregon election.

References

Ballotpedia. 2016. "Washington Superintendent of Schools election, 2016." *The
    Encyclopedia of American Politics.* ballotpedia.org/Washington_Superintendent_
    of_Schools_election,_2016.
Carter, Mike. 2016. "State Auditor Troy Kelley faces retrial on theft, money-
    laundering charges." *Seattle Times*, May 31, 2016. seattletimes.com/seattle-news/
    crime/prosecutors-plan-to-retry-state-auditor-troy-kelley-on-fraud-charges/.
Chuang, Aileen. 2017. "Washington Governor Inslee's Profile Rises With Trump-
    Thumping." *Roll Call*, February 22, 2017. rollcall.com/news/politics/washington-
    governor-inslees-profile-rises-trump-thumping.
Council of State Governments. 2014. *The Book of the States, 2014.* Lexington, KY:
    Council of State Governments.
Culverwell, Wendy. 2016. "Tri-Citian Duane Davidson breaks west-side monopoly
    on state executive offices." *Tri-City Herald,* November 20, 2016. tricityherald.com/
    news/local/article116126753.html.
Doe v. Reed 561 US 186 (2010).
Elway, Stuart H. 2012. "All eyes on Washington's independent voters." *Seattle Times*,
    June 23, 2012. seattletimes.com/opinion/all-eyes-on-washingtons-independent-
    voters.
Lee, Tara. 2016. "Inslee and Japan Ambassador sign agreement to strengthen trade
    ties and increase cooperation." News release, June 28, 2016. www.governor.wa.gov
    /news-media/Inslee-and-japan-ambassador-sign-agreement-strengthen-trade-
    ties-and-increase-cooperation.
McCarty, Nolan, Jonathan Rodden, Boris Shor, Chris Tausanovitch, and Chris
    Warshaw. 2015. "Geography, Uncertainty, and Polarization." SSRN, August 27,
    2015. ssrn.com/abstract=2477157.

McCleary, et al. v. State of Washington, 269 P.3d 227 (Wash. 2012).

National Federation of Independent Businesses v. Sebelius, 567 US 519 (2012).

Office of Public Affairs. 2013. "Justice Department Announces Update to Marijuana Enforcement Policy." U.S. Department of Justice, August 29, 2013. justice.gov/ opa/pr/justice-department-announces-update-marijuana-enforcement-policy.

Office of Superintendent of Public Instruction, Washington State. 2017. k12.wa.us/ AboutUs/default.aspx.

Office of the Insurance Commissioner, Washington State. 2017. insurance.wa.gov/ about-oic/what-we-do/.

Office of the Washington State Auditor. 2017. sao.wa.gov/about/Pages/default.aspx.

O'Sullivan, Joseph O. 2016a. "Troy Kelley Fires Senior Staffers at Auditor's Office." *Seattle Times*, May 7, 2016. seattletimes.com/seattle-news/politics/troy-kelley-fires-senior-staffers-at-state-auditors-office/.

———. 2016b. "When Lawmakers Can't Agree, Gov. Jay Inslee Takes Matters into His Own Hands." *Seattle Times*, May 8, 2016. seattletimes.com/seattle-news/ politics/inslee-takes-up-pen-whens-theres-a-legislative-deadlock/.

Thompson, Lynn. 2017. "Richland Florist Discriminated Against Gay Couple for Refusing Service, State Supreme Court Rules." *Seattle Times*, February 16, 2017. seattletimes.com/seattle-news/northwest/richland-florist-discriminated-against-gay-couple-for-refusing-service-states-highest-court-rules.

Washington State Grange v. Washington State Republican Party et al. 552 US 442 (208) (2007).

Washington State Office of the Lieutenant Governor. 2017. ltgov.wa.gov/ responsibilities/.

Washington State Office of the Treasurer. 2017. tre.wa.gov/aboutUs/coreFunctions. shtml.

CHAPTER 10

The Judicial System in the State of Washington

Michael F. Salamone and Carl McCurley

Introduction

The Washington State judiciary is at the center of a number of controversial policy issues. Recently, matters of public school funding, contraception, and gay rights—just to name a few—have all come before the state bench. We depend on our elected judges and justices to decide these and many other critical disputes. Although the state judicial system has been stable in terms of its institutional structure, caseload, and output, recent controversies surrounding judicial elections have some advocating that the system be reformed. In this chapter, we provide an overview of the state judiciary's hierarchy and structure, evaluate the controversies surrounding its selection methods, and discuss the challenges of its administration.

The Structure of the Judiciary

The Washington judicial system is structured as a four-tiered system consisting of two levels of trial courts at the lower end of the hierarchy and two levels of appellate courts at the upper end. The first and lowest tier of the judicial system consists of district and municipal courts, superior courts make up the second tier, the third tier is comprised of the Washington Court of Appeals, and at the top of the judicial hierarchy sits the Supreme Court of Washington. In this section, we describe the structure of the Washington judicial system in depth and explain the essential features and functions of each tier of the system.

Structure of Washington State Courts

Supreme Court of Washington
9 justices sit en banc
- Discretionary appellate jurisdiction over all Washington Court of Appeals decisions
- Discretionary appellate jurisdiction over all decisions involving state officers, decisions declaring a statute or ordinance unconstitutional, and decisions in cases presenting conflicts of law
- Exclusive jurisdiction over bar discipline
- Jurisdiction over certified questions
- Mandatory appellate jurisdiction over all decisions imposing the death penalty

Washington Court of Appeals (3 divisions)
22 judges sit in panels
- Mandatory appellate jurisdiction over all superior court decisions

Superior Courts (30 districts)
200 judges
- Original jurisdiction over all felony criminal cases, juvenile cases, and civil cases involving claims of greater than $100,000
- Appellate jurisdiction over all municipal court and district court decisions

Municipal Courts (127)
110 judges and commissioners
- Original jurisdiction over all cases involving violations of municipal ordinances

District Courts (49)
122 judges and commissioners
- Original jurisdiction over all misdemeanor criminal cases, civil cases involving claims of less than $50,000, small claims, petitions for protection and no contact orders, change of name petitions, and lien foreclosures

Trial Courts

District and municipal courts are known as "courts of limited jurisdiction" and serve as trial courts for misdemeanor criminal cases, cases involving traffic and parking infractions, civil cases involving claims of less than $100,000, and small claims. District courts, which have jurisdiction over both criminal and civil cases, are county courts that serve specific territories within counties. Municipal courts, which have jurisdiction over violations of municipal ordinances, serve specific municipalities. While all of the state's 107 district court judges are elected through nonpartisan elections to four-year terms, the state's 110 municipal court judges are appointed to four-year terms by mayors and confirmed by the city or town's legislative authority. Judges serving on courts of limited jurisdiction include both professional and lay judges (also known as commissioners). Courts of limited jurisdiction presided over by lay judges differ from other courts of limited jurisdiction in that they do not produce written records of their proceedings. Thus, any appellate review of their decisions is *de novo* (without reference to the previous ruling) and may involve review of issues of both fact and law. On the other hand, appellate review of the decisions of courts of limited jurisdiction presided over by professional judges is limited to issues of law. In 2009, the number of district and municipal court filings totaled 2,082,795 and the disposition of these cases generated approximately $257,523,054 through filing and other fees and through fines, forfeitures, and penalties; thus, these filings can be a major source of revenue for state and local governments. The imposition of heavy fines and fees in relatively minor cases has been controversial. In 2016 the Supreme Court's Minority and Justice Commission received a grant from the U.S. Department of Justice to develop an ability-to-pay calculator to address the problem of accumulation of unsustainable debt arising from court proceedings.

More serious cases are tried in the state's superior courts, which serve as trial courts for felony criminal cases, juvenile cases, and civil cases involving claims of greater than $100,000. Superior courts also hear appeals from courts of limited jurisdiction. The state of Washington has 30 superior court districts. While most counties comprise a single superior court district, some districts in sparsely populated areas of the state encompass two or more counties. The state's 172 superior court judges are professional judges elected to four-year terms and are required to be attorneys admitted to the state bar association and licensed to practice law in the state. In 2015, the number of superior court filings totaled 260,308. About two out of every five cases (42 percent) of these filings were civil matters involving tort claims, commercial cases, property rights, petitions for protection from civil harassment or domestic violence, and petitions to review rulings by state administrative agencies. Sixteen percent were criminal cases. The remaining cases consisted of adoption, domestic, guardianship, juvenile, mental illness, and probate cases.

Washington's district, municipal, and superior courts thus serve primarily as trial courts, whose function in the court system is distinct from that of appellate courts. In particular, trial courts are charged with making determinations regarding issues of fact and applying the law to their findings of fact. In a bench trial, a judge acts alone and is responsible for conducting the trial, making findings of fact, determining guilt or innocence, and imposing penalties in traffic and other minor cases. In more serious cases judges may preside over a jury trial in which the judge acts in concert with a jury of laypersons. In jury trials, the jurors serve as finders of fact while the judge oversees the trial by applying the law to make decisions regarding the admission of evidence and other procedural issues. Judges also provide jurors with instructions to help guide them in applying the law to their factual findings. The losing party at trial generally has the right to request appellate review of the trial court proceedings.

Although the trial courts are where cases originate, it is important to note that most legal disputes do not result in a trial. Most disputes are resolved through plea-bargains, settlements, dropped charges, dismissal, and other reasons. In most cases, the court of limited jurisdiction or superior court acts to approve or certify case results that do not involve actual trial. In 2015, about 2 percent of cases filed in Washington superior courts (including about 4 percent of felony criminal cases) and less than one-fourth of 1 percent of cases filed in limited jurisdiction courts culminated in either a jury or bench trial.

Courts of Appeals

Appellate courts—also referred to as "courts of appeals"—hear appeals from lower courts, usually brought by the losing party. Appellate review is ordinarily limited to issues of law. This is the case in Washington as well as most other jurisdictions in the United States. Appeals courts are primarily concerned with the proper application of legal provisions and precedents to the facts of the case, as determined by the trial court. Appellate courts in Washington must usually accept the findings of fact made in the superior court and review only whether the judge or jury applied the law correctly. Thus, appellate proceedings vary significantly from trials. Appellate courts generally do not hear witness testimony, accept new evidence, or make findings of fact. Instead, the parties to the appeal file legal briefs with the court identifying issues of law that may have been decided incorrectly by the trial court and make legal arguments regarding why the lower court ruling should be affirmed or reversed.

After the briefs have been filed and the judges have had the opportunity to read them, oral arguments are scheduled. During oral arguments, attorneys for both parties appear before a panel of three judges (selected at random) to make arguments and answer questions regarding the proper interpretation and application of the law. This differs from the Supreme Court level, where cases are heard *en banc*, or before the entire court. Following oral arguments, the panel of judges discuss the merits of both parties' argument and vote on an outcome. A simple majority is required to reach a decision. Ordinarily, one of the judges in the majority writes an opinion that explains the legal reasoning used to reach the court's decision. Other judges voting with the majority may write separate concurring opinions to explain their particular rationale or reasons for their decision. If the outcome is not unanimous, judges in the minority may write dissenting opinions explaining why they disagreed with the majority. The majority opinion is important not only because it dictates the outcome of the case, but also because the reasoning is supposed to guide future applications of the law by lower courts and other government actors. These opinions are regularly published in court reporters. The decisions of the Supreme Court of Washington are published in *Washington Reports* and *West's Pacific Reporter*, while decisions of the Washington Court of Appeals are published in *Washington Appellate Reports* and *West's Pacific Reporter*.

Most cases appealed from superior courts are heard at the first level of appellate review, the Washington Court of Appeals. This court is divided into three divisions that each serve multiple counties, and hence multiple superior courts. Division I, located in Seattle, and

Division II, located in Tacoma, serve the counties west of the Cascades, while Division III, located in Spokane, serves the counties east of the Cascades. These geographical divisions are important because a losing party in a superior court must file an appeal with the appropriate division of the Court of Appeals, that is, the division that includes in its geographical boundaries the county in which the trial occurred.

The caseloads of the three divisions vary significantly. Division I has consistently been the busiest of the three and reviewed 1,421 cases in 2015. In contrast, Division III has consistently had the lightest caseload, reviewing 929 cases in 2015, while Division II, which reviewed 1,245 cases in 2015, has had an intermediate caseload. Caseloads for all divisions have declined since 2009: Division I's caseload declined from 1,858 cases, Division II's from 1,447, and Division III's from 998 cases.

In general, civil and criminal cases represent approximately equal shares of the Washington Court of Appeals caseload, although it is common for criminal cases to make up a slight majority of the docket. This is notable because, among other things, criminal cases make up a much smaller percentage of filings than civil case filings in the trial courts. In other words, a much higher proportion of criminal trials result in appeals than do civil trials. In fact, criminal cases are about twice as likely to be appealed as civil cases.

The Washington Court of Appeals docket is "non-discretionary," meaning that it must accept all properly filed appeals. This practice exists because the losing parties in trial courts are guaranteed one appeal to ensure the trial court did not make a legal error that may have prejudiced the outcome of the trial. If an appellate court determines that a "reversible error" occurred during the trial, it may reverse the verdict or ruling in the lower court. Reversal may result in a new trial. On the other hand, if an appellate court finds no error or a "harmless error" (i.e., a minor mistake that even if remedied would not change the outcome), it will affirm the lower court's ruling or verdict.

There are 22 judges on the Washington Court of Appeals, each elected to six-year terms. The terms are staggered so only a subset of the court's membership is up for reelection in any single election year. Judges serving on the Washington Court of Appeals are required to have practiced law in the state of Washington for at least five years and must be residents of a county within their respective division for at least one year before taking office.

The State Supreme Court

The Supreme Court of Washington is at the top of the judicial hierarchy and hears appeals at its discretion. These include appeals of decisions of the Washington Court of Appeals and appeals of decisions at any level of the state court system that involve petitions against state officers, that declare a statute or ordinance unconstitutional, or that present a conflict of law. The court's "discretionary jurisdiction" is similar to that of the U.S. Supreme Court. A party that wishes to appeal to the Supreme Court of Washington is not guaranteed to have his or her case reviewed by the state's highest court. Rather, the party must file a petition for review that makes an argument for why the court should review the case. Petitions for review are considered by panels comprised of five members of the court. If the panel fails to reach a unanimous decision either to grant or reject the petition, the petition is considered by the entire court. In general, petitions are most likely to be granted when there is a conflict between different divisions of the Washington Court of Appeals about the proper interpretation of a law or when the justices on the court are otherwise convinced that the legal issue presented in the case is an important one that needs to be authoritatively resolved. The court also has mandatory jurisdiction in cases in which the death penalty has been imposed. This means the review is automatically granted and the justices do not have the discretion to reject it.

In addition, the court is specifically charged with the responsibility of making procedural rules for all state courts, with general administration of the state judicial system, and with disciplining attorneys. The court's exclusive power to make rules of procedure has been closely guarded and has occasionally led to conflicts with the legislature. These conflicts have produced a substantial body of separation-of-powers case law, with a recent addition being the court's 2010 decision in *Waples v. Yi.* In this case the court declared that legislatively imposed restrictions on the filing of medical malpractice claims were unconstitutional insofar as they conflicted with existing rules of procedure by barring cases that could otherwise be filed under the more permissive rules established by the court.

As the state's highest court, the Supreme Court of Washington is the final arbiter of the meaning of Washington State law. Its decisions interpreting the Washington State constitution, state statutes, and state administrative regulations therefore establish precedent that must be followed by lower courts in subsequent cases. The court's interpretations of state law are not subject to review by any higher court.[1]

There are nine justices on the Supreme Court of Washington, all of whom must be attorneys admitted to practice in the state of Washington. The justices are elected to serve six-year terms. The court is led by its chief justice, who is selected by the members of the court to serve a four-year term. The chief justice acts as the main spokesperson for the court, presides over the court's hearings and conferences, and co-chairs the state's Board for Judicial Administration (BJA). Justice Barbara Madsen was elected by her peers in 2009 and reelected in 2012 to serve as chief justice. In 2016, Justice Mary Fairhurst, who was first elected to the court in 2002, was elected to succeed her.

As one might surmise from the succession of two female chief justices in a row, the Supreme Court of Washington has long been among the most diverse state supreme courts in the nation in terms of gender. As of 2016, nationwide, women comprise 31 percent of state judiciaries and 35 percent of state supreme court justices (National Association of Women Judges 2016). In Washington, six of the court's nine current members are women, making it among the first states to have a female majority on its state supreme court.

The number of filings received by the court has remained relatively consistent over the last five years. In 2015, 1,565 cases were filed with the Supreme Court, a figure close to the 5-year average of 1,535 for the years 2011 to 2015. The number of cases resolved in 2015 was 1,400, slightly below the 5-year average from 2011 to 2015 of 1,460 cases.

Selecting Judges in Washington: Nonpartisan Elections

As mentioned in the previous section, judges in Washington are elected in nonpartisan elections. Thus, for any given judicial vacancy, voters select judges from a list of names of candidates similarly to how they select candidates for other offices. However, unlike executive and legislative elections, no political party affiliation appears next to a candidate's name on the ballot. If a vacancy occurs for a judgeship before the term ends, the governor may appoint a judge to fill the vacancy until the next election, at which time the governor's appointee must run for the office if he or she wishes to retain the position.

This nonpartisan election model was established by a constitutional amendment adopted in 1912, replacing an earlier system of partisan judicial elections. Like many states in the West, Washington's move to nonpartisan elections was influenced by the values of the Progressive Era. The move represented an effort to de-politicize the courts and to increase judicial independence by decreasing the influence of partisan politics without losing democratic accountability. The commitment to elect judges, rather than use the executive-appointment system utilized by the federal government and many Eastern states, reflects the populist values that pervaded Washington's political culture when the state was created (see also Chapter 7 in this volume).

Although Washington's system was intended to reduce the role of partisan politics in the judicial selection process, it does not function in that manner. The state's political parties have not only continued to blur the distinction between partisan and nonpartisan judicial elections by endorsing judicial candidates, they also engaged in active mobilization of party supporters on behalf of selected candidates (Modie 2002). This behavior comes from party organizations at all levels, with most county-level Democratic and Republican organizations endorsing judicial races on their websites. However, Washington is not unique in this respect. In a study of trial court elections in 25 states, Streb (2007) finds that party organizations are quite involved in nonpartisan judicial elections, particularly when it comes to candidate endorsements, candidate recruitment, fundraising, and voter turnout efforts.

In fact, there is evidence that the formal absence of parties from judicial elections in states like Washington actually makes these races more expensive. Bonneau and Hall (2009), for instance, show that, all else being equal, partisan races reduce the cost of campaigns. They attribute this difference to the fact that, in the absence of a party organization to educate and mobilize voters, candidates must bear the cost of these activities themselves. This is ironic given the fact that supporters of nonpartisan methods of selecting judges are generally critical of the increasing role of money in judicial elections (e.g., Brandenburg 2009).

Furthermore, in the absence of party labels as a heuristic to help voters make choices, voters may have to rely on other cues. The 2012 Washington Supreme Court election provides a troubling example.

Justice Steve Gonzalez won retention against his challenger, Kitsap County attorney Bruce Danielson. However, Danielson managed to receive 40 percent of the vote in spite of the fact that he did not campaign or raise any money. This led to speculation that many uninformed voters may have read Gonzalez's Latino surname as a cue not to vote for him (Miletich 2012).

In addition to worries about party involvement, there have also been concerns expressed about the role of "special interests" in judicial campaigns. Unease regarding interest group influence has been underscored by the fact that until 2006, contribution limits for candidates for statewide office did not apply to judicial candidates. As a result, interest groups played an especially significant role in funding judicial campaigns. The state's campaign finance laws were amended in 2006 in response to Justice James Johnson's 2002 and 2004 campaigns; this reform set contribution limits for judicial candidates equal to those running for other state offices. In both races, concerted mobilization on Johnson's behalf by business interests allowed Johnson to outspend his opponents decisively. Especially disconcerting was a $95,000 contribution from the Building Industry Association of Washington, for whom Johnson had previously performed legal work (Skolnik 2004). Although the ability of interest groups to contribute directly to a candidate for judicial office has subsequently been limited, independent expenditures on behalf of candidates by these groups are unlimited and have continued to generate controversy.

Critics of judicial elections argue that the growing role of interest groups in judicial campaigns nationwide might undermine public confidence in an independent judiciary. In Washington, some expressed concern after interest groups aired a series of attack ads in 2006 opposing the reelection of former Chief Justice Gerry Alexander. The tone of these ads were quite negative, and critics said they falsely characterized Alexander as "a dotty old man in sympathy with child killers and drunks" (Shannon 2006). While attack ads like these can be cause for concern, it is also worth noting that Justice Alexander won reelection in 2006, and that in the decade since, judicial elections in Washington did not see any televised advertising (neither by interest groups nor the candidates themselves). Further, while ads run by interest groups in judicial races tend to be more negative in tone than those run by the candidates themselves, they still tend to be more positive than those run by interest groups in gubernatorial and congressional races (Salamone, Yoesle, and Ridout 2017). Moreover, a number of studies have found that, even with the presence of attack advertising, judicial elections do not seem to detract from, and may actually bolster, public confidence in state supreme courts (Gibson 2008a, 2008b, 2009, 2012; Gibson et al. 2011).

Regardless, the role of interest group spending in judicial elections raises other concerns that elections may unduly sway the behavior of judges. As Deborah Goldberg (2007, 75) put it, "Sitting judges facing an imminent election…know that every decision is fodder for the opposition." Indeed, the public has held judges accountable for unpopular decisions (Wold and Culver 1987), and studies have shown that judicial elections make judges more punitive lest they be characterized as "soft on crime" (Gordon and Huber 2007; Huber and Gordon 2004).

Washington is certainly not immune to these pressures. As a result of the Washington Supreme Court's decisions in cases like *McCleary v. State of Washington*, all three justices up for reelection in 2016 faced an opponent, the first time in state history that all incumbent justices faced challenges (Camden 2016). In the decade prior (2004–2014) two-thirds of Washington's Supreme Court races were run unopposed. There was also an increase in spending on judicial elections in those races, with the challengers raising large sums from both the Washington Republican Party and from outside interest groups (Camden 2016). As it turned out, the three incumbents won handily: Justices Mary Yu and Charlie Wiggins each with 57 percent of the vote, and Justice Barbara Madsen with 62 percent. However, given the specter of electoral competition, it is not far-fetched to assume that political considerations play at least *some* part in each justice's internal decision-making calculus.

These concerns about the politicization of state judicial elections has led to nationwide reform efforts. One proposed reform is to publicly finance judicial elections, an effort that was successfully enacted in North Carolina in 2002 and Wisconsin in 2009 (National Center for State Courts 2017). The argument that regulations should be enacted to put distance between elected judges and their donors has gained traction. In fact, the U.S. Supreme Court, which in recent years has been fairly skeptical of the constitutionality of campaign finance regulation, ruled in *Williams-Yulee v. Florida Bar* (2015) that states have a compelling interest in restricting fundraising in judicial races. Moreover, there is evidence to show that these regulations are effective. One study found that North Carolina's campaign finance system caused publicly funded candidates to become less favorably inclined toward attorneys who donated to their campaigns (Hazelton, Montgomery, and Nyhan 2016).

Another popular reform among critics of judicial elections is to convert competitive electoral systems, like Washington's, to a "merit selection system," sometimes referred to as the "Missouri Plan." Under this system, currently used by more than a dozen states, the governor appoints a judge from a slate of qualified candidates presented by a nominating commission, and those judges subsequently face periodic non-competitive retention elections. As such, this method seeks to appeal to both professional and political audiences and attempts to balance the independence of appointed judges with the accountability of those who are elected. This plan is quite popular among reformers, including former U.S. Supreme Court Justice Sandra Day O'Connor (2010). In 2010, Minnesota and Nevada, states that utilize nonpartisan elections as Washington does, considered adopting this plan; however, the effort failed in both instances.

The empirical benefits of adopting the Missouri Plan are also unclear. For instance, there is no evidence that the merit selection system results in a more qualified or more diverse bench than that produced in partisan elections (Glick and Emmert 1987; Hurwitz and Lanier 2008). Moreover, Hall (2001) argues that, while retention elections may appear to be less partisan on their face, the reality is that they simply obscure—rather than remove—the overriding influence of partisanship. This is because the results of retention elections are closely linked to the fluctuations in the statewide electoral fortunes of political parties.

Administration and Decentralization of the "Judicial Branch"

The decentralized nature of the Washington state judicial system makes it difficult to call it the "judicial branch" relative to the more centralized nature of the federal judiciary. In this section, we begin by describing the somewhat limited central statewide administrative apparatus of the judiciary. As we discuss, there are several centralized features of the judicial system that do manage to keep it unified, albeit loosely so. Next, we explain how Washington's judicial system is subject to forces of decentralization, making it difficult to characterize it as a single "branch" of state government in the conventional sense of the meaning of that term.

The Supreme Court is one unifying force for the state judiciary. The high court serves to unify the judicial system through its ability to promulgate uniform rules of court procedure (rules describing, for example, how civil, criminal, and appellate matters are to be handled by the courts) and its power to appoint the leadership of other judicial-related offices, including the Administrative Office of the Courts (AOC), the Office of Public Defense (which operates the Parents Representation Program for child dependency cases, appellate indigent defense services, and criminal trial indigent defense services), and the Office of Civil Legal Aid (providing legal help to low-income residents with civil matters related to basic needs such as housing and family safety). The Supreme Court also leads the budget process for the judicial branch at the state level, supplying the legislature with biennial budget proposals.

The second major unifying body for the state judiciary is the Board for Judicial Administration. The BJA is the representative policy-making body for the courts and is authorized by Supreme Court rule. It is the balance between local and institutional interests. Membership of the BJA is comprised of representatives from the district and municipal courts, the superior courts, the courts of appeal, and the Washington State Supreme Court. The Board for Judicial Administration is chaired by the Chief Justice and a member chair who rotates leadership between the superior courts and courts of limited jurisdiction.

The BJA is charged with adopting policies and providing leadership for the administration of justice in Washington State. Included in their responsibilities are: 1) establishing judicial positions on legislation; 2) providing direction to the AOC on administrative matters; 3) fostering the local administration of justice by improving communication within the judicial branch; and 4) providing leadership for the courts at large by speaking with one voice. In 2014 the BJA was reorganized and four standing committees, essential to administering justice in the state, were formally established. Those committees are the Court Education Committee, the Budget and Funding Committee, the Legislative Committee, and the Policy and Planning Committee.

The Administrative Office of the Courts, located in Olympia, responds to the general needs of the judicial system, providing budgeting and accounting of state-funded expenses, automation of case records, and reporting on the caseload of Washington courts. The AOC also provides consultation on court business practices, analysis of staffing and resources, forecasts of the need for judges and court commissioners, and professional training and education of court staff and judges. The AOC also helps create a court community by bringing together judges, administrators, and staff from the cities and counties for state-level conferences.

In addition to its administrative support structure, the Washington State court system is also supported by the Task Force on Canons of Judicial Ethics and the Commission on Judicial Conduct, which are responsible for preserving judicial independence by ensuring that high standards of judicial conduct are observed. The commission has been the more active of the two bodies. The commission was established by constitutional amendment in 1980 in order to provide a less cumbersome alternative to impeachment for violations of judicial ethics by sitting judges. In cases in which misconduct is found, the commission may issue a formal reprimand or recommend to the Supreme Court of Washington that a judge be suspended or removed from office. The commission's most noteworthy recent imposition of discipline involved former Justice Richard Sanders of the Supreme Court of Washington. Sanders was found guilty of violating several canons of the Code of Judicial Conduct after he toured McNeil Island Corrections Center and met personally with a number of inmates, including some who unbeknownst to him had cases pending before the court. As a consequence, following the court's 2006 decision affirming the Commission on Judicial Conduct's sanction in *In re disciplinary proceeding against Sanders*, Sanders was formally reprimanded.

A variety of court associations draw their membership from across the courts and are charged with developing policy. Two associations represent judges—the District and Municipal Court Judges Association (for courts of limited jurisdiction) and the Superior Court Judges Association. Similar organizations exist for court administrators, such as the Washington Association of Juvenile Court Administrators, and for the clerks of court. These professional organizations help steer policy from a broader perspective, as has been the case with the Juvenile Court Administrators' state-level support for rigorous quality assurance standards to apply to all juvenile probation departments. Other groups created by order of the Supreme Court, in particular the Gender and Justice Commission, the Minority and Justice Commission, and the Commission on Children in Foster Care demonstrate that, although the courts are decentralized, they can at times work in unison as significant policy actors.

The day-to-day operations of the courts and other important matters, such as funding municipal, district, and superior court operations, are administered locally. Relative to other states, the level of state expenditure supporting this system is quite modest. While the full operating costs of the Supreme Court of Washington and the Washington Court of Appeals are paid out of the state budget, the state only funds half of the salaries and benefits paid to superior court judges, and a smaller percentage of the salaries and benefits paid to district and municipal court judges. According to figures for fiscal year 2012 published by the U.S. Department of Justice's Bureau of Justice Statistics, the average percentage of funding for judicial and legal services received from state general funds is 49 percent (Kyckelhahn 2015). Indeed, four states (Alaska, Delaware, Massachusetts, and Rhode Island) rely upon their general funds to provide 90 percent or more of the funding for their judicial systems. In contrast, the Washington judicial system received just 15 percent of its funding, mainly to operate the state's appellate courts and the AOC and to pay judicial salaries from the state general fund, while the other 85 percent was provided by county and municipal revenues. In fact, with only 0.4 percent of the most recent state budget devoted to the state's judicial system, Washington currently ranks 50th in the nation in state funding of judicial and legal services. In combination with local court administration that operates at the pleasure of locally and independently elected judges, reliance on local funding means that courts exercise considerable freedom in their operation. For example, local court administrators and judges have control over case calendaring, pre-trial hearings, services provided to self-represented litigants, use of problem-solving courts such as drug courts, and assignment of judges to specialized dockets. The administration of these and many other activities thus varies significantly from court to court all around the state.

The decentralization of Washington's courts poses challenges to coordination of policy and the development of standards for court operations. Disparity in practice can also arise with decentralized courts. Two examples of variation in practices are currently the object of widespread attention. The first example comes from juvenile detention centers. Analysis of 2015 juvenile detention by the Washington State Center for Court Research (2016) shows that county-level population-based rates of youth being admitted to juvenile detention facilities ranged from a low in San Juan County of 3 youths per every 1,000 youths age 10 to 17 with a detention stay in 2015, to a high in Okanogan County of 46 youths per 1,000. The second example relates to court-imposed fines and fees. In an analysis of fines and fees imposed by superior courts, Beckett, Harris, and Evans (2008) found that average amounts imposed ranged from a median of $600 in King County to over $7,000 in Whitman County. The disparities in courts' practices with regard to juvenile detention and to court-imposed fines and fees has led to requests for research and analysis of these practice, which, in turn, have motivated policy development activity in both areas.

New Responsiveness

The use of data as a lens to understand who is court-involved and how the courts act upon individuals is a pervasive new force in the administration of the larger justice system. The use of data is part of the gradually building wave of performance measurement and improvement in the public sector (see Behn 2014) but also driven by a highly publicized incident, such as the U.S. Department of Justice review of judicial fines and fees and policing in Ferguson, Missouri, after the death of Michael Brown in 2014. What is new and noteworthy is that courts in Washington State are variously feeling the effects of the new availability and use of data. At times, Washington's courts are on the forefront of data development and use.

For example, the State Supreme Court's Minority and Justice Commission received funds from the U.S. Department of Justice to further examine the pretrial use of bail and jail and post-conviction use of fees and fines, with the goal of developing an ability to pay calculator that will inform courts whether any particular level of financial penalty or fees would exceed an individual's ability to discharge the financial obligation. The Minority and Justice Commission, joined by other court associations such as the Superior Court Judges' Association and the District and Municipal Court Judges' Association, is also engaged in a broad-based effort to examine and improve pretrial justice. Two jurisdictions in particular, Yakima County and Spokane County, are using funds from private foundations to develop new data-driven approaches to pretrial operations that seek to align the level of risk for flight and to community safety with the level of restrictiveness (the amount of bail) assigned at pretrial hearings.

Conclusion

The Washington State judiciary is a populist and diffuse network of institutions. Though a few bodies act as a unifying force across the state's judicial system, many courts' activities are implemented independently of, and sometimes in contrast to, other courts. Likewise, Washington judges are separately elected and ultimately responsible to their diverse constituencies. Of course, this has both its costs and benefits.

As in many other parts of the country, Washington's judicial elections seem to be increasingly more competitive, and campaign contributions and expenditures in judicial races have been on the rise. The 2016 Supreme Court elections are a particularly salient example. While the increased spending by interest groups and political parties leaves some to worry about the independence of the judges, this phenomenon appears to be par for the course for elected judiciaries, which by design prioritize popular accountability over independence. That said, scholarly work has shown that some of these concerns may be overblown (e.g., Bonneau and Hall 2009). Moreover, the voters of Washington State have elected one of the more diverse state supreme courts in the nation.

Although there are some unifying features of the state's court system, it remains relatively decentralized. The Supreme Court of Washington and administrative units such as the AOC and the Office of Civil Legal Aid provide some degree of centralization and unification. However, a loose group of court associations around the state are also responsible for developing policies for the judiciary. Moreover, as noted above, funding and day-to-day operations of most individual courts around the state—especially trial courts—are administered locally. Only 15 percent of judicial funding comes from the state's general fund, which is much less than in other states.

Although the administration of the court system is uniquely decentralized, this has not prevented the judiciary, even at the local level, from being innovative and responding to problems. Courts around the state have adopted reforms in pre-trial procedures and various matters related to juvenile justice, while a range of problem-solving courts have been developed and instituted to help the courts better address specific problems within the justice system, such as finding ways to help drug offenders and reducing the harm of drugs in society.

Notes

1. The Supreme Court of Washington's rulings may be appealed to the United States Supreme Court if they involve an issue of federal law, such as a conflict between a state law and the U.S. Constitution. But the state's high court is the final arbiter of Washington State law.

References

Beckett, Katherine A., Alexes M. Harris, and Heather Evans. 2008. *The Assessment and Consequences of Legal Financial Obligations in Washington State*. Report commissioned by the Washington State Minority & Justice Commission.

Behn, Robert D. 2014. *The PerformanceStat Potential: A Leadership Strategy for Producing Results*. Washington, DC: Brookings Institution Press.

Brandenberg, Bert. 2009. "Is Justice for Sale?" *Experience* 19(3): 11–12.

Bonneau, Chris W., and Melinda Gann Hall. 2009. *In Defense of Judicial Elections*. New York: Routledge.

Camden, Jim. 2016. "Big Money Fuels Contentious Washington Supreme Court Races." *Spokesman-Review*, October 26, 2016.

Gibson, James L. 2008a. "Campaigning for the Bench: The Corrosive Effects of Campaign Speech?" *Law & Society Review* 42(4): 899–928.

_____. 2008b. "Challenges to the Impartiality of State Supreme Courts: Legitimacy Theory and 'New-Style' Judicial Campaigns." *American Political Science Review* 102(1): 59–75.

_____. 2009. "'New-Style' Judicial Campaigns and the Legitimacy of State High Courts." *Journal of Politics* 71(4): 1285–1304.

_____. 2012. *Electing Judges: The Surprising Effects of Campaigning on Judicial Legitimacy*. Chicago: University of Chicago Press.

Gibson, James L., Jeffrey A. Gottfried, Michael X. Delli Carpini, and Kathleen Hall Jamieson. 2016. "The Effects of Judicial Campaign Activity on the Legitimacy of Courts: A Survey-based Experiment." *Political Research Quarterly* 64(3): 545–558.

Glick, Henry R., and Craig F. Emmert. 1987. "Selection Systems and Judicial Characteristics: The Recruitment of State Supreme Court Judges." *Judiciature* 70(4): 229–235.

Goldberg, Deborah. 2007. "Interest Group Participation in Judicial Elections." In *Running for Judge: The Rising Political, Financial, and Legal Stakes of Judicial Elections*, edited by Matthew J. Streb, 73–95. New York: New York University Press.

Gordon, Sanford C., and Gregory A. Huber. 2007. "The Effect of Electoral Competitiveness on Incumbent Behavior." *Quarterly Journal of Political Science* 2(2): 107–138.

Hall, Melinda Gann. 2001. "State Supreme Courts in American Democracy: Probing the Myths of Judicial Reform." *American Political Science Review* 95(2): 315–330.

Hazelton, Morgan L.W., Jacob M. Montgomery, and Brendan Nyhan. 2016. "Does Public Financing Affect Judicial Behavior? Evidence From the North Carolina Supreme Court." *American Politics Research* 44(4): 587–617.

Huber, Gregory A., and Sanford C. Gordon. 2004. "Accountability and Coercion: Is Justice Blind when It Runs for Office?" *American Journal of Political Science* 48(2): 247–263.

Hurwitz, Mark S., and Drew Noble Lanier. 2008. "Diversity in State and Federal Appellate Courts: Change and Continuity Across 20 Years." *Justice System Journal* 29(1): 47–70.

Kyckelhahn, Tracey. 2015. "Justice Expenditure and Employment Extracts, 2012—Preliminary." *Bureau of Justice Statistics*. www.bjs.gov/index. cfm?ty=pbdetail&iid=5239.

Miletich, Steve. 2012. "Justice Gonzalez's Win Raises Questions about Role of Ethnicity." *Seattle Times*, August 9, 2012.

Modie, Neil. 2002. "Justice Johnson Trailing Opponent in Early Tally." *Seattle Post-Intelligencer*, September 17, 2002.

National Association of Women Judges. 2016. "2016 US State Court Women Judges." www.nawj.org/statistics/2016-us-state-court-women-judges.

National Center for State Courts. 2017. "History of Reform Efforts." www. judicialselection.com/judicial_selection/reform_efforts/formal_changes_since_ inception.cfm.

O'Connor, Sandra Day. 2010. "Take Justice Off the Ballot." *New York Times*, May 22, 2010.

Salamone, Michael F., Orion A. Yoesle, and Travis N. Ridout. 2017. "Judicial Norms and Campaigns: The Content of Televised Advertisements in State Supreme Court Races." *Justice System Journal* 38(1): 4–21.

Shannon, Brad. 2006. "This Isn't Your Usual Race for Supreme Court: Attack Ads Raise Campaign Stakes." *The Olympian*, September 17, 2016.

Skolnik, Sam. 2004. "Incumbent Judges, Becker Lead in Races." *Seattle Post-Intelligencer*, September 14, 2004.

Streb, Matthew J. 2007. "Partisan Involvement in Partisan and Nonpartisan Trial Court Elections." In *Running for Judge: The Rising Political, Financial, and Legal Stakes of Judicial Elections*, edited by Matthew J. Streb, 96–114. New York: New York University Press.

Washington State Center for Court Research. 2016. "Detained Youth and Detention Episodes in 2015." Presented at the annual fall conference of the Washington Association of Juvenile Court Administrators in Chelan, WA.

Wold, John T., and John H. Culver. 1987. "The Defeat of the California Justices: The Campaign, the Electorate, and the Issue of Judicial Accountability." *Judicature* 70(6): 348–355.

CHAPTER 11

Continuity and Change in Public Policy in Washington State

Steven D. Stehr, Season A. Hoard, and Christina M. Sanders

The public policy landscape in Washington can be viewed as a product of two oftentimes contradictory forces. The first is the ambivalence that citizens have regarding the size and scope of government activity and the belief that government authority should be constrained. This sentiment is reflected in a variety of institutional arrangements such as the use of the long ballot to elect statewide officials, as well as the active use of the initiative process to make state laws, and in the long-held resistance to establishing a state income tax. At the same time, however, Washington's economic and social development has been closely tied to active interventions on the part of both the state and federal governments. Washingtonians have greatly benefited from the influx of federal dollars to fund a vibrant national defense industry, health care, the construction and operation of the Hanford nuclear facility, the network of dams on the Columbia and Snake Rivers, and the Columbia Basin Irrigation and Reclamation Project, among other programs. Further, citizens have come to expect that the state will provide high levels of goods and services in the areas of education, environmental protection, transportation, and health care. In their centennial history of the state, Robert Ficken and Charles LeWarne recognize these contradictory forces when they write: "Government has always been a vital presence in Washington. Settlers and their entrepreneurial progeny might think of themselves as self-reliant and independent from public assistance, but the reality was otherwise" (Ficken and LeWarne 1988, 106).

Of course, the people of the State of Washington are not the only Americans who want both a small government along with high levels of government benefits. However, Washington policymakers face a particularly daunting environment when weighing tradeoffs between policy priorities. The state features a revenue system heavily reliant on sales and business taxes (like six other states, Washington does not levy an income tax) which makes the state particularly sensitive to economic down turns, and it disproportionately taxes citizens who have lower incomes. According to an analysis by the Office of Financial Management, tax revenues have been slow to recover to the levels that existed prior to the Great Recession of 2007–2009 (OFM 2014b). Adjusted for inflation, state and local tax revenues per capita were $4,558 in 2014 compared to $4,790 in 2007. In fact, revenue generation has been an issue in the state for some time. The Washington State Economic and Revenue Forecast Council calculates that over the past 30 years, state revenue collections as a share of the state economy have declined by nearly 30 percent (WSERFC 2016). Nor do the long term prospects for revenue enhancement look good in the absence of comprehensive tax reform because the current tax system was designed when the state's economy was based around manufacturing and the production of goods, not the current more service-based economy (Nicholas 2013).

State policy makers are also constrained on the expenditure side of the budgetary equation. In the 2015–2017 biennium, the total budget in Washington was $93.7 billion. "Human Services," such as medical and public assistance, represented approximately 38 percent of those expenditures, and many of these programs are partnerships between the state and federal government. Public schools—state funding for kindergarten through twelfth grade—is the next largest category of expenditures accounting for 22.7 percent. In practical terms approximately 60 percent of the state budget is thus protected from cuts either owing to constitutional provisions requiring expenditures in public education[1] or mandatory federal requirements in social service programs and health care. This means that all other functions of state government—higher education, protection of natural resources, transportation—must compete for the remaining funds.

Although there are many interdependencies between national and subnational governments in the United States, there is a relatively clear delineation between the functions undertaken by the federal government and those performed by the 50 state governments. Broadly speaking, the federal government's primary responsibilities are national defense (and the associated foreign policy activities) and redistributive programs such as Social Security, Medicare, and Medicaid. Indeed, these activities consumed well over 80 percent of federal expenditures in fiscal year 2015 (CBPP 2016). State governments, on the other hand, are primarily responsible for what have been called "developmental" programs (Garand, Ulrich, and Xu 2014). As the saying goes, the core functions of state governments are to "educate, medicate, and incarcerate." While this phrase is generally true in that every state expends the majority of its budget on these activities, extensive variation exists across states in their mixture of public policies. This raises the question of what forces explain variations in state level policy priorities over time.

This chapter examines the outputs of state policy making activities in Washington using budget data as the primary lens. It focuses on questions such as: What factors explain the outputs of public policy at the state level? What functions do state policy makers prioritize when faced with inevitable tradeoffs in budgetary choices? How and why have these priorities changed over time? How does the policy landscape in Washington compare with other states? This chapter proceeds as follows. We begin with a brief discussion of a framework developed by Robert Lowry that explains how and why policy outputs look the way they do at the state level. We then turn to examine some of the social and demographic trends that drive state policy making. Next the chapter looks at patterns in expenditures and how Washington compares to other western states, including Alaska, California, Hawaii, Nevada, Oregon, and Washington. Finally, we discuss several policy innovations recently introduced in Washington State, and briefly speculate on the near-term future of policy making in the state.

A Framework for Analysis

What explains the particular mix of public policies in individual states? Robert Lowry (2014) has suggested that state policy outputs at any given point in time are a function of four contextual factors: external constraints, resources, preferences, and institutions.

"External constraints" refer to factors outside of the direct control of state policy makers, chiefly the U.S. Constitution, and federal grants and mandates. In Washington, for example, the passage of the federal Affordable Care Act in 2010 and the decision by state lawmakers to expand the Medicaid program to newly eligible participants resulted in more state dollars being spent on health care. To the list of external constraints suggested by Lowry, we would add factors such as national economic conditions, demographic and social trends, voter approved initiatives (so-called "ballot box budgeting"), and state constitutional mandates that are difficult to change. Clearly, national economic factors help explain many of the revenue challenges facing contemporary state policy makers as Washington has struggled to recover from the Great Recession of 2007–2009. Prior versions of this volume have made a point of referencing budget challenges introduced either by the voters through the initiative process (LeLoup and Herzog 2004), or by a national economic recession (Holland and Lundin 2011). Additional demographic and social trends affecting policy making in Washington are discussed in the next section of this chapter.

"Resources" are another factor that can constrain the options of state policy makers according to Lowry. The most obvious resource is tax revenue raised by the state itself or through intergovernmental transfers to pay for public programs. In the absence of a state income tax, Washington is heavily reliant on sales and business taxes, and, like many states, grants from the federal government. In addition to the revenue challenges discussed earlier in this chapter, this tax system places a disproportionate burden on people with low incomes. According to a study conducted by the nonpartisan Institute on Taxation and Economic Policy in 2015, Washington has "by far" the most regressive tax system in the nation (ITPE 2015). Low income residents in Washington pay 16.8 percent of family income in state and local taxes while the wealthiest pay only 2.4 percent (see Table 1). By comparison, the equivalent percentages in Alaska are 7 percent and 2.5 percent, Idaho 8.5 percent and 6.4 percent, and Oregon 8.1 percent and 6.5 percent. Other researchers confirm the regressive nature of Washington's tax system. For instance, Virginia Gray developed a set of indexes to compare states on a variety of "conservative" and "liberal" positions and found that while Washington ranked 18th in "policy liberalism" it ranked 50th in "tax progressivity" (Gray 2008, 4).

Physical resources, such as oil and mineral reserves and human capital, can also provide resource advantages to states. In the case of Washington the availability of large, commercial seaports, the physical presence of large export-based firms such as Boeing, and the foreign demand for Washington's agricultural products makes foreign trade an important part of the state economy. However, the election of Donald Trump as president may introduce uncertainty to trade policy should he follow through on promises to renegotiate current trade deals and impose high tariffs on imported goods. In terms of human capital, Washington's population is more highly educated and generally scores high on "quality of life" measures such as overall health.

Table 1: Comparison of Selected State Tax Systems

	% of Family Income in State and Local Taxes	
	Low Income Residents	**Wealthiest 1%**
Washington	16.8%	2.4%
Alaska	7.0%	2.5%
Idaho	8.5%	6.4%
Oregon	8.1%	6.5%

Data from Gray 2008.

"Preferences" refers to the priorities of citizens, policy stakeholders, and elected officials. These preferences are articulated and implied through elections, public opinion, interest group and political party activities, and other mechanisms of political communication. Finally, "institutions" can be understood as "the rules of the game in a society" (North 1990, 3). These include both formal rules such as laws, regulations, and constitutions, as well as informal constraints such as conventions, customs, and norms that structure social behavior. Since other chapters in this volume are devoted to the preferences of Washingtonians and institutional structures in Washington, this chapter will focus on external constraints and resources as they relate to policy formation in the state.

Demographic Trends and Economic Drivers

The size and scope of public programs at the state level is highly contingent on social and demographic factors. Since states are largely responsible for public education, many health care programs, and corrections, the population size of the groups eligible for these services is important, as is the overall size of the population in the state.

Over the past 40 years, Washington experienced some of the highest population growth rates in the country (Holland and Lundin 2011). Since 2000, Washington's population has increased nearly 22 percent, from approximately 5,894,140 to 7,183,700 in 2016 (OFM 2016a) (see Figure 1). Moreover, the state's population increased in size at a higher rate in 2015 (+1.34 percent) and 2016 (+1.73 percent) than any other year since 2007 (OFM 2016a). Migration accounted for most of this recent growth, making up 71 percent (87,100 people) of the state's population growth in 2016 and 62 percent in 2015. During the ten years prior to this time the increase from migration averaged 45,000 people per year (OFM 2016b; Sauter, Comen, and Stebbins 2016).

Figure 1: Washington State Population Increase 2008-2016

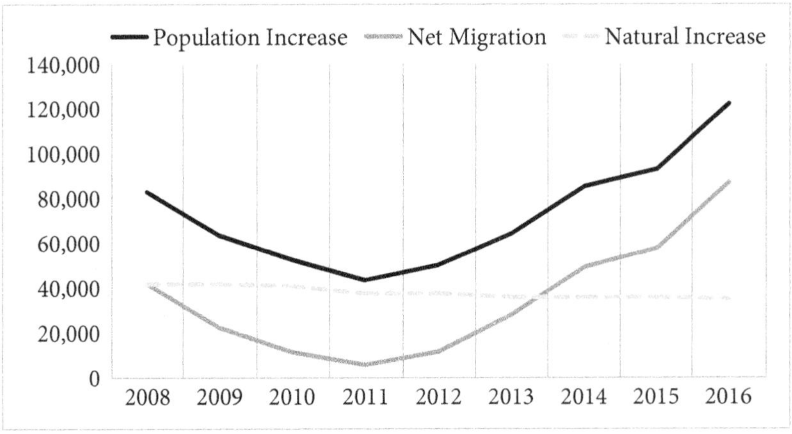

Data from OFM (2016a, 2016b); Sauter, Comen and Stebbins (2016).

As of 2015, 22.5 percent of the population of Washington State was under 18 years of age (Census Bureau 2016). This demographic group has a particularly large impact on the state's budget and this impact will likely increase in the foreseeable future (For information on budget drivers, see Table 2). For instance, public school (K–12) enrollment increased 17 percent between 1990 and 2001 (Stehr and Ellwanger 2004). K–12 enrollment continued to increase from 2001 to 2016 but at a lower rate of 7.3 percent and it is projected to increase by another 4.9 percent by 2019 (OFM 2016c). Besides increasing enrollments, K–12 education funding has been subject to high profile litigation. To address budget shortfalls during the national economic recession that began in 2008, Washington State suspended K-12 programs designed to reduce class sizes and to offer professional development opportunities for teachers (Holland and Lundin 2011). In 2012, the Washington State Supreme Court ruled in *McCleary et al. v. State of Washington* that the state had violated its "paramount duty" under the state constitution by not providing sufficient funding for public education (see Chapter 7). Although the legislature made efforts to address the problem, in 2014 the court held it in contempt for not developing an adequate plan to fund K-12 education, sanctioning the state with a fine of $100,000 per day until it comes into compliance. The court ruling, in combination with increasing K-12 enrollment (an average increase of 8,500 per year according to OFM), has thus made public school funding a top priority for the governor and legislative leaders, and it will heavily impact budget allocations in the future.

Another group that disproportionately impacts state finances are the elderly. Individuals 65 years or older use social and health services at a much higher rate than younger citizens. This group currently accounts for 14.4 percent of Washington's population (Census Bureau 2016). The medical assistance caseload in the state has increased 67 percent since 2000 as a result of the growth of this group in the population (OFM 2016d). Although passage of the federal Affordable Care Act led to larger enrollment in medical assistance in the state, it had little impact on the state's budget because the federal government provided 100 percent of the funds for the expansion, although this will change in the future (OFM 2016d). The Office of Financial Management (OFM 2016e) also projects that the "Long-Term Care" population (85 and over), will increase by 5.9 percent between 2015 and 2019, and that state-supported nursing homes will not be able to meet the demand of this growing population, necessitating in-home assistance and community programs to address the gap. The number of individuals receiving home and community services in the state has already increased 76 percent since 2000 (OFM 2016f), so as the population 85 years and older continues to grow and federal funds likely decrease, these services will have a growing impact on state finances.

The unemployment rate, which was as high as 10 percent in 2010, fell to 5.3 percent by the end of 2016 (Department of Numbers 2016). This is slightly higher than in the past, when unemployment in the state averaged around 4 percent during the 1990s and early 2000s

Table 2: Washington State Select Budget Driver Populations

	2010	2011	2012	2013	2014	2015	2016
K-12 Enrollment	1,038,219	1,037,703	1,040,077	1,046,962	1,057,388	1,067,998	1,080,027
Public Higher Education Enrollment	315,231	303,484	295,508	290,281	287,613	290,105	286,795
Income Assistance Caseload	64,451	65,140	54,436	48,679	42,572	35,160	31,286
Home & Community Services	44,080	46,038	48,143	49,057	50,105	51,680	N/A
Medical Assistance Caseload	1,055,995	1,107,768	1,125,391	1,136,317	1,156,643	1,203,163	1,243,280
Prison Inmate Population	17,096	17,058	17,087	17,404	17,502	17,433	17,578

Data from OFM (2016c, 2016d, 2016e, 2016f)

Note: OFM data not available for Home and Community Services for 2016.

(Holland and Lundin 2011), and higher than the national average of 4.6 percent (Department of Numbers 2016). While Washington State has made significant gains in employment since the Great Recession, these figures indicate that the state has yet to fully recover and remains susceptible to national economic trends. Moreover, while Washington State outranked every other state in combined wage and job growth in early 2016 (Torres 2016), Boeing, a major contributor to the state economy, cut its workforce over 8 percent in 2016 (over 6,600 jobs), and announced additional workforce cuts for 2017 (Gates 2016). Additionally, Microsoft has reduced its workforce during the past three years (Callaham 2016). It remains to be seen if these job reductions presage a more fragile state economy.

In addition to these common drivers of state budgets, wildfires in Washington have also increased in recent years, exacting a larger toll on the state's economy. The number of large (over 500 acres) wildfires in Washington increased from an average of six per year during the 1970s to more than twenty-one per year after the year 2000 (Washington State Department of Natural Resources 2015). Washington State's Department of Ecology (DOE) expects the cost of fighting wildfires to exceed $75 million per year by the 2020s, a figure that does not take into account the value of the lost timber (DOE 2006). The increase in fires is likely linked to long-term changes in climate, population growth, and human interaction with the environment, all factors that are unlikely to change and so fire control will continue to have a growing impact on the state's economy.

Patterns in State Program Expenditures

The state of Washington will spend approximately $93.7 billion during its 2015–2017 biennium (Senate Ways and Means Committee 2016). Of this total about 84 percent was allocated to the operating budget ($78.9 billion), which pays for the day-to-day operating expenses of state government. About 8.8 percent was allocated to the transportation budget ($8.3 billion) to fund operating and capital costs. Finally, 7.0 percent of expenditures will be spent through the capital budget ($6.6 billion), used to build, acquire and maintain buildings, public lands, and other physical assets. Approximately 30 percent of the funding for the state budget is provided by the federal government with the remaining funding coming from taxes (42.9 percent), licenses, permits, and fees (19.2 percent), and borrowing (4.2 percent).

What programmatic functions were covered by this nearly $94 billion budget? As noted earlier, a little more than 60 percent of the budget was spent on human services (37.9 percent) and public schools (kindergarten through grade 12) (22.7 percent). Human services include a variety of medical and public assistance programs, most of which are partnerships between the state and federal governments. Spending for higher education amounted to 15.9 percent of the budget, with the remaining monies expended on transportation projects (7.4 percent), government operations (6.3 percent) and natural resources (4.4 percent) (See Figure 2 below). In terms of their relative share of the total state budget, the three largest functional categories have not changed dramatically in the past ten years. Comparable percentages for the 2007–2009 biennium were: human services (35.8 percent), public schools (23.2 percent), and higher education (14.9 percent) (Senate Ways and Means 2016). These relatively stable distributions actually mask some rather dramatic changes in these three categories of expenditures.

Figure 2: Washington State Programmatic Functions

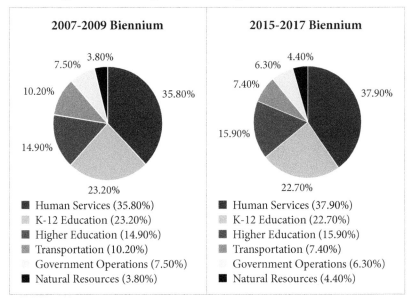

Note: Percentages do not add up to 100 percent owing to small amounts budgeted for other programmatic functions not included in the charts.

One change that has impacted the budget was the passage of the federal Affordable Care Act in 2010. Among its provisions were the options for states to expand coverage under Medicaid and the Children's Health Insurance Program (CHIP). Medicaid, established by the U.S. Congress in 1965, is a health care program for poor people. CHIP was created in 1997 to provide health care coverage for children in families with incomes too high to qualify for Medicaid. Medicaid and CHIP are administered by the states and are jointly funded by the state and federal governments. Washington was one of 27 states that chose to expand eligibility for these health care programs and the results have been dramatic (the expanded Medicaid program in Washington is named "Apple Health"). As of September 2016, Washington has enrolled 1,785,189 individuals in Medicaid and CHIP—a net increase of almost 60 percent since 2013 (Medicaid.gov 2016). According to data gathered by the Kaiser Family Foundation, the state paid 35 percent of the Medicaid benefits in fiscal year 2015, and the federal government paid the remaining 65 percent (Kaiser Foundation 2015a). Nationwide, states receive roughly one-third of their total budgets from the federal government. These funds help to pay for health care, schools, roads, public safety, and a range of other programs. Between 2008 and 2016, federal support for state level programs changed. For example, grants for health care programs have grown 57 percent in real terms while grants for other areas such as transportation (-10 percent) and education (-11 percent) have declined during this time period (Pew 2015).

Another large component of the state budget is funding for public schools. Nationwide state spending on K–12 schools has declined over the last decade. According to the Center for Budget and Policy Priorities, 23 states will provide less "formula" or "general" funding in 2017 than they did before the Great Recession in 2008 (Leachman, Masterson, and Wallace 2016). In many cases, declining property values meant that local (school district level) funding of public education could not make up the decline in state support. In contrast to the many other states, Washington has grown its investment in public schools in recent years.[2] Indeed, between 2008 and 2014, total state funding per student (inflation adjusted) fell by only 1.0 percent in Washington, compared to much steeper declines in other states, such as Arizona (-37 percent), Idaho (-23 percent), and Alabama (-22 percent) (Leachman,

Masterson, and Wallace 2016). Then, illustrating the impacts of the *McCleary* decision, state general fund spending per student on public education grew by 8.3 percent in 2015–16. Overall, state general funding per student (inflation adjusted) in Washington has actually increased by 16.5 percent from 2008 to 2017 (Leachman, Masterson, and Wallace 2016). Only Alaska (+18.2 percent) and North Dakota (+25.9 percent) increased by more during this period.

The Great Recession had perhaps its largest impact on state spending in higher education. During the 2015–2016 school year, 46 states spent less per student than when the recession began in 2008 (Mitchel, Leachman, and Masterson 2016). Nationwide, average state spending per student (inflation adjusted) was 18 percent less in 2016 than before the recession. In Washington, state spending per student in the two and four year colleges declined by 20 percent between 2008 and 2016 (Mitchel, Leachman, and Masterson 2016). This amounted to a decline in spending of $1,826 per student.[3] To make up for the decline in state support, public colleges and universities across the country increased tuition by an average of 33 percent since 2007. In Washington, the percent change in average tuition at public colleges (inflation adjusted) was a little over 50 percent between 2008 and 2016 (see Figure 3). Only nine states had larger percentage increases during that time period. Tuition increased in Washington by $3,446 (inflation adjusted) between 2008 and 2016. Again, only nine states had greater tuition increases. However, in the 2015–17 budget, Washington State cut tuition for four-year universities by 15 to 20 percent, the only state to announce tuition cuts that year (Long 2015). It seems clear, that when faced with tradeoffs between human services, K–12 schools, and higher education, public colleges and universities typically bore the brunt of the fiscal pain. It remains to be seen whether the tuition cuts announced in 2015 reflect a longer term trend, or merely a temporary reprieve.

Washington State Budget in Comparative Perspective

As noted earlier, Washington State differs from most states in the Western region of the United States (Alaska, California, Hawaii, Nevada, Oregon, and Washington) and nationally, owing to its heavy reliance on sales and gross receipts taxes for revenue. Washington ranked 29th in total state and local taxes per capita in fiscal year 2014,

Figure 3: Average Tuition Increase at 4 year Public Universities 2008-2016

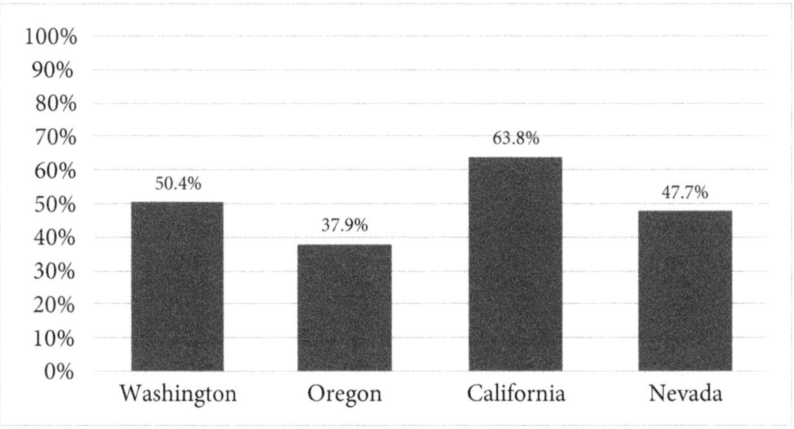

Data from Mitchel, Leachman and Masterson (2016).

and sales and business taxes accounted for nearly 40 percent of state revenue, compared to the national average of approximately 25 percent (OFM 2014a). Highlighting the state's dependence on these forms of revenue, Washington ranked third in the nation in per capita collection of state and local sales tax in fiscal year 2014 (OFM 2014b), and they comprised 78.2 percent of all tax collections by source (Ballotpedia 2014). In comparison to other states in the West, income taxes comprised 73.8 percent of total tax collections in Oregon, and 55.7 percent in California. Of Western states, only Nevada derived more of its total tax collections (80 percent) from sales and gross receipts (Ballotpedia 2014). This reliance on sales and business taxes means that Washington State is particularly susceptible to economic downturns in comparison to nearby states.

There is evidence that Washington State citizens receive higher levels of public services than citizens in other states, but trends also suggest that this may be changing. For example, Stehr and Gaffney noted that spending per capita in 2007 was $5,741, ranking Washington 20th among all 50 states (2011). By fiscal year 2015, spending per capita had decreased to approximately $5,590, ranking it 33rd among all 50 states and below the U.S. average (Kaiser Family Foundation 2015b). Spending per capita is also now less than all other states in the U.S. west region with the exception of Nevada (NASBO 2016). Examining spending per capita by function (see Table 3 below), Washington spends slightly more per capita on elementary and secondary education compared to other Western states with the exception of California and Alaska. In 2014, Washington ranked 15th in total public elementary and secondary school system expenditures (Census Bureau 2014), but 29th in spending per pupil at $10,202 (Maciag 2016). Per pupil spending in Washington State is higher than California, Oregon, and Nevada. Higher education spending per capita is also considerably higher in Washington compared to other states in the U.S. west, and higher than the national average (although, as noted previously, spending per student is 20 percent below 2008 levels) (Mitchel, Leachman, and Masterson 2016). Of nearby states, only Nevada reduced per student funding more between 2008 and 2016, cutting $3,147 per student (Mitchel, Leachman and Masterson 2016) (see Table 3 below). With current budget obligations, it is unlikely that state funding for higher education will return to pre-2008 levels in the near future. Washington State also spends more on transportation per capita than California and Nevada, but spends less per capita on total public assistance, Medicaid, and corrections with the exception of Nevada.

Table 3: Expenditures by Function Per Capita— Selected State Comparisons*

	Total	Elementary & Secondary Education	Total Public Assistance	Medicaid	Corrections	Medicaid
Washington	$5,590	$1,269	$29	$1,082	$137	$1,082
Oregon	$9,235	$1,106	$36	$2,158	$227	$2,158
Nevada	$4,023	$649	$17	$1,029	$100	$1,029
California	$6,395	$1,350	$255	$2,143	$316	$2,143
All U.S. States	$5,711	$1,122	$79	$1,625	$177	$1,625

*Calculated by dividing total expenditure (NASBO 2016) by 2015 population data (Census Quick Facts 2015).

Washington's mix of policy priorities display both similarities and differences compared to other states (see Table 4). For instance, total education spending (elementary and secondary education, and higher education) was approximately 29.6 percent of total expenditures nationally in fiscal year 2015, while Washington spent 36.4 percent in this category (NASBO 2016). Further, among the western states, Washington's percentages of state expenditures in this area was the highest. Oregon, the most comparable state to Washington in terms of size, geography, and political culture, expended only 13.1 percent of total expenditures in this area. As mentioned, the *McCleary* ruling, which declared K-12 spending in the state inadequate to meet its constitutional obligation, is a considerable constraint on state lawmakers in this regard, and will likely lead to even higher expenditures in this area in the future. While Washington's percentage spent on education was higher than the national average, the state was considerably lower in the percent spent on Medicaid. Washington's Medicaid spending as percentage of total expenditures was 19.4 percent, compared to the national average of 28.2 percent, and ranking third in the west above only Alaska and Hawaii (NASBO 2016). However, Medicaid spending in Washington is heavily reliant on federal funding.

Table 4: Percentage of Total State Expenditures by Function Comparison*

	Education	Public Assistance	Medicaid	Corrections	Transportation	All Other
Washington	36.1%	0.5%	19.4%	2.4%	7.7%	33.6%
Oregon	13.1%	0.4%	23.4%	2.5%	7.5%	53.1%
Nevada	22.9%	0.4%	25.6%	2.5%	5.4%	43.2%
California	28.3%	4.0%	33.5%	4.9%	5.4%	23.9%
All U.S. States	29.6%	1.4%	28.2%	3.1%	7.7%	30.0%

*Data from National Association of Budget Officers (2016, 13).

When examining total spending by funding source, Washington State's percentage of total spending from federal sources is less than most western states with the exception of Oregon (NASBO 2016). However, total spending per capita from federal sources is actually higher in Oregon (see Table 5). Washington's total federal spending per capita is less than other western states, with the exception of Nevada, and the national average. With less than a third of Washington State's percentage of total spending coming from federal sources, and reductions of federal monies to states that might result from changes in federal budget policy after the 2016 presidential election, Washington may be impacted less than its neighboring states. However, Washington has a higher percentage of federal spending in total public assistance than nearby states and higher than the national average, and 67 percent of its spending on Medicaid was from federal money in fiscal year 2015 (NASBO 2016). While Washington's percentage of federal spending on Medicare is less than Nevada and Oregon, it is higher than California and the national average. Thus a repeal of the Affordable Care Act would significantly impact the state's spending in Medicaid, the second largest area of the state budget.

**Table 5: FY 2015 Spending From Federal Funds—
Selected State Comparisons***

	% of Total Spending	Total Per Capita	Elementary & Secondary Education	Medicaid	Public Assistance	Transportation
Washington	28.7%	$1,604	9%	67%	67%	25.0%
Oregon	26.9%	$2,488	15%	77%	62%	1.7%
Nevada	32.6%	$1,312	14%	76%	50%	49.0%
California	36.0%	$2,300	12%	63%	45%	38.0%
All U.S. States	30.7%	$1,769	14%	61%	55%	28.0%

*Calculated by dividing Federal Fund spending (NASBO 2016), by 2015 population data (Census Quick Facts 2015).

Washington and State Policy Innovations

There are no agreed upon metrics in determining what accounts for innovation in public policy, but Washington is nevertheless typically thought of as a policy "innovator." In fact, Bloomberg News ranked Washington third (behind Massachusetts and California) in their 2016 U.S. State Innovation Index (Jamrisko and Lu 2016). Two exemplars of policy innovation in Washington are the Voluntary Stewardship Program and the recent legalization of recreational marijuana use.

Voluntary Stewardship Program

One of the recent policy decisions with budget implications in Washington State was the creation of the Voluntary Stewardship Program (VSP). Established in 2011 by the State Conservation Commission, the program aims at resolving ongoing legal disputes between the environmental community, agriculture stakeholders, and counties over protecting critical environmental areas while maintaining agricultural viability. Of Washington's 39 counties, 28 have opted into the program, and funding for the first two pilot counties, Thurston and Chelan, was provided in the 2013–15 operating budget ($246,000). The remaining 26 counties were subsequently funded in the 2015–17 budget with a $7.6 million allocation (OFM 2013–15).

Intended to resolve years of legal disputes over Washington's Growth Management Act (GMA), the VSP is an incentive-based framework providing opportunities for counties, farmers, environmental groups, and other stakeholders to work collaboratively to develop plans for protecting and enhancing critical areas where agricultural activities are conducted, while maintaining and improving the long-term viability of agriculture (WSCC 2014). Participating counties develop and submit their plans to WSCC for approval, and submit progress reports every five years. However, there is concern that without continued funding for the program, the protection of critical areas where agricultural activities are conducted will revert to protracted legal battles in the state (WSCC 2014).

Legalizing Recreational Marijuana

Another area where Washington is pioneering policy innovations involves legalization of recreational marijuana. In 2012, Washington voters approved ballot initiative 502, which provided for state licensing and regulation of marijuana production, distribution, and possession for people over the age of twenty-one, and removed state criminal and civil penalties for initiative-approved marijuana activities. It also established a new tax from marijuana-related sales. Washington State voters have a history of supporting change in drug law as the legalization of the use of medical marijuana was passed by voters back in 1998. Unlike other states that have legalized recreational marijuana use, Washington's statute provides resources for collecting information on societal impacts, which will allow for ongoing data collection and analysis of the effects of legalization (Benjamin, Chavez, and Lovrich 2016). Under the law, the Washington State Institute for Public Policy (WSIPP) is funded through marijuana production and sales revenue to conduct cost/benefit analyses annually until 2032 using data collected by the Washington State Department of Health, the Office of the Superintendent of Public Schools, the Department of Social and Health Services, the Administrative Office of the Courts, and the Washington State Association of Sheriffs and Police Chiefs.

The initiative created three new excise taxes to generate additional revenue which is specifically dedicated to education, health care, and research. The taxes include a 25 percent tax on sales between licensed producers and processors, a 25 percent tax on sales between licensed processor and retailors, and a 25 percent tax on retail sales. These taxes are generating substantial additional revenue for the state that may help provide funding for other public services such as education and health care. For instance, the state Department of Revenue (2017) estimates a total of $26,708,525 state sales tax collections from December to July 2016. However, it is unclear how subsequent legalization in nearby states such as Oregon and California will impact this revenue source in the future. Additionally, as of early 2017, the Trump administration has sent mixed signals regarding whether the federal government's marijuana enforcement posture will change and whether it will continue to allow states to experiment in this area of policy. These factors will greatly impact any future revenues from Initiative 502 and Washington's policy innovation.

Conclusions

The contemporary policy environment in Washington State is beset by uncertainty. In December 2016, Governor Jay Inslee revealed a plan to increase taxes by $5.5 billion for fiscal years 2017–2019. The two year budget plan would increase state spending by approximately 20 percent, funded by new taxes on carbon pollution ($2.1 billion), service industries ($2.3 billion), capital gains ($821 million), and through the elimination of some tax exemptions ($320 million) (O'Sullivan 2016; O'Sullivan and Brunner 2015). With Republicans holding a narrow majority in the state Senate and the Democrats holding a narrow majority in the House, the budget debate promises to be contentious as the governor and legislature seek a solution to the school funding issue.

The election in November 2016 of President Donald Trump introduces another source of uncertainty. Candidate Trump made altering or eliminating global trade agreements such as the North American Free Trade Agreement (NAFTA) and the Trans Pacific Trade Agreement (TPTT) a center piece of his campaign. The Washington State economy is heavily reliant on trade with Pacific Rim countries (particularly China and Japan) and Mexico. According to the Business Roundtable, international trade accounted for over 900,000 jobs in the state in 2013, which is approximately 25 percent of total state employment. In that same year, exports were responsible for approximately 18 percent of the value of the total state economy. Indeed, only three states (California, Texas, and New York) export more goods than does Washington (Business Roundtable 2015). Fundamental changes in U.S. trade policy could have deep effects on the state economy, and with it, state policy options. Proposed changes in federal immigration policy—making it more difficult to employ both skilled and unskilled labor from other countries—also has the potential of disrupting the large and dynamic agriculture and technology sectors of the state economy.

In many respects, state lawmakers wrestling with such economic and policy uncertainty is nothing new. In 2004, Lance LeLoup and Christina Herzog offered the following assessment regarding policy making in Washington:

> The budget choices facing the state during the coming decade are among the most critical policy decisions that elected officials will face. Those decisions will shape the economic environment of the state, i.e., whether Washington retains an infrastructure that supports economic and population growth. The will determine what kind of education system emerges and what kinds of opportunities for higher education that the state's high school students will find. Budget decisions, such as continuing to rely heavily on sales taxes rather than income taxes, will determine whether the tax system changes or not. These choices will take place in a political context of close partisan division in government, and a healthy dose of citizen mistrust of elected officials (LeLoup and Herzog 2004).

This passage is as true today as it was nearly 15 years ago.

Notes

1. For a discussion of the constitutional mandates involving public school funding under the State Supreme Court's decisions in *McCleary v. State* see Chapter 7.
2. Certainly the threat of *McCleary* ruling has played a major role in this state of affairs.
3. In a report for the American Council on Education, Mortenson (2012) estimates that if current trends continue, Washington State will provide zero funding for higher education by the year 2045.

References

Ballotpedia. 2014. "Washington State Budget and Finances." ballotpedia.org/Washington_state_budget_and_finances.

_____. 2016. "Washington Marijuana Legislation and Regulation, Initiative 502." ballotpedia.org/Washington_Marijuana_Legalization_and_Regulation,_Initiative_502_(2012).

Benjamin, Francis, Maria Chavez, and Nicholas Lovrich. 2016. "2014 Washington State Budget." *California Journal of Politics and Policy* 8(1).

Business Roundtable. 2015. "How Washington's Economy Benefits from International Trade and Investment." tradepartnership.com/wp-content/uploads/2015/01/WA_TRADE_2013.pdf.

Callaham, John. September 17, 2016. "Microsoft confirms 300 more employee layoffs, largely in Redmond, Washington." *Windows Central.* www.windowscentral.com/microsoft-confirms-300-more-employee-layoffs-largely-in-redmond-washington.

CBPP. March 4, 2016. Center on Budget and Policy Priorities. "Policy Basics: Where do our Federal Tax Dollars Go?" www.cbpp.org/research/federal-budget/policy-basics-where-do-our-federal-tax-dollars-go.

Census Bureau. 2014. "Public Education Finances: 2014." Washington, DC: U.S. Government Printing Office, G14-ASPEF. www2.census.gov/govs/school/14f33pub.pdf.

_____. 2016. "QuickFacts: Washington." www.census.gov/quickfacts/table/PST045215/53.

Department of Numbers. 2016. "Washington State Unemployment Rate and Total Unemployed." www.deptofnumbers.com/unemployment/washington.

Ficken, Robert E., and Charles P. LeWarne. 1988. *Washington: A Centennial History.* Seattle: University of Washington Press.

Garand, James C., Justin Ulrich, and Ping Xu. 2014. "Fiscal Policy in the American States." In *The Oxford Handbook of State and Local Government*, edited by Donald P. Haider-Markel. Oxford University Press: Oxford, 611–642.

Gates, Dominic. 2016. "More Boeing Job Cuts Ahead in the New Year." *Seattle Times*, December 19, 2016. www.seattletimes.com/business/boeing-aerospace/boeing-cuts.

Gray, Virginia. 2008. "The Socioeconomic and Political Context of States." In *Politics in the American States*, 9th edition, edited by Virginia Gray and Russel L. Hanson, 1–29. Washington, DC: CQ Press.

Holland, Jenny and Steve Lundin. 2011. "Public Financing and Budgeting in Washington State." In *Governing Washington: Politics and Government in the Evergreen State,* edited by Cornell W. Clayton and Nicholas P. Lovrich, 232–58. Pullman: Washington State University Press.

ITPE. 2015. Institute on Taxation and Economic Policy. "Who Pays: A Distributional Analysis of the Tax Systems in all 50 States Policy," 5th edition. itep.org/whopays.

Jamrisko, Michelle, and Wei Lu. 2016. "Here are the Most Innovative States in America in 2016." Bloomberg.com, December 22, 2016. www.bloomberg.com/news/articles/2016-12-22/here-are-the-most-innovative-states-in-america-in-2016.

Kaiser Family Foundation. 2015a. "Federal and State Share of Medicaid Spending." kff.org/medicaid/state-indicator/federalstate-share-of-spending/?currentTimeframe=0.

————. 2015b. "Total State Expenditures per Capital." kff.org/other/state-indicator/per-capita-state-spending.

Leachman, Michael, Kathleen Masterson, and Marlana Wallace. 2016. "After Nearly a Decade, School Investments Still Way Down in Some States." Center on Budget and Policy Priorities, October 20, 201. www.cbpp.org/research/state-budget-and-tax/after-nearly-a-decade-school-investments-still-way-down-in-some-states.

LeLoup, Lance T., and Christina Herzog. 2004. "Budgeting and Public Finance in Washington." In *Washington State Government and Politics*, edited by Cornell W. Clayton, Lance T. LeLoup, and Nicholas P. Lovrich, 189–207. Pullman: Washington State University Press.

Lowry, Robert C. 2014. "The Context of State Policy Policymaking." In *The Oxford Handbook of State and Local Government*, edited by Donald P. Haider-Markel. Oxford: Oxford University Press, 534–560.

Long, K. 2015. "'Historic' tuition cut sets state apart from rest of U.S." *Seattle Times*, June 30, 2015. www.seattletimes.com/seattle-news/education/historic-tuition-cut-sets-state-apart-from-rest-of-us.

Lueck, Dean and Jonathan Yoder. 2016. *Clearing the Smoke from Wildfire Policy: An Economic Perspective*. Bozeman: PERC Policy Series.

Maciag, Mike. August 2016. "The States that Spend the Most (and the Least on Education)." *Governing*. www.governing.com/topics/education/gov-education-funding-states.html.

Medicaid.gov. 2016. "Medicaid & CHIP in Washington." www.medicaid.gov/medicaid/by-state/stateprofile.html?state=washington.

Mitchel, Michael, Michael Leachman, and Kathleen Masterson. 2016. "Funding Down, Tuition Up." Center on Budget and Policy Priorities, August 15, 2016. www.cbpp.org/research/state-budget-and-tax/funding-down-tuition-up.

Mortenson, Thomas G. 2012. "State Funding: A Race to the Bottom." American Council on Education. www.acenet.edu/the-presidency/columns-and-features/Pages/state-funding-a-race-to-the-bottom.aspx

NASBO. 2016. "State Expenditure Report." National Association of State Budget Officers. www.nasbo.org/mainsite/reports-data/state-expenditure-report.

Nicholas, Andrew. 2013. "Washington State's 1930's Tax System Doesn't Work in a 21st Century Economy." Washington State Center for Budget and Policy. budgetandpolicy.org/reports/washington-state2019s-1930s-tax-system-doesn2019t-work-in-a-21st-century-economy.

North, Douglas C. 1990. *Institutions: Institutional Change and Economic Performance.* New York: Cambridge University Press.

O'Sullivan, Joseph. 2016. "McCleary Fix? Inslee Proposes Billions in New Taxes to Pay Teacher." *Seattle Times*, December 16, 2016. www.seattletimes.com/seattle-news/politics/gov-jay-inslee-to-announce-k-12-school-funding-plan.

O'Sullivan, Joseph, and J. Brunner, 2015. "School funding back on table as court fines state $100,000 a day." *Seattle Times*, August 13, 2015. www.seattletimes.com/seattle-news/education/supreme-court-orders-100000-per-day-fines-in-mccleary-case.

OFM. 2013–15. Office of Financial Management. "2013–15 Enacted Budgets." www.ofm.wa.gov/budget/legbudgets/1315biennial.asp.

_____. 2014a. Office of Financial Management. 2014. "State & Local Revenue Sources." www.ofm.wa.gov/trends/revenue/fig503.asp.

_____. 2014b. Office of Financial Management. "State and Local Government Revenues Per Capita, Washington State." www.ofm.wa.gov/trends/revenue/fig501.asp.

_____. 2016a. Office of Financial Management. "Total Population and Percent Change." www.ofm.wa.gov/trends/population/fig301.asp.

_____. 2016b. Office of Financial Management. "Population Change: Natural Increase and Net Migration." www.ofm.wa.gov/trends/population/fig302.asp.

_____. 2016c. Office of Financial Management. "Kindergarten through Grade 12 (K-12) Enrollment." www.ofm.wa.gov/trends/budget/fig402.asp.

_____. 2016d. Office of Financial Management. "Medical Assistance Caseload." www.ofm.wa.gov/trends/budget/fig407.asp.

_____. 2016e. Office of Financial Management. "Projected Change in Budget Driver Populations." www.ofm.wa.gov/trends/budget/fig410.asp.

_____. 2016f. Office of Financial Management. "State-Supported Nursing Home Caseload." www.ofm.wa.gov/trends/budget/fig406.asp.

Pew Charitable Trusts. September 21, 2015. "Federal Spending Decisions Affect State Budgets." www.pewtrusts.org/en/research-and-analysis/fact-sheets/2015/09/federal-spending-decisions-affect-state-budgets.

Sauter, M., Evan Comen, and Samuel Stebbins. 2016. *The Fastest Growing (and Shrinking) States.* 24/7 Wall St., January 22, 2016. 247wallst.com/special-report/2016/01/22/the-fastest-growing-and-shrinking-states.

Senate Ways and Means Committee. 2016. "A Citizen's Guide to the Washington State Budget." www.leg.wa.gov/Senate/Committees/WM/Pages/defalut.aspx.

Stehr, Steven D., and Steven J. Ellwanger. 2004. "The Executive Branch in Washington State Government." In *Washington State Government and Politics*. Pullman, WA: Washington State University Press.

Stehr, Steven D., and Gaffney, Michael J. 2011. "The Executive Branch in Washington State Government." In *Governing Washington: Politics and Government in the Evergreen State*, edited by Cornell W. Clayton and Nicholas P. Lovrich. Pullman, WA: Washington State University Press.

Torres, Blanca. 2016. "Washington State Ranks No. 1 for Combined Job and Wage Growth." *Seattle Times*, February 15, 2016. www.seattletimes.com/business/economy/employment-and-wage-growth-in-washington-outpacing-other-states.

Washington State Department of Ecology. 2006. *2006 Economic Impacts Report*. www.ecy.wa.gov/climatechange/economic_impacts2006.htm

Washington State Department of Natural Resources. 2015. *EM Wildfire Summary*. Olympia: Washington State Department of Natural Resources.

Washington State Department of Revenue. 2017. *Recreational Marijuana Taxes*. dor. dor.wa.gov/about/statistics-reports/recreational-and-medical-marijuana-taxes.

Washington State Employment Security Department. July 2015. "2015 Employment Projections." https://fortress.wa.gov/esd/employmentdata/docs/industry-reports/employment-projections-2015.pdf.

WSCC. 2014. Washington State Conservation Commission. "Voluntary Stewardship Program." scc.wa.gov/wp-content/uploads/2014/03/VSP_FINAL.pdf.

WSERFC. 2016. Washington State Economic Research and Forecasting Council. "Final November 2016 Economic Forecast." erfc.wa.gov/sites/default/files/files/public/documents/forecasts/p1116.pdf.

CHAPTER 12

Environmental and Natural Resource Policy in the Evergreen State

Edward P. Weber and Ellen Rogers

The Pacific Northwest has been known historically as a region blessed with an abundance of natural resources—millions of acres of evergreen forests, tens of millions of salmon and steelhead in its rivers, pristine waters, and diverse flora and fauna. However, the region's natural resource and species abundance, pristine waters, and healthy ecosystems encountered severe challenges in the twentieth century. Massive population growth, large scale industrialization, damming of most major rivers, and a series of public policies designed to encourage the "efficient" exploitation of natural resources in support of human settlement and economic growth decimated native species and forests alike, while also over-allocating many streamflows and harming water quality. The widespread damage done to nature in the Northwest and across the entire United States spurred a backlash, a reaction made manifest in the emergence of a national environmental movement starting in the mid-1960s that successfully pushed for federal and state pollution control and natural resource protection laws.

The State of Washington was front and center in the environmental movement, rapidly earning a label as a leader among the 50 states in adopting policies to protect nature and humans from harm. From its initial willingness in the 1960s and 1970s to create and empower extensive new institutional capacity and to adopt a broad array of programmatic initiatives, to its ongoing political and financial support for environmental policy, Washington justifiably has earned a reputation as a national leader in environmental affairs. As such, the state was much better prepared than most for the shift toward environmental federalism starting with President Reagan, with its concomitant devolution of considerable policy authority to the states and the added demands it places on the building of state capacity (Lester 1994; Weber and Lysak 2004).

In the intervening decades Washington State has maintained its environmental policy leadership role, passing significant and innovative new legislation in areas such as watershed planning (1998), urban growth management (1990), salmon recovery (1998), forests and fish protection law (1999), clean "renewable" energy (2006), and electric fleet vehicles (2015), among others (Weber and Lysak 2004; ACEEE 2016).

It is important to note that the policies adopted to protect the environment embraced by policymakers over the course of the past 25 years look much different from the policies favored in the 1960s and 1970s. Traditional top-down, government-goes-it-alone, coercive, command-and-control approaches to environmental policy are not the dominant storyline in Washington, nor elsewhere across the country. In what some have called the "next generation" of environmental policy, the emphasis now is placed on developing institutional capacity grounded in devolution, collaboration, citizen participation, and area-based (e.g., watersheds), comprehensive, integrated approaches to public problems (Fiorino 2006; Weber 2000). The overall message coming from policymakers is also changing. Instead of "save the environment at all costs," it is more often a positive sum environment and economy message that seeks to promote ecological health *and* traditional economic livelihoods, while also building sustainable communities for the future (Sustainable Northwest 2016).

Moreover, the character of policies has been increasingly affected by the growing political pressure to incorporate the challenges of expected climate changes into a broad array of public policies in the state. Few were talking about the need for a "green" economy reliant on renewable energy, energy efficient technologies, "green" buildings, and so on a decade ago. And only a handful of elites within the world of forestry management and policy formation were overly concerned with the new challenges and threats to forests, species, and human health posed by global climate change. Further, while more attention has been paid to policies reducing carbon consumption, the recent successes of California, British Columbia, and a few other states in implementing carbon emissions trading markets has prompted state leaders to promote similar, albeit thus far unsuccessful, legislation and citizen initiatives in 2015 and again in 2016.

This chapter explores the environmental policy dynamic in Washington through a series of illustrative, and innovative, new state-based efforts initiated to promote renewable energy and build a "green" economy, and respond to the challenges of climate change for forest management. We chronicle the political struggles which have arisen in recent years to pass and codify legislation, and discuss citizens' initiatives targeting carbon emission reductions using carbon taxes and market-based "cap and trade" programs. The examples discussed show how Washington policymakers are either maintaining their leadership, or in the case of the thus far failed carbon reduction initiatives, seeking to maintain their leadership role in the area of environmental policy.

Promoting a Green State and Economy

State governments are uniquely positioned to advance environmental and energy policies and programs that impact many sectors of society, including private manufacturers (e.g., cars, phones, etc.), utilities (energy producers), transportation and construction businesses, and government agencies. They can also shape the individual choices of citizens in the areas of transportation, energy (e.g., lighting, appliances, vehicles), water, and waste, among many others by the adoption of a combination of taxation and exemption policies that incentivize choices that promote sustainability (Simon, Steel and Lovrich 2010).

As noted, Washington State has long enjoyed a leadership role among the states when it comes to policies promoting a green state and economy. Wingfield and Marcus (2007) measured the "greenest" states according to six equally-weighted categories: carbon footprint, air quality, water quality, hazardous waste management, policy initiatives, and energy consumption. The top three states on their measure were Vermont, Oregon, and Washington. All have low carbon dioxide emissions per capita, strong policies to promote energy efficiency, and high air quality as indicated by their major metro areas that are low in smog and ozone pollution. They also are among the states with the most buildings (on a per capita basis) awarded the U.S. Green Building Council's benchmark LEED certification, for Leadership in Energy and Environmental Design. The American Council for an Energy Efficient Economy ranked states in 2016 on a variety of measures. Washington tied for first place with a perfect 7 out of 7 score for "green" buildings (ACEEE 2016).

Washington also is one of only nine U.S. states wherein over 90 percent of its energy production is sourced from renewable fuels. With 92.25 percent of its energy coming from renewable sources, the state provides 10.96 percent of the U.S. total. The state's energy mix is comprised of 80 percent hydropower, 9 percent biomass, and 3.25 percent wind, with negligible contributions from geothermal and solar to date, and only one coal-fired power plant located in Centralia (Energy Information Agency 2016).

In addition, Washington ranks quite high as an energy efficient economy according to the annual ranking of states on their energy policies and program efforts by the American Council for an Energy Efficient Economy. Ranked in 8th place in the 2016 rankings, Washington has never ranked lower than 10th since these annual rankings started in 2006. A key strength for Washington in 2016 was the set of significant incentives offered by the state for energy efficiency investments. In this case, the state government leads by example by requiring energy-efficient public buildings and vehicle fleets, benchmarking energy use, and encouraging the broad use of energy savings performance contracts. Washington is one of the few states to require commercial building energy use disclosure. In addition, research focused on energy-efficiency is conducted at the state's Smart Buildings Center and at WSU's Energy Program (U.S. DOE 2016). Specific policies include:

- Efficiency Grants for Higher Education and Local Governments: Program provides $38 million in funding for energy efficiency improvements.
- Energy Revolving Loan Fund Grants: Approximately $15 million was awarded to Craft3 (commercial and residential) and Puget Sound Cooperative Credit Union (residential). Projects included residential and commercial energy retrofits, residential- and commercial-scale solar installations, anaerobic digesters to treat dairy and organic waste, and combined heat and power projects using woody biomass as a fuel source.
- Community Energy Efficiency Program (CEEP): Community-based program that funds pilot projects for community-wide urban residential and commercial energy efficiency retrofits and upgrades estimated to produce $1.7 million annual energy cost savings (U.S. DOE 2016).

The most recent ranking of the "greenest" states, from spring 2016, finds Washington maintaining its leadership role. Based on 17 relevant metrics across three categories—environmental quality, eco-friendly behaviors, and climate-change contributions—Washington ranks second with clear strengths in environmental quality (third overall) and eco-friendly behaviors (third) (Table 1). However, and as the case study outlining the state's efforts on behalf of carbon taxes and emissions trading policies will demonstrate, Washington struggles more with its climate-change contributions, ranking in the middle of the pack in 24th place (Kiernan 2016).

Table 1. Top Ten Greenest State Scores, 2016 (Kiernan 2016)

Overall Rank	State	Total Score	'Environmental Quality' Rank	'Eco-Friendly Behaviors' Rank	'Climate-Change Contributions' Rank
1	Vermont	78.67	2	2	10
2	Washington	74.88	3	3	24
3	Massachusetts	73.28	6	10	7
4	Oregon	72.77	9	1	28
5	Minnesota	70.93	1	12	30
6	Maine	70.40	13	5	9
7	Connecticut	70.02	5	23	2
8	New York	69.34	16	8	8
9	New Hampshire	68.67	30	7	3
10	New Jersey	68.42	26	9	5

Climate Change, Forest Fires, and Forest Resilience

Washington has some of the nation's largest, most majestic forests, with 22 million acres overall split between 12.6 million acres owned by state, federal, and local entities, and 9.4 million acres belonging to large industrial private timber companies, tribes, and small family forestland owners (Washington Department of National Resources 2007). In 2014, sadly, an estimated 387,000 acres of forest fires burned in Washington, including the devastating Carlton Complex fire involving a record 256,000 acres. The 2014 "acres burned" figure was twice the annual average over the period 2005 to 2014, and was considered by many to be the worst wildfire season on record (National Forest Protection Association 2015). *Then came 2015.* The 2015 forest fire season in the states of Oregon and Washington was the most severe in modern history in terms of both the total number of fires, which reached 3,800 (almost 2,300 in Oregon and more than 1,500 in Washington), and the 1,730,000 acres burned (Gabbert 2016). The fires also created human health hazards for persons with respiratory diseases because they led to dozens of exceedance events (i.e., unhealthy to hazardous readings) with respect to the EPA's Clean Air Act-based Air Quality Index for small particulate matter (PM-2) in population centers in central Washington (e.g., Omak, Twisp), as well as violations to the east and south (e.g., Clarkston, Colville, Pullman). In addition, forest fires contribute to greenhouse gas emissions associated with climate change. For example, in 2006 Washington's forest fire greenhouse gas emissions exceeded the total annual emissions from the state's electric power system (Mason et al. 2009).

Washington's catastrophic 2015 season of fire was part of over 10 million acres burned across the United States, the most acreage burned since reliable records began to be assembled in 1960. The size and severity of these fires are part of a recent national trend of more frequent, larger, and often rather catastrophic fire events, with years 2006 (9.9M acres), 2007 (9.3M acres), and 2012 (9.3M acres) recording the 2nd, 3rd, and 4th highest totals since 1960, according to the National Interagency Fire Center (Gabbert 2016).

For many climate change scientists, the accelerating loss of forests to fire is not surprising. The first six months of 2015 were the warmest of any year across much of Oregon and Washington since temperature record keeping began in 1895. These record-warm temperatures, coupled with below-average precipitation, led to very poor snowpack, which is important because it insulates and moistens the landscape. The warmer, dryer climate also contributes to an increase in the prevalence of forest pests (e.g., pine beetle) and diseases that drain moisture from trees and ultimately kill them. Moreover, the expectation for the future is that the general trend of warmer temperatures, a dryer climate, and changing precipitation patterns (more rain, less snow) throughout the Pacific Northwest will create wildfire-prone forest conditions.

A dryer, hotter climate is not the only factor contributing to the increasing potential for wildfire; some public policies and changing forest management practices are often creating massive increases in forests' fuel loads. As Franklin and Agee (2003) note: "A substantial amount of scientific evidence indicates that, in many North American forests, accumulations of fuels have reached levels far exceeding those found under 'natural' or pre-European settlement conditions." In the first case, the growth in two primary fuel sources, forest understories— the highly flammable brush, grass, and saplings growing between the forest canopy and the forest floor—and downed and dead woody debris, is directly associated with the widespread application over the past 70 years of fire suppression policies on both state and federal public forests by the U.S. Forest Service (USFS) and state agencies. Perhaps best known through the USFS's Smokey the Bear campaigns starting in 1944, which emphasized how "only you can prevent forest fires," forestry management has long treated fire as an evil, one that needs to be stopped at all costs. The regular occurrence of fires, however, is a natural phenomenon that historically served, among other things, as a way to clear forests of the potentially dangerous fuel buildups that are the feedstock of the catastrophic-scale fires that have become the virtual norm in recent fire seasons. Over the past 50 years, despite "some deviations from [fire suppression] policies, chiefly the adoption of natural fire and prescribed burning programs, particularly in national parks and wilderness areas… aggressive suppression policies have continued to dominate" (Franklin and Agee 2003).

In addition, little timber is now cut in both state and national forests in the region. Environmental advocates have successfully used the federal National Environmental Policy Act (NEPA) of 1970 and the Endangered Species Act of 1973 to slow and even stop timber harvests, including salvage logging projects designed to remove "non-green" trees as a method for gaining some economic value from said trees while also reducing the fuel load of dead woody debris. The state also enacted the Forests and Fish Rule in 2001, creating stream buffers to protect riparian zones and threatened fish (e.g., salmon, steelhead), effectively removing from production approximately 10 percent of Washington's timberland. Finally, the state Department of Natural Resources (DNR) negotiated the Forest Practices Habitat Conservation Plan (FPHCP) in 2005 with the U.S. Fish and Wildlife Service and the U.S. National Oceanic and Atmospheric Administration, National Marine Fisheries Service (NOAA Fisheries) designed to protect five different species of endangered or threatened fish. The plan covers 9.3 million acres of forestland in Washington, with 6.1 million acres west of the Cascades and 3.2 million acres in eastern Washington, with roughly 20 percent of this area set aside as ecologically sensitive and off limits to logging.

The end result has been an enormous decline in timber production from pre-1990 levels (see Table 2). The largest declines have come on federal forestlands, which have seen a 97 percent decrease in western Washington forests and an 85 percent decline in eastern Washington. State forests have experienced a 41 percent decline in timber production in western Washington and a 34 percent decrease east of the Cascades (Washington DNR 2007, 22). The point here is not to disparage policies offering additional protection to ecosystems and species in need, but rather it is to describe the manner in which Washington's public forests have accumulated the kinds of fuel loads that factor into more frequent and more intense forest fires.

Table 2. Change in Washington State Timber Harvests, Pre-1990 (1986–89) to 1998–2002 Years

	Pre-1990	1998–2002	Percentage Change
Western Washington			
Federal forests	906 MBF	31 MBF	- 97 %
State forests	826 MBF	487 MBF	- 41 %
Private & Tribal	3,836 MBF	2,518 MBF	- 34 %
Eastern Washington			
Federal forests	431 MBF	133 MBF	- 85 %
State forests	122 MBF	81 MBF	- 34 %
Private & Tribal	751 MBF	782 MBF	+ 4 %

MBF=1,000 board-feet. The American Council for an Energy Efficient Economy ranked states in 2016 on a variety of measures. Washington tied for first place with a perfect 7 out of 7 score for "green" buildings (ACEEE 2016).

Given the condition of Washington's public forests, what can be done and what have Washington policymakers done to try to manage the situation, especially in the face of climate change? To date, there have been two important innovative policy responses. One response is focused on turning the overabundance in forest fuel loads and excess biomass waste from timber removal processes into renewable heat, energy, and liquid biofuels. The other response is legislation passed in 2016 to promote forest resiliency through the use of prescribed fire.

Biomass as a Source of Renewable Energy.

As noted, Washington is already almost 100 percent dependent on traditional renewable energy sources—hydropower, wind, solar—for its electricity generating capacity. Therefore, "changes in electricity generation have comparatively limited potential to reduce greenhouse emissions" (Mason et al. 2009, ii). Biomass from forests, however, can not only increase supplies of renewable energy for heating, power, and liquid fuel purposes and provide reductions in greenhouse gases, it can simultaneously reduce the fuel loads associated with catastrophic forest fires. In an advisory report prepared for the Washington legislature, University of Washington scientists highlighted the demonstrable facts that "the forest industry represents the State's largest biomass collection system" and that "thinning forests to avoid CO_2 emissions from catastrophic wildfires while providing wood resources for green building materials and renewable biofuels will deliver greenhouse gas emission reduction benefits while sustaining forest ecosystems" (Mason et al. 2009, ii).

Pressed hard by Peter Goldmark, Commissioner of Public Lands, state legislators passed House Bill 2165, the Biomass Initiative, in 2009 (Washington DNR 2009). Starting with several pilot projects, the program has grown into an annual program which allots 5-year contracts to successful bidders and is spread across more than a dozen counties. Within the first two years, $539 million was invested in biomass plants, jobs, and production resulting in 373.3 megawatts of energy capacity, with expectations that this capacity will expand exponentially in the next decade (Northwest Energy Coalition 2012).

Project activities conducted under the auspices of the Biomass Initiative include:

- Co-producing electricity, bio-oil, and "syngas" at one integrated facility using pyrolysis technology.
- Heating systems for public facilities, including public schools.
- Mobile production of bio-oil and bio-char using "fast pyrolysis" technology.
- Pellet or "bio-brick" production for heating applications.

- Combined heat and power systems for existing forest products manufacturing facilities.
- Production of electricity for sale to utilities with renewable energy requirements.

The aviation biofuels project likewise is noteworthy. In 2011, the University of Washington and Washington State University (WSU) partnered with private companies and five other universities to secure a five-year, $80 million research grant from the U.S. Department of Agriculture to develop aviation biofuels from both newly planted poplar forests and residue wood, including wood typically burned after timber harvests and removed during thinning to improve forest health. With an emphasis on commercialization, sustainability, and renewable energy jobs, this work is designed to ensure that biorefineries and their feedstock are considered as integrated renewable systems (Hines 2011). Toward these ends, the project will construct and operate five commercial bio-refineries, cultivate over 500,000 acres of poplars, and result in 1,500 jobs created in rural areas of the state. As Dr. John Gardner, then WSU Vice President of Advancement, noted:

> We see this as a move in the right direction, aligning Washington's public and private sector that are emerging world leaders in this new sector.... [We] stand ready to provide the critical research and development, as well as bring our broad network together [that is] already working on sustainable, next generation biofuels (Timber West 2009).

Whatever the project, the program requires that forest biomass is burned in an advanced technology "controlled" boiler, a method releasing far less air pollution than burning the same amount in a home wood stove or fireplace, and generating less greenhouse gas and small particulate matter than wildfires or the burning of forest slash (waste) on the ground (Mason et al. 2009). The biomass sales do not include any wood from "old growth" forests. Another critical feature of the biomass law is that it contains an offset, or sequestration capacity, a provision wherein the Legislature recognized that standing trees can and do absorb CO_2, thus offsetting the carbon emissions produced by the biomass boilers.

Prescribed Burning for Resilient Forests

In 2015, Jerry Franklin, a nationally prominent forest scientist at the University of Washington, argued that "it's very clear that our current policies aren't working. We need to change our policies to recognize the use of more prescribed and natural fire to deal with the conditions we're seeing in our forests today as well as to greatly accelerate restoration of more resilient conditions in accessible forests that have been dramatically altered over the past century" (Ma 2015). As for Washington, the Washington Prescribed Fire Council (2016) finds conditions deteriorating due to "unhealthy forests [and] unfightable fires" and the organization lobbies for more prescribed fire. Prescribed fire regimes employ planned, low intensity, controlled fires in order to relieve the unhealthy stress to trees arising from overcrowded, dense stands, maintain fire-dependent species, and reduce flammable, hazardous fuel buildup. In addition, "the right fire at the right place at the right time":
- Reduces hazardous fuels, protecting human communities from extreme fires;
- Minimizes the spread of pest insects and disease;
- Removes unwanted species that threaten species native to an ecosystem;
- Provides forage for game;
- Improves habitat for threatened and endangered species;
- Recycles nutrients back to the soil; and
- Promotes the growth of trees, wildflowers, and other plants (U.S. Forest Service 2016).

Combined with strategic timber management and thinning, prescribed burns can make forests and neighboring communities more resilient to wildfire, and help protect clean water, wildlife habitat, and timber.

In response to these challenges and opportunities, the Washington State Legislature passed House Bill 2928, the Forest Resiliency Burning Act, in 2016. Washington's new prescribed burning law provides several million dollars of funding and the legal authority to:
- Identify priority areas and safely complete controlled burns;
- Inform the public in advance of planned burns as to their purpose and projected effects;

- Monitor smoke forecasts and actual smoke results created by prescribed burns in order to develop recommendations for updating the state's existing DNR Smoke Management Plan;
- Analyze and monitor fuel reductions and conditions of the forest stands before and after prescribed burns;
- Track outcomes and make recommendations for future prescribed burns to achieve more resilient forest conditions and reduce wildfire risks to communities across the state.
  (Washington Prescribed Fire Council 2016)

The law places the responsibility for executing and monitoring the Forest Resilience projects with three regional forest "collaboratives"— the Tapash Sustainable Forest Collaborative (south central), the North Central Washington Forest Health Collaborative, the Northeast Washington Forestry Coalition—and the Washington Prescribed Fire Council, a statewide organization. In the first stage of the resiliency projects, fifteen sites covering almost 10,000 acres were subjected to controlled burns in the fall of 2016.

Finally, given that the smoke from prescribed fires necessarily affects air quality standards protected under the federal Clean Air Act (CAA), particularly for small particulate matter, otherwise known as PM-2, any such policy must be sensitive to the potential for human health problems in the immediate area. Therefore, the Washington State policy, to the greatest extent possible, plans prescribed fires for days and nights when winds and weather will push smoke away from populated areas. The air quality issue is also the reason why the biomass policy required the installation of nine new air quality monitors to supplement Washington's existing statewide system of air quality monitoring operated by the Washington Department of Ecology; state officials want to be sure that the policy's controlled burns are not causing too many avoidable CAA violations (Washington Smoke 2016).

Struggling to Lead on Climate and Carbon Emissions

When Democrat Jay Inslee campaigned for Washington State Governor in 2012, climate change was a primary focus. As a result, he was hailed by environmentalists as a "Climate Hero" and a "Climate Hawk" (Schiffman 2012). Upon election he was appointed to President Obama's Task Force on Climate Preparedness and Resilience (Smith 2013).

Governor Inslee inherited a state that had taken numerous early policy steps in the battle against climate change. In 2006, voters passed Initiative 937, which imposed standards for energy efficiency and set strict renewable energy targets for utilities (Sims 2013). In 2007, Democratic Governor Christine Gregoire imposed carbon reduction goals for the state through the "Climate Change Challenge" Executive Order (Roberts 2016), and under her firm guidance Washington worked collaboratively to craft a strategy for climate change via the Climate Action Team process (Manning and Wilkerson 2008). However, towards the end of Governor Gregoire's term, her climate change agenda met increasingly stiff resistance and faltered despite having sizable Democratic Party majorities in both houses of the legislature. In the 2008–2010 biennium, the legislature failed to pass the carbon reduction programs needed to meet the goals of the 2007 Climate Change Challenge policy (Roberts 2016). In 2011, Governor Gregoire herself pushed for and successfully passed the Coal Transition Energy Bill, a statute which essentially deferred the process of entirely removing coal-fired electric power from Washington's statewide energy portfolio (Washington State Legislature 2011).

Enter Governor Inslee. Immediately upon taking office in 2013, Governor Inslee encountered a fair amount of collaborative success on his climate change agenda, although mostly through executive agreements with other states and countries rather than by legislative enactments. For example, Inslee joined forces with the United Kingdom to work cooperatively to combat climate change on their two continents (Smith 2014). He also signed onto the Pacific Coast Action Plan on Climate and Energy along with California, Oregon, and British Columbia (Postman 2013). Inslee had some success working with the Washington legislature. In March 2013 the legislature passed his Climate Action Bill (SB 5802), which established the Climate Legislative and Executive Work (CLEW) Group to make recommendations for meeting Washington State greenhouse gas reduction goals (Pearl and Elenbas 2013).

In his second year, Inslee decided to push a more comprehensive climate change agenda through the legislature. In April of 2014 he issued an executive order outlining his policy agenda to reduce carbon emissions (pollution) in Washington State. These preferences included using market mechanisms to reduce carbon use, reducing dependence on coal-fired electricity, expanding clean technology and transportation, and increasing energy efficiency in state-owned buildings (Inslee 2014a). He followed up his executive order the next year by presenting the legislature with a specific agenda to combat climate change, headlined by the Carbon Pollution Accountability Act (Postman 2014). This act was designed to enable Washington to meet the carbon reduction goals from 2008 (25 percent reduction by 2035, and 50 percent by 2050 of 1990 levels) using a market-based "cap and trade" system, which involved the sale and exchange of carbon emission "allowances" between various polluting entities. Over time the "cap" on emissions would be reduced, and with them the available allowances, allowing the state to reach the specified limits. Much like a similar "cap and trade" program adopted in California, the revenues from the sale of "allowances" would be collected by the Washington government, and the proceeds would be reinvested into further carbon, and other greenhouse gas, reduction projects (Inslee 2014b). Governor Inslee's bill was met with immediate skepticism from legislators in both political parties, primarily due to concerns with the complexity and uncertainty involved in estimating statewide emissions (*Woodinville Weekly* Staff 2015). These concerns ultimately led to its failure in both legislative chambers (Washington State Legislature 2015).

In the 2016 legislative session, the relationship between Governor Inslee and the legislature continued to sour on the issue of climate change, in large part because the Republicans now controlled the state Senate and the Democratic majority in the House had dwindled from a 55–43 vote advantage to 51–47. In addition, geographic "bifurcation" is visible in both houses, with the Seattle and west side of the state remaining Democratic while the rest of the state is becoming majority Republican. Oppositional legislators inserted a poison pill into the Washington Department of Transportation department's budget that tied Inslee's hands in terms of implementing low carbon fuel standards (LCFS). The budget bill specified that if any legislation or executive order was passed related to LCFS, all of the alternative, or non-auto transportation projects (light rail, bike lanes, etc.) would lose funding (Camden 2015; Deshais 2015).

The new legislative environment forced Inslee to take a regulatory and administrative approach to climate change dubbed "cap and reduce." The new Clean Air Rule (CAR) developed by the Department of Ecology would allow emitters (initially only 24 organizations in the state) to either gradually reduce their emissions and/or buy into carbon reduction programs over time (Le 2016). The CAR was adopted in September 2016 to go into effect in October 2017.

The limited progress on climate change initiatives by Washington's elected officials frustrated many. In response, an independent grassroots group, Carbon Washington, formed in order to push a ballot initiative, I-732, in the November 2016 election that would have been the U.S.'s first state-level carbon tax. Based on the carbon tax model enacted in British Columbia in 2008, which has been largely successful (Ip 2016; Roberts 2016), I-732 was touted as a revenue-neutral way to gradually reduce the state's reliance on fossil fuels by taxing carbon emissions. The initiative was designed to tax all carbon emissions initially at $15/ton of carbon dioxide, with the tax rising over time and hopefully reducing demand for carbon-based goods even further. A 1 percent state sales tax decrement would offset the increases in the cost of carbon-based goods for consumers. I-732 also promised a tax rebate to 460,000 low income workers (Roberts 2016; Hsu, Schwedel, and Meng 2016). The underlying logic was that the combination of carbon tax increments and sales tax decrements and rebates would make the overall effect "revenue neutral" and increase its appeal to a broad coalition of groups, including conservatives who typically oppose climate change initiatives as well as environmentalists and Democrats who would traditionally support such measures (Roberts 2016; Hsu, Schwedel, and Meng 2016).

In the end, Washington voters rejected I-732 59 percent to 41 percent. Only in King County, the area encompassing Seattle, did voters narrowly approve the initiative with a 51.4 percent "yes" vote (*New York Times* 2016). The hoped-for broad-based coalition never fully materialized for a number of reasons. First, I-732 was dealt an early blow when the Washington State Department of Revenue found the package to be revenue negative in its impact on government (Harvey 2016; Roberts 2016). Second, Carbon Washington was criticized by many as being "too grassroots" and lacked the political party backing and necessary connections the high-level state power brokers required to succeed. The I-732 architects structured the initiative without consulting either powerful environmental groups or the Alliance for Jobs and Clean Energy, a key group representing communities of color and low income interests. As a result, and even though the alliance was on the record in favor of "cap and trade" in the past, the alliance did not support I-732 (Roberts 2016; Hsu, Schwedel, and Meng 2016). Third, environmental advocacy groups in recent years have tended to throw their support behind revenue *positive* cap and trade policies that allow revenue from emission "allowance" sales to go directly to government, which then gives them greater control, and the ability to spend the new tax revenues on a "clean energy economy." Fourth, some Republicans and conservatives opposed the carbon tax given their general philosophical opposition to new taxes (Ip 2016). Finally, many energy-intensive businesses and manufacturers would have been heavily hit by the tax, and therefore they openly opposed it (Coombs 2016).

The question that remains, given the political balance of power in Washington into the near future, is whether environmentalists and other liberal progressives, in their opposition to I-732, have made the "classic progressive mistake: waiting for the ideal policy instead of taking the small steps that can be transformative over time" (Johnson 2016). In any case, and unlike in so many other environmental policy areas, Washington has struggled to lead on carbon emissions policy.

Conclusion

Over the past two decades and more Washington has adopted a number of innovative programs for managing the state's environmental problems. The governor, senior legislators, organized interests, and ordinary citizens have all repeatedly pressed for new policies in response to the challenges of a warming earth and expected global climate changes. In fact, as this chapter has made clear, the primary environmental policymaking dynamic in Washington State now, and most likely over the next few decades, is and will be focused heavily on the challenges associated with climate change. Whether it is speeding the transition from carbon-heavy fossil fuels to a "greener" energy economy, effectively managing all the critical aspects of the state's massive forest resources, adjusting to rising sea levels, or seeking to more effectively tackle and implement public policies to reduce greenhouse gas emissions such as carbon dioxide and reactive nitrogen, Washington is in the forefront of research and public policy development. Interestingly, while Washington State has for many decades been a proven leader among the 50 states in passing and implementing cutting edge approaches to environmental and natural resource problems, its recent struggles in the area of carbon cap and trade programs and carbon taxes threaten to tarnish this well-earned reputation.

Yet, Washington is not alone in these struggles. Most U.S. states and the federal government as well have struggled to make significant headway in the battle against global climate change. It may be because the overall scope, complexity, and abstractness (i.e., it is hard to "see" climate change) of the climate change puzzle militates strongly against stronger, more comprehensive policies precisely because the economic and convenience costs of action over time will be direct, extremely large, widespread, often immediate, and quite tangible. This mix of consequences necessarily increases the political difficulty of building lasting majority coalitions in favor of stronger climate change policies. The challenge of successful coalition building is made all the more difficult by the fact that the promised benefits of action will occur at some point in the rather distant future, all of which are accompanied by varying degrees of uncertainty. Just as importantly, and also closely mimicking the larger stage of U.S. national politics, the political balance of power in Washington State is fairly evenly divided between Democrats and Republicans, with an edge to Democrats. In a democracy with separate institutions—legislature, courts, executive branch—sharing power, and with considerable checks and balances built in to ensure careful consideration of policy alternatives and ample representation for minority interests, unless this balance changes significantly toward the Democrats the struggle to pass stronger, comprehensive, and enduring protections against climate change will likely continue to languish. If such a conclusion is dismaying to readers, they should keep in mind that Washington as a whole, given its almost complete reliance on renewable energy for its power, is, when all is said and done, a fairly minor contributor to the overall global emissions at the heart of the climate change issue.

References

ACEEE. 2016. American Council for an Energy Efficient Economy. 2016. State and Local Policy Database: Washington. database.aceee.org/state/washington.

Camden, Jim. 2015. "State OKs $38.2B Spending Package: Budget Goes to Inslee, Gas Tax Bill to House." *Spokesman Review* (June 30).

Coombs, Casey. 2016. "Washington Rejects the Initiative 732 Carbon Tax—Here's What's Next." *Puget Sound Business Journal*, November 9, 2016. bizjournals.com/ seattle/news/2016/11/08/washington-rejects-the-initiative-732-carbon-tax.html.

Deshais, Nicholas. 2015. "Inslee Weighing Climate Action, Transportation Funding at Risk from 'Poison Pill.'" *Spokesman Review*, July 25, 2015.

Energy Information Agency. 2016. "State Energy Data System." energy.gov/maps/ renewable-energy-production-state.

Fiorino, Daniel J. 2006. *The New Environmental Regulation*. Cambridge, MA: The MIT Press.

Franklin, Jerry F., and James K. Agee. 2003. "Forging a Science-Based National Forest Fire Policy," *Issues in Science and Technology* 20 (1). issues.org/20-1/franklin.

Gabbert, Bill. 2016. "Review of the 2015 wildfire season in the Northwest," *Wildfire Today*, February 14, 2016. wildfiretoday.com/2016/02/14/review-of-the-2015-wildfire-season-in-the-northwest/.

Harvey, Chelsea. 2016. "It Could Be the Nation's First Carbon Tax." *Washington Post*, November 29, 2016. www.washingtonpost.com/news/energy-environment/ wp/2016/10/17/it-could-be-the-nations-first-carbon-tax-and-environmentalists-are-fighting-over-it.

Hines, Sandra. 2011. "NW biofuels coming of age with $80 million in separate projects led by UW, WSU," *UW Today*, September 28, 2011. www.washington.edu /news/2011/09/28/nw-biofuels-coming-of-age-with-80-million-in-separate-projects-led-by-uw-wsu.

Hsu, Shi-Ling, Heather Schwedel, and Kyle Meng. 2016. "Environmentalists' Disdain for Washington's Carbon Tax." *Slate*, October 20, 2016. www.slate.com/articles/ health_and_science/science/2016/10/environmentalists_are_against_i_732_ washington_s_carbon_tax.html.

Inslee, Jay. 2014a. "Policy Brief: Cutting Carbon Pollution and Taking Clean Energy Action: Washington Will Lead the Way." Olympia, WA: Governor's Legislative Affairs and Policy Office. www.governor.wa.gov/sites/default/files/policy_briefs/ pb_Climate_2014.pdf.

_____. 2014b. "Policy Brief: Carbon Pollution Accountability Act of 2015." Policy Brief: December 2014. Olympia, WA: Office of the Governor. www.governor. wa.gov/sites/default/files/policy_briefs/pb_Carbon_market_policy.pdf.

Ip, Greg. 2016. "A Growth-Friendly Climate Change Proposal." *Wall Street Journal* (September 28). www.wsj.com/articles/a-growth-friendly-climate-change-proposal-1475079939.

Johnson, Peter. 2016. "Are Washingtonians About to Vote Down a Chance to Fight Climate Change?" *The Atlantic*, November 7, 2016. www.theatlantic.com/ business/archive/2016/11/washington-carbon-tax/506771/.

Kiernan, John S. 2016. "2016's Greenest States." (April 19). wallethub.com/edu/ greenest-states/11987/#main-findings.

Le, Phuong. 2016. "Ecology: New Rule Limits Big Polluters: Washington State Agency Won't Charge Emissions Fees." *Spokesman Review*, September 15, 2016.

Lester, James P. 1994. "A New Federalism? Environmental Policy in the States." In *Environmental Policy in the 1990s,* 2nd ed., edited by N. J. Vig and M. E. Kraft. Washington, DC: CQ Press: 51–68.

Ma, Michelle. 2015. "Scientists: Let wildfires burn when prudent." *UW Today*, September 17, 2015.

Manning, Jay, and Juli Wilkerson. 2008. "Leading the Way: Implementing Practical Solutions to the Climate Change Challenge." Olympia, WA: Climate Action Team. www.ecy.wa.gov/climatechange/2008CATdocs/ltw_app_v2.pdf.

Mason, C. Larry, Richard Gustafson, John Calhoun, Bruce R. Lippke, and Natalia Raffaeli. 2009. "Wood to Energy in Washington: Imperatives, Opportunities, and Obstacles to Progress," Report to the Washington State Legislature, The College of Forest Resources University of Washington (Seattle, Washington) (June). www. igert.org/system/content_item_assets/files/300/Wood_to_Energy_full_report. pdf?1257273850.

National Forest Protection Association. November 2, 2015. "The Year in Fire," *NFPA Journal*. www.nfpa.org/news-and-research/publications/nfpa-journal/2015/ november-december-2015/features/the-year-in-wildfire.

New York Times. 2016. "Washington Initiative 732—Create Carbon Emission Tax— Results: Rejected." *New York Times*. www.nytimes.com/elections/results/ washington-ballot-measure-732-create-carbon-emission-tax.

Northwest Energy Coalition. 2012. "RNP releases new report: Renewable investments near $8 billion in Washington state." www.nwenergy.org/news/rnp- releases-new-report-renewable-investments-near-8-billion-in-washington-state.

Pearl, Abigail, and Hunter Elenbas. 2013. "Washington Environmental Law Year in Review." *Washington Journal of Environmental Law and Policy* 3 (2): 348–70.

Postman, David. 2013. "British Columbia, California, Oregon & Washington Join Forces to Combat Climate Change" Washington Governor Jay Inslee: News & Media (October 28). www.governor.wa.gov/news-media/british-columbia- california-oregon-washington-join-forces-combat-climate-change.

———. 2014. "Inslee Proposes Sustainable, Responsible, Fair Budget to 'reinvest in Washington'" Governor Jay Inslee: News & Media (December 18). www. governor.wa.gov/news-media/inslee-proposes-sustainable-responsible-fair- budget-reinvest-washington.

Roberts, David. 2016. "The Left vs. a Carbon Tax." *Vox.com*. www.vox.com/2016/10/ 18/13012394/i-732-carbon-tax-washington.

Schiffman, Richard. 2012. "Election 2012: America's New Mandate on Climate Change." *Guardian.com* (November 10).

Simon, Christopher, Brent Steel, and Nicholas Lovrich. 2010. *State and Local Government and Politics: Prospects for Sustainability*. New York & Oxford: Oxford University Press.

Sims, Ron. 2013. "Initiative 937: People Power Means Clean Power for the People of Washington State." *Seattle Times*, March 31, 2013. www.seattletimes.com/opinion/ initiative-937-people-power-means-clean-power-for-the-people-of-washington- state/.

Smith, Jaime. 2013. "Statement from Governor Jay Inslee about His Appointment to President Barack Obama's Task Force on Climate Preparedness and Resilience" Washington Governor Jay Inslee: News & Media. (November 1). www.governor. wa.gov/news-media/statement-governor-jay-inslee-about-his-appointment-president-barack-obamas-task-force.

_____.2014. "Gov. Inslee and UK Minister of Energy and Climate Change Sign Agreement to Extend Collaboration on Climate Action" Washington Governor Jay Inslee: News & Media (July 14). www.governor.wa.gov/news-media/gov-inslee-and-uk-minister-energy-and-climate-change-sign-agreement-extend-collaboration.

Sustainable Northwest. 2016. "Pioneering natural resource solutions that work for people and nature." www.sustainablenorthwest.org/what-we-do.

Timber West. 2009. "Aviation Biofuel." http://forestnet.com/TWissues/jan_11/In_the_News.pdf.

U.S. Department of Energy. 2016. "Database of State Incentives for Renewables and Efficiency (DSIRE Washington)." programs.dsireusa.org/system/program?state=WA.

U.S. Forest Service. 2016. "Managing Wildland Fires: Prescribed Burning." www.fs.fed.us/fire/management/rx.html.

Washington Department of Natural Resources. 2007. "Washington's Forests, Timber Supplies, and Forest-Related Industries." file.dnr.wa.gov/publications/em_fwfeconomiclow1.pdf.

_____. 2009. "Biomass Initiative." file.dnr.wa.gov/publications/em_fs09_007.pdf.

Washington Prescribed Fire Council. 2016. "Unhealthy Forests, Unfightable Fires." www.putfiretowork.org.

Washington Smoke (blog). 2016. "Using Prescribed Fire and Measuring Impacts to Air Quality," (September 13). wasmoke.blogspot.com/2016/09/9132016-using-prescribed-fire-and.html.

Washington State Legislature. 2011. Coal-Transition Energy Bill. ESSSB 5769.

_____. 2015. Implementing a Carbon Pollution Market Program to Reduce Greenhouse Gas Emissions. SB 5283/HB 1314. app.leg.wa.gov/billsummary?BillNumber=5283&Year=2015.

Weber, Edward P. 2000. "A New Vanguard for the Environment: Grass-Roots Ecosystem Management as a New Environmental Movement." *Society and Natural Resources* 13: 237–59.

Weber, Edward P., and Tetyana Lysak. 2004. "Environmental and Natural Resource Policy in Washington State," in Cornell Clayton, Lance Leloup, and Nicholas Lovrich, eds. *Washington State Politics*. Pullman, WA: Washington State University Press: 209–231.

Wingfield, Brian, and Miriam Marcus. 2007. "America's Greenest States," *Forbes* (October 17). www.forbes.com/2007/10/16/environment-energy-vermont-biz-beltway-cx_bw_mm_1017greenstates.html.

Woodinville Weekly Staff. 2015. "Gov. Inslee's Pollution Control Proposal: Carbon Emissions Reduction Plan Could Generate Funds for Education, Transportation" *The Woodinville Weekly* (February 12).

Contributors

Gerry Alexander retired from the Washington Supreme Court in 2011 after a 17-year tenure. During nine of those years he served as Chief Justice, giving him the distinction of being the longest serving Chief Justice in state history. Prior to being elected to the Supreme Court he served as a judge of the Superior Court for Thurston and Mason Counties for 11 years, followed by ten years as a judge of the Washington Court of Appeals. Since early 2012 he has been "of counsel" to the Olympia law firm of Bean, Gentry, Wheeler and Peternell.

David Ammons, a journalism and political science graduate of the University of Washington, spent 46 years reporting on and working in Washington state government. He was longtime political writer/columnist for the Associated Press, host of TVW's *Inside Olympia*, and communications and policy adviser to two secretaries of state. He is a member of the Public Disclosure Commission.

Jim Camden has been a newspaper reporter for more than 40 years, most of them covering some level of government and politics. He was hired by the *Spokesman-Review* in 1981, assigned to the political beat in 1984, and became the paper's Olympia bureau chief in 2009. At the *Spokesman-Review* he covers the legislature and state government, writes a weekly column, and blogs. While in Spokane he taught advanced reporting as an adjunct instructor at Whitworth College and Gonzaga University.

María Chávez is associate professor in the Department of Politics and Government at Pacific Lutheran University in Tacoma, Washington. Her research interests include the politics of race and ethnicity focused on Latinos and public policy, especially immigration policy and education policy.

Cornell W. Clayton is the director of the Thomas S. Foley Institute of Public Policy and Public Service at Washington State University, where he also serves as the Thomas S. Foley Distinguished Professor of Government. Professor Clayton received his DPhil from Oxford University and has published widely in the area of American politics, judicial politics, and constitutional law.

Todd Donovan is a professor in the Department of Political Science at Western Washington University in Bellingham, Washington. His research areas include public opinion, electoral rules, representation, and direct democracy. He studies elections in the United States, United Kingdom, Australia, Canada, and New Zealand, and has worked as an expert witness on election matters in state and federal courts.

Richard Elgar is the assistant director of the Thomas S. Foley Institute for Public Policy and Public Service, the executive director of the Pacific Northwest Political Science Association, and a doctoral candidate in the School of Politics, Philosophy, and Public Affairs at Washington State University.

H. Stuart Elway is president of Elway Research, Inc. and, since 1992, publisher of *The Elway Poll,* a nonpartisan analysis of public opinion in Washington State. He has a PhD from the University of Washington and has taught public opinion and civic engagement in the graduate public affairs programs at the University of Washington and The Evergreen State College.

Season A. Hoard is an assistant professor at Washington State University, jointly appointed in the Division of Governmental Studies and Services (DGSS), and the School of Politics, Philosophy, and Public Affairs. At the DGSS, she serves as research coordinator for applied policy research in the Pacific Northwest. Professor Hoard received her PhD from Washington State University and has published in the areas of public policy, gender and politics, and criminal justice policy.

Robin Dale Jacobson is associate professor in the Department of Politics and Government at University of Puget Sound in Tacoma, Washington. She publishes and speaks on the role of race and religion in the politics of immigration. She received her BA from Johns Hopkins University and her PhD in Political Science from the University of Oregon.

Carolyn N. Long is the Director for Strategic Partnerships at Washington State University Vancouver, where she is also the Sam Reed Distinguished Professor in Civic Education and Public Civility. She received her Ph. from Rutgers University and has published books and articles in American politics and public law.

Nicholas P. Lovrich is Regent Professor Emeritus and Claudius O. and Mary W. Johnson Distinguished Professor of Political Science at Washington State University. He served as the director of the Division of Governmental Studies and Services from 1977 to 2010, and as interim chancellor of WSU Spokane. He earned his BA at Stanford University, and PhD from UCLA.

Carl McCurley is the manager of the Washington State Center for Court Research at the Administrative Office of the Courts, and co-director of the Center for the Study and Advancement of Justice Effectiveness. He received his PhD from Indiana University, Bloomington. Improving justice administration through better use of performance measurement and transparency is the central focus of his work.

John C. Pierce is lecturer in the School of Public Affairs and Administration at the University of Kansas. Formerly he served as chair of the Department of Political Science and dean of the College of Liberal Arts at Washington State University, as well as vice chancellor for Academic Affairs at the University of Colorado at Colorado Springs.

Kevin Pirch is associate professor and chair of the Department of Political Science and International Affairs at Eastern Washington University. He is also director of the Center for the Studies of Northwest Politics at EWU and has published work in voting behavior, redistricting, and state and local governance.

Sanne A. M. Rijkhoff is adjunct assistant professor of political science at Portland State University. She holds a PhD in political science from Washington State University, and master's degrees in social and organizational psychology and political science from Leiden University, the Netherlands. She received the 2017 Best Dissertation Award from the Western Political Science Association. Dr. Rijkhoff's work has been published in numerous journals and she is a contributor to the forthcoming book, *Oregon State and Local Politics*.

Ellen Rogers is an adjunct instructor in the school of Politics, Philosophy and Public Affairs at Washington State University Vancouver, where she also serves as the associate director of the Initiative for Public Deliberation.

Michael F. Salamone is an assistant professor of political science in the School of Politics, Philosophy, and Public Affairs at Washington State University. He received his PhD from the University of California, Berkeley. His research focuses on the public perception of judicial decision-making.

Christina M. Sanders is currently the acting director for the Division of Governmental Studies and Services (DGSS) at Washington State University. DGSS provides applied research, technical assistance, and training services for governmental agencies and non-profits throughout the Northwest. Sanders received her MPA at the University of Idaho and has published in the areas of criminal justice, public policy and disaster recovery.

Sara Singleton is associate professor of political science at Western Washington University, where she teaches courses in environmental politics, political economy, and the politics of inequality. She has served several times as the faculty legislative representative to the state legislature.

Steven D. Stehr is associate professor and interim director of the School of Politics, Philosophy, and Public Affairs at Washington State University. He received a BS degree in Economics from the University of Nebraska, Lincoln, and a PhD from the University of California, Berkeley. His work in the fields of public policy and public administration has appeared in a variety of scholarly outlets.

Clive S. Thomas is a senior fellow at the Thomas S. Foley Institute for Public Policy and Public Service at Washington State University. From 1981 to 2011 he taught political science at the University of Alaska in

Juneau. He has published extensively on U.S. national and state politics as well as comparative politics, particularly in the areas of interest
groups and political parties. He also runs the consulting firm Political
Advocacy Strategies (PAS).

Edward P. Weber is the Ulysses G. Dubach Professor of Political
Science in the School of Public Policy at Oregon State University. He
has published widely on natural resource and environmental policymaking, democratic accountability, and the operation of alternative
governing institutions, particularly collaborative governance arrangements. He is also the chair of the Committee for Family Forestlands for
the Oregon Department of Forestry.

Hans Zeiger is a Washington State Senator representing Pierce
County's 25th District, and he serves as chair of the Senate Early
Learning and K–12 Education Committee. He previously served for
three terms in the Washington State House of Representatives, where
he was ranking member on the House Higher Education Committee.
He is director of the Chapman Center for Citizen Leadership at the
Seattle-based Discovery Institute.